Springer Proceedings in Business and Economics

More information about this series at http://www.springer.com/series/11960

Angelo Sifaleras • Konstantinos Petridis
Editors

Operational Research in the Digital Era – ICT Challenges

6th International Symposium and 28th National Conference on Operational Research, Thessaloniki, Greece, June 2017

 Springer

Editors
Angelo Sifaleras
Department of Applied Informatics
University of Macedonia
Thessaloniki, Greece

Konstantinos Petridis
Department of Applied Informatics
University of Macedonia
Thessaloniki, Greece

ISSN 2198-7246 ISSN 2198-7254 (electronic)
Springer Proceedings in Business and Economics
ISBN 978-3-319-95665-7 ISBN 978-3-319-95666-4 (eBook)
https://doi.org/10.1007/978-3-319-95666-4

Library of Congress Control Number: 2018955699

This Springer imprint is published by the registered company Springer Nature Switzerland AG
The registered company address is: Gewerbestrasse 11, 6330 Cham, Switzerland

Foreword

I am very pleased to introduce this volume of proceedings from the above event, co-organized by the Hellenic Operational Research Society (HELORS) and the Department of Applied Informatics of the University of Macedonia, Thessaloniki, Greece.

The papers in this volume are a sample of the dynamic and varied research taking place in the broad fields of operational research and informatics in Greece.

Two of the papers address the issue of forecasting using neural networks, one in the field of energy consumption and the other in the field of employment. Neural networks are an alternative to the more traditional time series and econometrically based forecasting methods, obviating the need for model specification in the latter and the inherent risk of misspecification. Neural networks show much promise in the field of forecasting.

Two papers examine cloud computing, one from a traditional and the other from a less usual perspective. In the first case, the importance of cloud computing in e-government is explored. In the second case, cloud computing is seen from a game-theoretic-perspective. Pricing strategies for cloud systems can be addressed using a game theoretic approach. Both papers show how the two fields of informatics and operational research can be used jointly to address governance and business issues. Another interesting paper holding the prospect of interdisciplinary research, is that addressing the issue of condition-based maintenance (CBM). It deals with the very issues addressed in servitization where the object traded is not a physical asset, such as an aircraft engine, but rather the service of it, with the engine remaining the property of the manufacturer A link between CBM and servitization is clearly worth exploring further.

There are also in this volume, papers on social media analysis and on digital currency adoption. These two areas are growing in use exponentially offering a productive seam for further research. Another paper offering an interesting perspective is that on the distinction between soft and technical skills and their importance for prospective employers of graduates from Management Science and Informatics departments.

I congratulate the organizers on putting together an informative conference and encourage the authors featured in this volume to pursue with vigor their interesting research agendas.

Professor in Management Sciences   Emmanuel Thanassoulis
Aston Business School
Aston University
Birmingham B4 7ET
United Kingdom

Preface

It is our great pleasure to introduce this book entitled *Operational Research in the Digital Era: ICT Challenges*, of the series Springer Proceedings in Business and Economics, which contains selected, refereed proceedings from the 6th International Symposium & 28th National Conference on Operational Research (HELORS 2017). This conference is an established annual event attended by a large number of operational research (OR) scientists, instructors, and students, mainly from Greece but also from all over Europe.

The purpose of the Conference is to disseminate recent scientific advances in the field of operational research and management science in Greece and to promote international cooperation among researchers and practitioners working in the field. The specific aim of this year's Conference is to highlight the role and importance of OR in the digital era and the underlying ICT challenges (*Operational Research in the Digital Era: ICT Challenges*).

Three plenary talks were given by eminent researchers in the field of operational research. Professor John N. Tsitsiklis opened the conference by presenting an overview of dynamic programming. Professor Georgios Doukidis addressed business transformation strategies using data-driven innovations in the retail supply-chains. Finally Professor Panos M. Pardalos demonstrated how to use quantification of network dissimilarities and its practical implications in several research areas that include bioinformatics, climate dynamics, percolation in networks, network robustness, and model selection.

Apart from the funds provided by the co-organizers, the conference attracted the sponsorship of well-known companies, such as Marathon Data Systems, Open Technology Services (OTS), ATLANTIS Consulting SA, Egnatia Odos AE, and Geotechnical Chamber of Greece. Other partners of the conference include the Greek Ministry of Macedonia and Thrace, OK!Thess, and the Aristotle University of Thessaloniki.

This year the conference was co-organized by the Department of Applied Informatics of the University of Macedonia and the Hellenic Operational Research Society (HELORS). It took place in the University of Macedonia, Greece, 8–10 June 2017. The conference chairs were Professor M. Vlachopoulou, G. Kalfakakou, and B. Manos. Around 94 papers were presented in 20 streams, including meta-heuristics, multicriteria decision-making, data envelopment analysis, supply chain optimization, etc. Apart from Greece, the conference received submissions from Algeria, Finland, Serbia, Slovakia, Spain, Turkey, United Arab Emirates, the United Kingdom, and the United States. After the reviewing process, the following 13 papers were eventually accepted for publication:

The book begins with the manuscript "Final Energy Consumption Forecasting by Applying Artificial Intelligence Models" by G.N. Kouziokas, A. Chatzigeorgiou, and K. Perakis. The authors apply artificial neural networks in order to build and compare neural network forecasting models for predicting the final energy consumption.

The second paper presents a short survey of recent game-theoretic approaches applied in P2P networks and cloud systems, and it is titled "Game theoretic approaches in cloud and P2P networks: Issues and challenges." G. Koloniari and A. Sifaleras provide a classification of game-theoretic approaches dealing with a variety of problems encountered in the design and deployment of P2P and cloud systems.

Bousdekis and G. Mentzas, in the paper "A proactive model for joint maintenance and logistics optimization in the frame of Industrial Internet of Things," propose a proactive event-driven model for joint maintenance and logistics optimization in a sensor-based, data-rich industrial environment. The authors have validated their approach in a real industrial environment (oil and gas industry) and also evaluated their results using a comparative and sensitivity analysis.

The fourth paper studies the actual use of digital currency by companies and freelancers globally with an emphasis in the European Union. I. Roussou and E. Stiakakis in their paper titled "Adoption of Digital Currencies: The Companies Perspective" present the results of an online academic survey and apply a combination of Diffusion of Innovation (DOI) Theory (mainly Innovation Decision Process Model, IDPM) and Technology Acceptance Model (TAM), in order to investigate the actual use of digital currency.

In the paper by G.N. Kouziokas titled "Unemployment Prediction in UK by Using a Feedforward Multilayer Perceptron," the aim is to implement prediction models by using artificial neural networks in order to forecast unemployment. The author considered several socioeconomic factors and evaluated their findings using real data collected from the official website of the UK Office for National Statistics.

The sixth paper is titled "Performance Evaluation of Routing Protocols for BIG Data application" and authored by E. Balasas, K. Psannis, and M. Roumeliotis. It illustrates how dynamic routing protocols perform in real-time applications. The proposed study assess the use of three interior gateway routing protocols for video conferencing and VoIP.

S.P. Gayialis, G.D. Konstantakopoulos, and I.P. Tatsiopoulos, in the paper "Vehicle Routing Problem for Urban Freight Transportation: A Review," present a literature review from Scopus scientific database of the vehicle routing problem (VRP) for urban freight transportation. The authors discuss some critical insights of the study and analyze the trends of the VRP for urban freight transportation.

The eighth paper is titled "Development of a framework for the assessment of soft skills in the ICT sector" and authored by V.A. Valavosiki, E. Stiakakis, and A. Chatzigeorgiou. The authors aim to develop a framework for the assessment of both technical and nontechnical skills in the information technology and communications sector.

In the paper by I. Nanos, V. Manthou, and E. Androutsou titled "Cloud Computing Adoption Decision in E-government," the relationship between cloud computing and e-government is investigated. The authors highlight the importance of cloud computing adoption in public administration and offer insights on the way that cloud computing can contribute to the successful deployment of e-government services.

The book closes with the manuscript "A unified framework for decision-making process on social media analytics" by N. Misirlis and Maro Vlachopoulou. The authors consider the procedures that have to be followed in order to achieve the most optimized choice of social media analytics methodology initiating the 4P's procedure (people, purpose, platform, and process).

Thessaloniki, Greece   Angelo Sifaleras
Thessaloniki, Greece   Konstantinos Petridis
April 2018

Organization

Conference Chairs

Maro Vlachopoulou	University of Macedonia, Greece
Glykeria Kalfakakou	Aristotle University of Thessaloniki, Greece
Basil Manos	Aristotle University of Thessaloniki, Greece

Organizing Committee

Emmanouil Stiakakis	University of Macedonia, Greece
Fotis Kitsios	University of Macedonia, Greece
Michael Madas	University of Macedonia, Greece
Konstantinos Petridis	University of Macedonia, Greece
Nikolaos Petridis	Aristotle University of Thessaloniki, Greece
Angelo Sifaleras	University of Macedonia, Greece
Kostas Vergidis	University of Macedonia, Greece
Christos Ziakis	University of Macedonia, Greece

Contents

Final Energy Consumption Forecasting by Applying Artificial Intelligence Models

Georgios N. Kouziokas, Alexander Chatzigeorgiou, and Konstantinos Perakis

Abstract The application of artificial neural networks has been increased in many scientific sectors the last years, with the development of new machine learning techniques and methodologies. In this research, neural networks are applied in order to build and compare neural network forecasting models for predicting the final energy consumption. Predicting the energy consumption can be very significant in public management at improving the energy management and also at designing the optimal energy planning strategies. The final energy consumption covers the energy consumption in sectors such as industry, households, transport, commerce and public management. Several architectures were examined in order to construct the optimal neural network forecasting model. The results have shown a very good prediction accuracy according to the mean squared error. The proposed methodology can provide more accurate energy consumption predictions in public and environmental decision making, and they can be used in order to help the authorities at adopting proactive measures in energy management.

Keywords Artificial intelligence · Energy management · Environmental management · Neural networks · Public management

1 Introduction

Considering the increased amount of information in public management, the latest years, it is significant for the authorities to adopt new information technologies in order to manage multiple kinds of information in a more computerized way

G. N. Kouziokas (✉) · K. Perakis
Department of Planning and Regional Development, School of Engineering,
University of Thessaly, Volos, Greece
e-mail: gekouzio@uth.gr

A. Chatzigeorgiou
Department of Applied Informatics, University of Macedonia, Thessaloniki, Greece

© Springer Nature Switzerland AG 2019
A. Sifaleras, K. Petridis (eds.), *Operational Research in the Digital Era – ICT Challenges*, Springer Proceedings in Business and Economics,
https://doi.org/10.1007/978-3-319-95666-4_1

(Dunleavy et al. 2006; Kouziokas 2016b, c, 2017b). Information and Communication Technology has a significant role in public management, especially in processing and managing information of increased importance related to decision-making issues and technology-based practices in order to improve the public management strategies.

Neural networks have been used in many studies as an advanced tool for forecasting data in several sectors of public administration such as environmental management (Kouziokas et al. 2016, 2017), public transportation (Kouziokas 2016a, 2017c) and decision support systems (Cortès et al. 2000; Efendigil et al. 2009; Kouziokas 2017a; Kouziokas and Perakis 2017).

The application of artificial neural networks has been studied by several researchers in the field of energy consumption forecasting (Azadeh et al. 2013; Ekonomou 2010; Khoshnevisan et al. 2013; Khosravani et al. 2016; Zeng et al. 2017).

Ekonomou (2010) has implemented artificial neural networks so as to predict the long-term energy consumption prediction in Greece. The results of the research have been more precise compared to the ones produced by a linear regression model. Khosravani et al. (2016) have studied the comparison of neural network forecasting models regarding energy consumption. The results of the research have shown a very good forecasting accuracy. Zeng et al. (2017) have implemented a back-propagation neural network in order to construct forecasting models in order to predict the energy consumption. The results have shown a very good prediction accuracy.

In this study, the implementation of neural network forecasting models is investigated for predicting the final energy consumption, which covers the final energy consumption in many sectors: industry, transport, households, public administration, commerce and other sectors. This research has taken into consideration several factors that affect the final energy consumption levels according to the literature. Several tests were performed with multiple network topologies so as to discover the optimal prediction model. In the following sections, the methodology, the results and the discussion are described.

2 Theoretical Background

2.1 Artificial Neural Networks

The artificial intelligence is used in many studies as an emerging technique for performing predictions in several kinds of problems. The artificial neural networks (ANNs) can be defined as artificial computational systems that simulate the neural structure of the human brain. A neural network processes the information from the input parameters. The input information traverses through the established neuron connections, and after being processed, the output predictions are computed

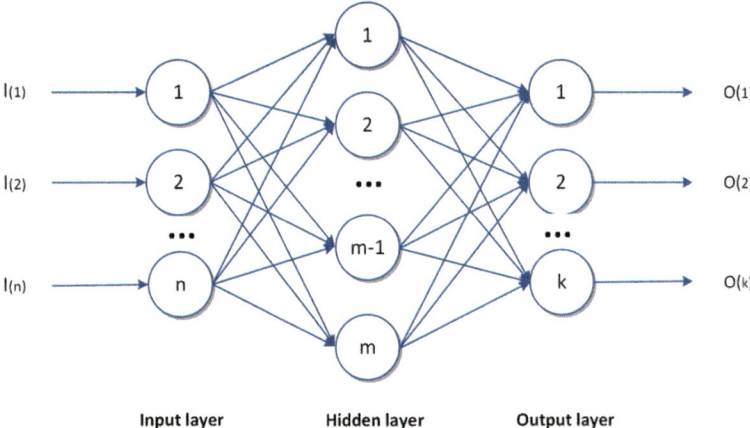

Fig. 1 The architecture of a feedforward neural network, where n is the number of the neurons in the input layer, $I_{(n)}$ represents the input value, m is the number of the neurons in the hidden layer, k is the number of the neurons in the output layer and $O_{(k)}$ represents the output value

according to the input (Svozil et al. 1997). The artificial neural networks (ANNs) were utilized in this study in order to forecast the values of the final energy consumption.

A feedforward multilayer neural network was used in this research. In a feedforward multilayer neural network, the neurons between the layers are connected only in a forward direction and the typical structure consists of an input layer, an output layer and a hidden layer. Each layer is composed of neurons (Koskela et al. 1996). A Feedforward Multilayer Perceptron (FFMLP) was utilized in this study, as it is considered as the most appropriate for time series issues according to the literature. The architecture of a typical feedforward neural network is illustrated in Fig. 1.

2.2   Levenberg Marquardt Algorithm

The Levenberg Marquardt Algorithm is the most suitable training algorithm for problems that have to do with time series predictions according to the literature. That is the main reason for using this algorithm in this research. Another reason for choosing the Levenberg Marquardt Algorithm as the learning algorithm for training the feedforward multilayer neural network is that according to the literature, it is one of the fastest learning algorithms compared to other algorithms (Lourakis 2005). The Levenberg Marquardt Algorithm combines all the minimization advantages of two algorithms: the steepest descent algorithm and also the Gauss-Newton algorithm used for solving many non-linear least-squares problems (Marquardt 1963).

	1990	1995	2000	2005	2010	2011	2012	2013	2014	Share in EU-28, 2014 (%)
EU-28	1 667.9	1 674.7	1 730.0	1 831.0	1 763.7	1 698.1	1 684.7	1 566.7	1 605.9	100.0
Belgium	48.5	53.8	59.3	59.1	61.2	57.0	54.6	56.5	53.4	3.3
Bulgaria	27.6	22.7	18.5	19.8	17.8	19.1	18.2	16.8	17.7	1.1
Czech Republic	49.9	41.7	41.1	45.1	44.7	43.0	42.8	42.2	41.5	2.6
Denmark	17.9	20.2	19.7	19.6	20.0	18.6	17.9	18.2	16.9	1.1
Germany	356.3	341.6	342.3	341.9	333.0	316.7	318.6	324.5	313.0	19.5
Estonia	9.9	5.5	5.0	5.6	6.2	6.2	6.1	6.7	6.7	0.4
Ireland	10.3	11.1	14.4	15.3	15.2	13.9	13.8	13.7	13.6	0.8
Greece	22.3	23.9	28.3	31.4	28.8	27.0	27.7	24.3	24.4	1.5
Spain	90.1	102.1	123.6	144.2	130.3	128.5	128.1	119.3	116.7	7.3
France	227.8	241.8	257.5	276.6	267.1	257.5	257.8	258.9	248.5	15.5
Croatia	9.5	7.9	8.4	9.8	9.4	9.3	8.9	8.6	8.2	0.5
Italy	153.5	161.8	174.2	190.1	177.9	172.5	165.7	159.5	151.0	9.4
Cyprus	1.6	2.0	2.4	2.5	2.7	2.7	2.5	2.2	2.2	0.1
Latvia	7.9	4.6	3.9	4.6	4.6	4.4	4.5	4.5	4.5	0.3
Lithuania	15.9	8.6	7.1	8.7	6.8	7.0	7.1	6.7	6.7	0.4
Luxembourg	3.5	3.3	3.7	4.8	4.6	4.6	4.5	4.3	4.2	0.3
Hungary	28.8	26.2	25.3	27.6	25.7	25.0	23.5	22.7	22.8	1.4
Malta	0.6	0.8	0.8	1.0	0.9	0.9	1.0	0.9	0.9	0.1
Netherlands	66.7	75.4	78.1	84.4	86.1	80.4	80.8	80.4	76.8	4.8
Austria	25.0	27.1	29.0	34.2	34.3	33.3	33.2	33.7	32.7	2.0
Poland	103.3	98.8	88.6	92.2	100.7	100.8	97.6	98.0	94.3	5.9
Portugal	18.2	20.6	25.3	27.5	24.3	23.6	22.2	22.4	22.1	1.4
Romania	58.1	46.3	36.6	39.2	35.8	36.6	35.4	32.4	32.3	2.0
Slovenia	5.7	6.1	6.5	7.3	7.3	7.3	7.1	6.9	6.7	0.4
Slovakia	21.8	17.7	18.3	19.0	17.9	17.4	16.7	17.0	16.2	1.0
Finland	28.8	29.4	32.4	34.5	37.1	35.9	34.7	34.1	34.6	2.2
Sweden	47.4	51.5	48.9	51.0	50.8	49.7	49.8	49.1	48.2	3.0
United Kingdom	210.6	222.3	230.6	234.0	212.5	198.2	204.0	202.2	189.3	11.8
Iceland	2.4	2.3	3.3	3.4	5.9	6.3	5.8	6.1	6.1	–
Norway	21.4	23.8	26.4	27.2	34.3	28.4	30.1	33.7	29.2	–
Montenegro	–	–	–	1.1	1.2	1.1	1.1	1.0	1.0	–
FYR of Macedonia	2.4	2.5	2.7	2.8	2.8	3.1	3.0	2.7	2.6	–
Albania	2.6	1.3	1.8	2.2	2.1	2.2	2.1	2.4	2.3	–
Serbia	19.6	13.6	13.7	15.7	15.6	16.2	14.5	14.9	13.3	–
Turkey	52.3	62.1	76.7	85.6	106.9	113.9	119.8	118.5	124.0	–
Bosnia and Herzegovina	5.0	0.9	3.2	3.9	4.7	5.4	5.1	5.0	7.8	–
Kosovo (under UNSCR 1244/99)	–	–	1.5	1.9	2.5	2.5	2.4	2.3	2.1	–

Source: Eurostat (online data code: nrg_100a)

Fig. 2 The final energy consumption in Europe from 1990 to 2014 (million tonnes of oil equivalent). Source: Eurostat (http://ec.europa.eu/eurostat/statistics-explained/index.php/Energy_ saving_statistics)

2.3 Final Energy Consumption

The final energy consumption covers the total energy that is consumed by the end users, such as households, industry, agriculture, transport, households, public administration, commerce and other sectors (Alcántara and Padilla 2003). Figure 2 shows the final energy consumption in Europe (million tonnes of oil equivalent) from 1990 to 2014.

3 Research Methodology

The followed research methodology consists of four stages: data collection, data preparation and cleansing, neural network prediction model development and the application of the optimal neural network model to predict the values of energy consumption. In the first stage, final energy consumption data were collected, and in the second stage, the data were prepared and cleansed in order to feed the constructed neural network models. In the third stage, multiple neural network structures were investigated so as to develop the optimal neural network forecasting model. In the last stage, the optimal artificial neural network model was implemented to

Fig. 3 Overview of the
followed methodology

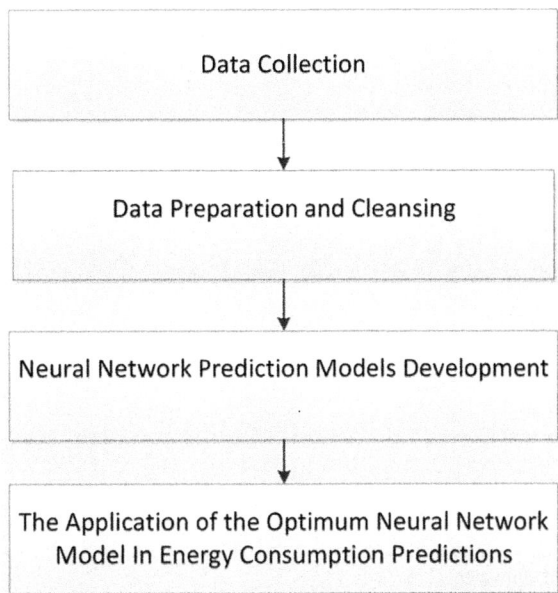

predict the values of the final energy consumption. An overview of the followed
methodology is illustrated in Fig. 3.

4   Results

4.1   Data Collection and Preparation

The information about the population, the population change rate and the GDP
(Growth Domestic Product) annual percentage growth were collected from the
official website of the UK Office for National Statistics (ONS). The energy
consumption data were collected from the official website of the UK Department
for Business, Energy and Industrial Strategy in the UK.

The data that were collected for the time period from 1970 to 2013 were
processed and prepared to be utilized as inputs in the artificial neural network
models. The data were checked for gaps and duplicates. Figure 4 shows the final
energy consumption [Thousand tonnes of oil equivalent (ktoe)] in the United
Kingdom for the time period from 1970 to 2013.

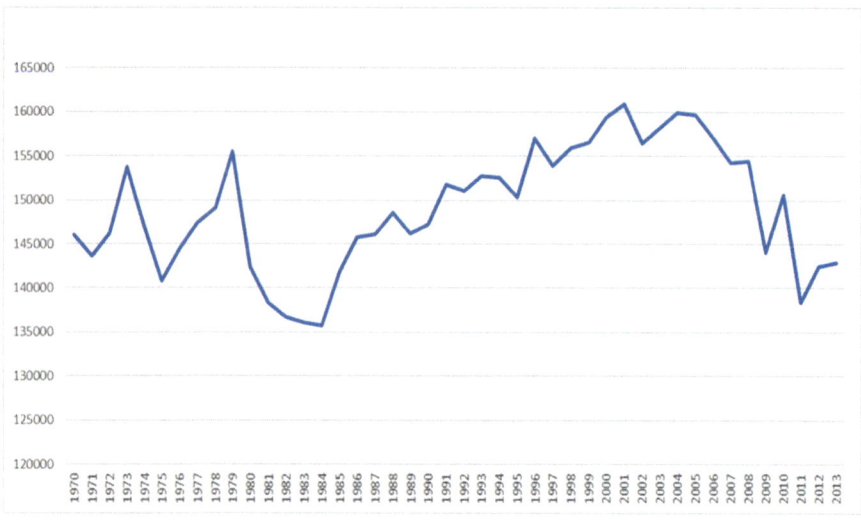

Fig. 4 Energy consumption in the UK for the time period from 1970 to 2013 [thousand tonnes of oil equivalent (ktoe)]

4.2 Artificial Neural Network Models

First, the input variables were selected by studying the literature in order to find the most important factors that affect the final energy consumption. Several researchers have shown the increased influence of the population, the population growth and of the GDP (Growth Domestic Product) growth in energy consumption (Ramanathan 2006; York 2007). Consequently, these factors were selected as input variables for constructing the neural network models. The artificial neural network models were developed and tested by using as input variables the prementioned variables that influence the levels of the final energy consumption and also the historical values of the energy consumption. Finally, the input values are the annual energy consumption, the population, the population percentage growth and the GDP (Growth Domestic Product) percentage growth (annual). The artificial neural network output produces the forecasted values of annual final energy consumption.

The collected data was divided into three different parts. The 70% of the data was used for the training set, 15% for the validation set and 15% for the test set. The training data set was used so as to train the neural network with input data. The validation set was utilized to assess the neural network model performance. The Levenberg Marquardt Algorithm was selected as the learning algorithm for training the neural network models, since according to the literature, it is the most appropriate for time series problems (Lourakis 2005).

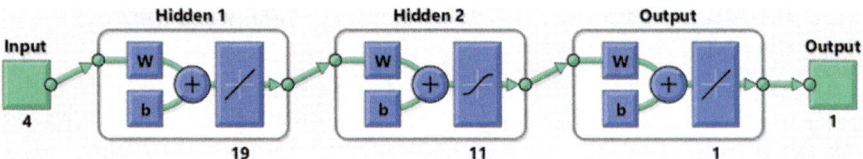

Fig. 5 The topology of the optimal neural network model

4.3 Optimal Neural Network Forecasting Model

The performance of each tested prediction model was used in order to find the best network topology. Several topologies of artificial neural network models were tested regarding the number of the hidden layers (one to two) and also the nature of the tested transfer functions in the hidden layers. The optimal topology that produced the best forecasting results was the one with two hidden layers in this case study. The most commonly used transfer functions were tested in the hidden layers: the Log-Sigmoid Transfer Function (LSTF), the Tanh-Sigmoid Transfer Function (TSTF) and the Linear Transfer Function (LTF).

The optimal model was evaluated according to the produced mean squared error (MSE) between all the other constructed neural network models. The mean squared error (MSE) was calculated by utilizing the following equation:

$$MSE = \frac{\sum_{i=1}^{N} \left(y_{p_i} - y_{r_i}\right)^2}{N} \tag{1}$$

where y_{pi} is the predicted value, y_{r_i} represents the real value and N is the number of the output values.

The optimal network topology was the one with 19 neurons in the first hidden layer and 11 neurons in the second hidden layer. The transfer functions in the hidden layers that yielded the best results were The Linear Transfer Function (LTF) in the first hidden layer and the Tanh-Sigmoid Transfer Function (TSTF) in the second hidden layer.

The mean squared error (MSE) of the optimal neural network model was 54.9509 at epoch 17 and the root mean squared error (RMSE) was 7.4129. The results have shown a very precise forecasting accuracy. In Fig. 5 the neural network topology of the optimal model is shown.

The linear regression method was utilized to evaluate the prediction accuracy of the optimal neural network model. The regression plot which is illustrated in Fig. 5 shows the relationship between the output values of the network and the target values of the final energy consumption. The R value represents the relationship between the targets and outputs. Figure 6 shows that the predictions are very accurate according to the R value of the test set that was found to be 0.99997.

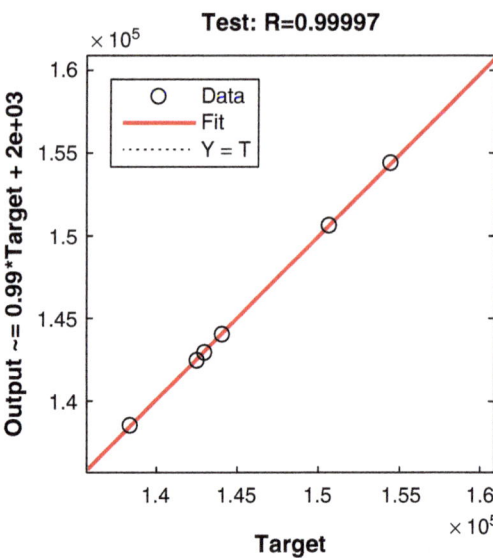

Fig. 6 The regression plot of the test set by using the constructed optimal neural network model according to the minimum mean squared error (MSE)

5 Conclusions and Discussion

The artificial intelligence has been applied in many studies by several researchers as an emerging technique for performing predictions in several kinds of time series problems. In this paper, artificial intelligence was implemented in order to develop neural network models for forecasting the levels of the final energy consumption, which covers the energy consumption in industry, transport, households, public administration, commerce and other sectors.

This study takes into consideration multiple factors that affect final energy consumption levels, as input variables, that have utilized neural networks to forecast the final energy consumption, and tests multiple network topologies regarding the number of neurons in every hidden layer and also the nature of the transfer functions that were tested so as to develop the optimal neural network prediction model.

The results have shown a very precise forecasting accuracy of the values of the final energy consumption that were selected to be predicted in the study area which was the United Kingdom. The optimal neural network forecasting model was constructed by investigating different neural network topologies in order to find the optimal one and also by taking into consideration several variables that influence the values of the final energy consumption.

The final energy consumption forecasting can be very valuable in adopting strategies regarding the energy management and also in designing and planning national energy practices. The results have shown that the proposed technique can provide energy consumption predictions with a very precise prediction accuracy which can be very valuable in public and environmental management since they can be used by the pubic stakeholders at adopting proactive strategies in energy management and planning.

Acknowledgments The UK Office for National Statistics and the UK Department for Business, Energy and Industrial Strategy websites for retrieving the data.

References

Alcántara, V., & Padilla, E. (2003). "Key" sectors in final energy consumption: An input–output application to the Spanish case. *Energy Policy, 31*(15), 1673–1678.

Azadeh, A., Babazadeh, R., & Asadzadeh, S. (2013). Optimum estimation and forecasting of renewable energy consumption by artificial neural networks. *Renewable and Sustainable Energy Reviews, 27*, 605–612.

Cortès, U., Sànchez-Marrè, M., Ceccaroni, L., R-Roda, I., & Poch, M. (2000). Artificial intelligence and environmental decision support systems. *Applied Intelligence, 13*(1), 77–91.

Dunleavy, P., Margetts, H., Bastow, S., & Tinkler, J. (2006). New public management is dead— long live digital-era governance. *Journal of Public Administration Research and Theory, 16*(3), 467–494.

Efendigil, T., Önüt, S., & Kahraman, C. (2009). A decision support system for demand forecasting with artificial neural networks and neuro-fuzzy models: A comparative analysis. *Expert Systems with Applications, 36*(3), 6697–6707.

Ekonomou, L. (2010). Greek long-term energy consumption prediction using artificial neural networks. *Energy, 35*(2), 512–517.

Khoshnevisan, B., Rafiee, S., Omid, M., Yousefi, M., & Movahedi, M. (2013). Modeling of energy consumption and GHG (greenhouse gas) emissions in wheat production in Esfahan province of Iran using artificial neural networks. *Energy, 52*, 333–338.

Khosravani, H. R., Castilla, M. D. M., Berenguel, M., Ruano, A. E., & Ferreira, P. M. (2016). A comparison of energy consumption prediction models based on neural networks of a bioclimatic building. *Energies, 9*(1), 57.

Koskela, T., Lehtokangas, M., Saarinen, J., & Kaski, K. (1996). Time series prediction with multilayer perceptron, FIR and Elman neural networks. In: *Proceedings of the World Congress on Neural Networks, 1996* (pp. 491–496). Citeseer.

Kouziokas, G. N. (2016a). Artificial intelligence and crime prediction in public management of transportation safety in urban environment. In: *Proceedings of the 3rd Conference on Sustainable Urban Mobility, Volos, Greece, 2016* (pp. 534–539). University of Thessaly.

Kouziokas, G. N. (2016b). Geospatial based information system development in public administration for sustainable development and planning in urban environment. *European Journal of Sustainable Development, 5*(4), 347–352. https://doi.org/10.14207/ejsd.2016.v5n4p347.

Kouziokas, G. N. (2016c). Technology-based management of environmental organizations using an Environmental Management Information System (EMIS): Design and development. *Environmental Technology & Innovation, 5*, 106–116. https://doi.org/10.1016/j.eti.2016.01.006.

Kouziokas, G. N. (2017a). An information system for judicial and public administration using artificial intelligence and geospatial data. In: *Proceedings of the 21st Pan-Hellenic Conference on Informatics, Larissa, Greece* (pp. 1–2). ACM, 3139402. doi:https://doi.org/10.1145/3139367.3139402

Kouziokas, G. N. (2017b). Machine learning technique in time series prediction of gross domestic product. In: *Proceedings of the 21st Pan-Hellenic Conference on Informatics, Larissa, Greece* (pp. 1–2). ACM, 3139443. doi:https://doi.org/10.1145/3139367.3139443

Kouziokas, G. N. (2017c). The application of artificial intelligence in public administration for forecasting high crime risk transportation areas in urban environment. *Transportation Research Procedia, 24*, 467–473. https://doi.org/10.1016/j.trpro.2017.05.083.

Kouziokas, G. N., Chatzigeorgiou, A., & Perakis, K. (2016). Predicting environmental data in public management by using artificial intelligence. In: *Proceedings of the 11th International Scientific Conference eRA-11, Piraeus, Greece, September 2016* (pp. 39–46). Piraeus University of Applied Sciences.

Kouziokas, G. N., Chatzigeorgiou, A., & Perakis, K. (2017). Artificial intelligence and regression in predicting ground water levels in public administration. *European Water*, (57), 361–366.

Kouziokas, G. N., & Perakis, K. (2017). Decision support system based on artificial intelligence, GIS and remote sensing for sustainable public and judicial management. *European Journal of Sustainable Development, 6*(3), 397–404. https://doi.org/10.14207/ejsd.2017.v6n3p397.

Lourakis, M. I. A. (2005). A brief description of the Levenberg-Marquardt algorithm implemented by levmar. *Foundation of Research and Technology, 4*, 1–6.

Marquardt, D. W. (1963). An algorithm for least-squares estimation of nonlinear parameters. *Journal of the Society for Industrial and Applied Mathematics, 11*(2), 431–441.

Ramanathan, R. (2006). A multi-factor efficiency perspective to the relationships among world GDP, energy consumption and carbon dioxide emissions. *Technological Forecasting and Social Change, 73*(5), 483–494.

Svozil, D., Kvasnicka, V., & Pospichal, J. (1997). Introduction to multi-layer feed-forward neural networks. *Chemometrics and Intelligent Laboratory Systems, 39*(1), 43–62.

York, R. (2007). Demographic trends and energy consumption in European Union Nations, 1960–2025. *Social Science Research, 36*(3), 855–872.

Zeng, Y.-R., Zeng, Y., Choi, B., & Wang, L. (2017). Multifactor-influenced energy consumption forecasting using enhanced back-propagation neural network. *Energy, 127*, 381–396. https://doi.org/10.1016/j.energy.2017.03.094.

Game-Theoretic Approaches in Cloud and P2P Networks: Issues and Challenges

Georgia Koloniari and Angelo Sifaleras

Abstract Game theory constitutes a mathematical method for rational decision making in competitive and conflicting situations under specified rules, and thus is closely associated with decision theory. The applicability and usefulness of game theory has been already proved in the research area of peer-to-peer (P2P) networks and network optimization in general. P2P networks consist of autonomous nodes that not only collaborate for sharing and consuming resources, but also act independently and are governed by selfish motives. Thus, game-theoretic solutions lend themselves well for problems arising in P2P networks. Also, game-theoretic approaches have recently been employed in order to exploit the benefits of cloud infrastructures. The proposed work surveys the recent developments on game-theoretic approaches in P2P networks and cloud systems, and provides a classification of approaches dealing with a variety of problems encountered in the design and deployment of P2P and cloud systems.

Keywords Network optimization · Game theory · Cloud pricing strategies

1 Introduction

Game theory is a formal framework with a set of mathematical tools to study the complex interactions among interdependent rational players. Strategic games have found a number of important applications in economics, politics, sociology, etc. During the past decade, there has been a surge in research activities that employ game theory to model and analyze modern communication systems, due to (1) the emergence of Internet as a global platform for computation and communication, (2) the development of large-scale, distributed, and heterogeneous communication systems, and (3) the need for robust designs against uncertainties.

G. Koloniari · A. Sifaleras (✉)
Department of Applied Informatics, University of Macedonia, Thessaloniki, Greece
e-mail: gkoloniari@uom.gr; sifalera@uom.gr

© Springer Nature Switzerland AG 2019
A. Sifaleras, K. Petridis (eds.), *Operational Research in the Digital Era – ICT Challenges*, Springer Proceedings in Business and Economics,
https://doi.org/10.1007/978-3-319-95666-4_2

11

P2P networks consist of autonomous nodes that not only collaborate for sharing and consuming resources but also act independently and are governed by selfish motives. Users are generally selfish in nature, for instance, distributed mobile users tend to maximize their own performance, regardless of the other users, subsequently giving rise to competitive scenarios. Consequently, game-theoretic solutions are suitable for problems arising in P2P systems.

Cloud systems (Xinogalos et al. 2012) is another environment in which game-theoretic models find a natural application. In such systems, the cloud provider tries to maximize its profit and cloud users also expect to have the best resources available under their budget and time constraints. Therefore the allocation problem and the pricing strategies is one of the problems encountered in cloud systems that has been modeled using a game-theoretic approach.

Game-theoretic approaches have been widely studied in the context of design of communication networks (Akkarajitsakul et al. 2011; Niyato and Saad 2011; Shah et al. 2012), design of wireless sensor networks (Sengupta et al. 2010; Shi et al. 2012; Voulkidis et al. 2013), and other applications in network optimization (e.g., traffic networks) (Alpcan and Başar 2010; Laporte et al. 2010; Pozo et al. 2011). However, although there is work on game-theoretic models for P2P and cloud systems, there is a lack of a systematic classification.

In this paper, we survey recent developments in applying game-theoretic models and techniques to deal with problems encountered in P2P systems and cloud infrastructures. Our goal is to categorize the different approaches with respect to the problems they solve, in order to show the wide spectrum of issues involved in both P2P and cloud systems that are appropriate for game-theoretic solutions. By showcasing this wide variety, beyond a categorization of the related approaches, we also aim at indicating future application areas of game-theoretic approaches both in P2P and cloud systems, and other emerging domains exhibiting similar characteristics such as the Internet of Things (IoT) (Psannis et al. 2014).

The rest of the paper is structured as follows. In Sect. 2, we present recent developments in game-theoretic approaches grouped according to the sub-domains of P2P networks and cloud systems. Finally, Sect. 3 concludes the paper.

2   Recent Developments

This section presents the recent developments in a number of problems in P2P and cloud systems, namely (1) network formation, (2) content sharing and resource allocation, (3) routing and replication, (4) incentives, (5) video transmission over P2P, (6) security, (7) trust, and (8) privacy.

2.1 Network Formation

One of the first problems that was addressed based on game-theoretic modeling is the problem of P2P network formation. In P2P systems, each node (peer) in the network forms logical links to a selected subset of other nodes, its neighbors. Particularly in unstructured P2P systems, neighbor selection was initially random. However, as the routing and resource sharing algorithms use mainly variations of flooding and random walks to locate interesting resources, the neighbors of each node play a significant role in the performance of such algorithms.

Therefore, peer selection is modeled as a strategic game, in which each player (the peers) selects which peers to connect to so as to maximize their own lookup performance (Moscibroda et al. 2011). Though most works consider only selfish motives, altruistic ones have also been studied (Zhang et al. 2015). Alternative games aim at forming an overlay network consisting of groups (clusters) of peers (Koloniari and Pitoura 2012) which considers both selfish and altruistic peers or selecting super-peers in a hybrid P2P topology (Pitoura et al. 2013).

In all works, the cost function is the lookup performance and many factors are incorporated into its modeling such as the hop distance, network latency, the cost of links maintenance, the load distribution, availability, content locality, and also trust and even personal preferences if they are available.

The combination of the strategies each peer selects yields the final P2P topology. To measure the performance of the game-theoretic models, the price of anarchy is evaluated and also the existence of equilibria when those arise. Under selfish models there may or not be possible to attain one (Koloniari and Pitoura 2012; Moscibroda et al. 2011). Recent work has also explored the idea of bounded rationality players so as to better simulate the real-world context in which most decisions are based on limited information and the players have limited cognitive abilities (Kasthurirathna et al. 2016).

The game of peer selection has also been applied in slightly different networks that follow the P2P paradigm, especially wireless and mobile networks. In Namvar et al. (2015), the problem of peer selection is applied in Device-to-Device communications, where the goal is similarly to optimize the traffic offloading from the cellular level to the devices. Thus, the game is formulated as finding the optimal pairs of devices to link with each other.

2.2 Content Sharing and Resource Allocation

Content sharing is also a problem closely related to the network topology one we discussed above. After receiving or downloading a file, a peer needs to determine whether to share or cache the file. Each peer has to select between two strategies, either to share or not share the given file (Tao et al. 2010). The factors that influence the strategy selection take into account the upload capacity of each node, the available bandwidth, fairness among peers, and others. A complementary problem regards the incentives to limit selfish behaviors and is studied also when considering the strategies for sharing or not sharing resources (Wang et al. 2012). Also reputation models have been combined to the same end (Goswami et al. 2017). The problem becomes even more difficult considering the heterogeneity of the shared files. All files are not equally important or popular and each file may induce a different cost when cached.

Most approaches use evolutionary games to model the behavior of peers. Micro-macro dynamics reveal how the interactions about file caching among peers affect the caching condition in the whole system and agent-based dynamics are deployed (Matsuda et al. 2010). Superior strategies now spread on a hop-by-hop basis, through neighbors interactions.

In cloud environments, a similar problem is that of resource allocation where game-theoretic models are deployed for modeling dynamic resource allocation algorithms (Yuan et al. 2017; Thakur et al. 2015) that maximize the cloud providers profits.

In Garmehi and Analoui (2016), a hybrid system combining the benefits of P2P systems and content delivery networks utilizes an auction-based resource scheduling mechanism that is envy-free and relies on the economic modeling of the hybrid system and its users. The objective function that is maximized is defined as the net profit of the content providers.

A non-cooperative game is used to model the problem of content delivery between peer swarms belonging to different ISPs. Content delivery deploys a proportional-fairness mechanism and the authors prove that their system reaches equilibrium states that are suboptimal but adequate as the price of anarchy remains bounded (Parag et al. 2012).

2.3 Routing and Replication

Other issues related to content sharing and resource allocation that also determine the performance of a peer-to-peer system are routing and replication. The routing problem of discovering resources of interest is also closely related to the problem of network formation, as the network topology is what determines the routing algorithms deployed. The game consists of peers cooperating to discover desired resources. The peers decide between cooperation or not based on the costs involved and their potential rewards and various approaches modeling variations have been proposed (Mandapati and Kishore 2016; Khethavath et al. 2017).

A repeated game for modeling a distributed service discovery process is proposed in Mart-nez-Cnovas et al. (2016).The utility function of the players is based on network topological criteria and the distance to the search target. Also, an incentives-based mechanism is also used to avoid free-riding phenomenas. The authors show that under specific conditions the game between the collaborative players that discover and consume services reaches a Nash equilibrium.

Replica placement when done with global knowledge can optimally make decisions to improve the overall system performance. Game modeling has been applied to cope with local decisions based on limited knowledge, the selfish behavior of peers (Rzadca et al. 2010; Zuo and Zhang 2012), and even malicious behaviors (Guo and Bhattacharya 2016). Similar games have been deployed for other large-scale distributed networks that exhibit common characteristics with P2P systems (Rzadca et al. 2015; Liu et al. 2016).

2.4 Incentives

It is widely known that selfish behavior of peers leads to free-riders. Thus, in order to cope with free-riding usually incentives are offered to peers for increasing their contribution to the system. Such approaches include the following:

- *Punishment-based schemes: tit-for-tat* approach for file-sharing
- *Reward-based schemes*: money rebate from the service fee, virtual credits, reputation record

Other rewards schemes are as follows:

- *Payment-based schemes*: a pricing scheme is optimal if it induces a Pareto non-cooperative equilibrium, e.g., linear pricing.
- *Differential service*: in which peers obtain different qualities of service depending on their contribution levels.
- *Repeated game*: peers can reciprocate service to each other based on private or public history.
- *Intervention*: the system treats peers differentially based on their contribution to the system.

Recently, Sun et al. (2017) proposed a novel incentive mechanism using Accumulated-Payoff-Based Snowdrift Game (APBSG) model for the improvement of the cooperation frequency for P2P networks. Their study showed that their proposed APBSG model was able to reduce the sensitivity of cooperation to the selfishness of nodes, thus promoting the cooperative behavior in P2P network.

Also, Cui et al. (2015) verified the effectiveness of a reciprocation-based incentive mechanism, based on spatial evolutionary game theory. The authors proposed a transaction overlay network for modeling the transaction relationships of peers and tested various scenarios with heterogeneous and homogeneous benefits of services.

Furthermore, Kang and Wu (2015) formulated a Stackelberg game for maximizing the utilities of the downloaders and the revenue of the uploader, by considering peers' heterogeneity and selfish nature. The proposed resource allocation scheme was shown to be effective in stimulating the peers to make contribution to the P2P streaming system.

Other recent game-theoretic approaches regarding incentives include the works by Jin et al. (2015), Park and van der Schaar (2010), Wang et al. (2010), and Wu et al. (2013).

2.5   Video Transmission over P2P

There are peer-to-peer systems that are specifically designed for multimedia sharing. These systems take into account multimedia characteristics, and thus stringent delay constraints appear. Furthermore, video quality is not simply a function of the download rate. Regarding the upload credit rate, different pieces of the bitstream may have significantly different impact on the video quality. Also, credits allow peers to offer different prices for various parts of their multimedia content based on their perceived importance. A foresighted resource reciprocation game includes:

- A state of peer i represents the set of discretized received resources (in credits per state) from the peers in its group, i.e., its neighbors
- An action of peer i is its resource allocation (in credits per state) to the peers in its group
- The transition from a current state to a future state through an action is governed by the state transition probability that is learned online through the behavior of peers
- Reward R_i: The utility of peer i downloading its desired multimedia content from other peers in its group is defined as the total credit downloading rate.
- Reciprocation policy: Each individual peer's ultimate goal is to maximize the sum of its expected rewards to determine the best strategy

Such a game deals with the following issues:

- Free riders: free-riders are cut out using a credit line mechanism
- Delays: minimum-delay streaming is achieved by uploading data to the most deprived peers

Hu et al. (2017) formulated problems, raised in mobile social video sharing, as decentralized social utility maximization games. The authors presented a general framework for modeling the information diffusion and utility function of users on a public cloud-assisted architecture.

A game-based Adaptive Bitrate Streaming (ABR) method was recently proposed by Lin and Shen (2015). The authors formulated the bitrate adaptation problem in ABR as a non-cooperative Stackelberg game, where video-on-demand (VoD) service provider and the users are players. According to the presented experimental results it was shown that the proposed game-based method can save cloud bandwidth consumption and provide high user satisfaction, compared to other existing methods.

Mahini et al. (2016) suggested a new game-theoretic mechanism for P2P live video streaming. The objectives of the proposed framework are the minimization of loss rate in video data transmission and the prevention of free-riding. By analyzing the proposed game, the authors obtained a Nash equilibrium for the determination of a peer's best strategic response for participation in the video chunk distribution.

Other recent game-theoretic approaches regarding video transmission over P2P include the works by Asioli et al. (2012a,b), Maani et al. (2012), and Mostafavi and Dehghan (2016).

2.6 Security

P2P systems leverage network topology information to optimize performance. Nodes rely on information reported by a subset of participating nodes and on latency measurements. Malicious nodes can lie in the reports about their own latencies, or they can influence the measurements conducted by other nodes. A game-theoretical model allows us to assess the strategic interactions between the attacks and defenses, and to model an advanced adversary who knows how and what defense strategies are used, and can adjust his attack strategies accordingly.

Chen et al. (2012) suggested a two-player game-theoretic framework for modeling the fragments exchanging behavior between neighboring mobile peers. The goal of their work is to prevent Message Dropping Attacks (MDAs) in mobile P2P live streaming systems. Based on the experimental results, the authors showed that their strategy can prohibit mobile peers from cheating on their private information and dropping messages.

A randomized, game-theoretic approach for computing the optimal positioning of Intrusion Detection Systems (IDSs) in a P2P network was recently proposed by Narang and Hota (2015). Their method aims at minimizing the probability of a successful attack by randomly distributing the responsibility of running the IDSs between the peers.

Jin et al. (2017) implemented a repeated two-layer single-leader multi-follower game for obtaining a quantitative understanding of the fundamental tradeoff between the organizations' privacy and the intrusion detection accuracy. According to the findings of their game-theoretic analysis, the authors derived the expected behaviors of both the IDSs and the attacker and obtained the utility-privacy tradeoff curve.

Other recent game-theoretic approaches regarding security include the works by Becker et al. (2011) and Siwe and Tembine (2016).

2.7 Trust

Domingo-Ferrer et al. (2016) introduced the notion of co-utility and studied how existing protocols can become self-enforcing by including reputation mechanisms.

Also, the authors demonstrated a case study about a co-utile P2P privacy-preserving query submission to a database or web search engine.

Wang et al. (2015) proposed a trust measurement model based on game theory for addressing the problem of accurately calculating the trust degree in social networks. The effectiveness of the proposed trust measurement model was verified by simulation results. Furthermore, the authors also suggested a punishment mechanism for solving the free-riding problem in social networks.

Hawlitschek et al. (2016) presented an experimental framework with several applications regarding the trust game mechanics, (e.g., repeated interactions, experience, learning effects, or endowments and payment protocol) in the sharing economy.

Recently, Gao et al. (2017) applied a game theory approach in order to investigate the acceptance of a cloud data access control system based on reputation. Their findings indicate that the effectiveness of the proposed compensation and punishment mechanisms increased cloud storage rate and restrained dishonest system entities.

Other recent game-theoretic approaches regarding trust issues include the works by Chen et al. (2010), Gao and Guo (2012), and Xiang et al. (2010).

2.8 Privacy

As content sharing among the peers is one of the core functionalities of P2P systems, the problem of privacy perseverance is also a very important one. Cloud systems that offer storage and searching functionalities also deal with the same problem and privacy concerns also arise in cloud environments particularly in federated clouds.

Some limited work shows that game-theoretic models show promise when modeling the privacy problem as well. For preserving the privacy of location-based services a game that models a privacy-performance tradeoff has been designed (Jung et al. 2015). The main idea is using game theory to deal with free-riding phenomenas appearing during collaborative caching, where redundant query results need to be shared among users so as to achieve k-anonymity.

Another application is for multi-party secure computation to deal with collusion attacks (Wang and Cheung 2016). The paper presents a collusion deterrence game while modeling different players preferences so as to account for heterogeneous participants.

Also, combined with other methods such as cryptography, game-theoretic concepts have been exploited to deal with the problems of privacy in P2P systems focusing on the collaboration of the players and aiming for private content sharing (Bhaduri et al. 2007; Hong et al. 2016). In particular, in Bhaduri et al. (2007), data mining applications that may trigger privacy concerns are considered. The applications are modeled as multi-party games where each node selects different strategies for communication, computation, collusion, or privacy attacks depending on their expected gain.

In Hong et al. (2016), the authors consider devices on a microgrid and utilize a P2P energy exchange system to better utilize the available energy without burdening the main grid. The problem is modeled as a series of optimization problems, in which the peers aim to preserve their privacy using a secure communication protocol.

3 Conclusions and Future Work

A short survey of recent game-theoretic approaches applied in P2P networks was presented. The approaches were grouped according to the different application sub-domain of P2P networks and cloud systems. A variety of issues was presented, starting from issues in network design, resource allocation, and routing to issues related to security, trust, and privacy showing how versatile game-theoretic solutions can be.

Furthermore, the study of game-theoretic applications with an emphasis in the research area of Internet-of-Things (IoT) could be a very interesting future extension of this work.

References

Akkarajitsakul, K., Hossain, E., Niyato, D., & Kim, D.I. (2011). Game theoretic approaches for multiple access in wireless networks: A survey. *IEEE Communications Surveys & Tutorials, 13*(3), 372–395.

Alpcan, T., & Başar, T. (2010). Network security: A decision and game-theoretic approach. Cambridge: Cambridge University Press.

Asioli, S., Ramzan, N., & Izquierdo, E. (2012a). Exploiting social relationships for free-riders detection in minimum-delay P2P scalable video streaming. In *Proceedings of the 19th IEEE International Conference on Image Processing* (pp. 2257–2260). IEEE.

Asioli, S., Ramzan, N., & Izquierdo, E. (2012b). A game theoretic approach to minimum-delay scalable video transmission over P2P. *Signal Processing: Image Communication, 27*(5), 513–521.

Becker, S., Seibert, J., Zage, D., Nita-Rotaru, C., & State, R. (2011). Applying game theory to analyze attacks and defenses in virtual coordinate systems. In *Proceedings of the 41st IEEE/IFIP International Conference on Dependable Systems & Networks* (pp. 133–144).

Bhaduri, K., Das, K., & Kargupta, H. (2007). Peer-to-peer data mining, privacy issues, and games. In V. Gorodetsky, C. Zhang, V.A. Skormin, & L. Cao (Eds.), *Lecture Notes in Computer Science: Vol. 4476. Autonomous Intelligent Systems: Multi-Agents and Data Mining. AIS-ADM 2007*. Berlin: Springer.

Chen, L., Chen, H.w., Zhou, K., & Chen, J.X. (2010). A study of trust based on game theory in P2P networks. *Journal of Hubei University of Technology, 5*, 15.

Chen, J., Li, L., Zhang, Z., & Dong, X. (2012). Game theory analysis for message dropping attacks prevention strategy in mobile P2P live streaming system. In *Proceedings of the 3rd IEEE International Conference on Software Engineering and Service Science* (pp. 359–363).

Cui, G., Li, M., Wang, Z., Ren, J., Jiao, D., & Ma, J. (2015). Analysis and evaluation of incentive mechanisms in P2P networks: A spatial evolutionary game theory perspective. *Concurrency and Computation: Practice and Experience, 27*(12), 3044–3064.

Domingo-Ferrer, J., Farrs, O., Martnez, S., Snchez, D., & Soria-Comas, J. (2016). Self-enforcing protocols via co-utile reputation management. *Information Sciences, 367*, 159–175.

Gao, J., & Guo, Y. (2012). Research on P2P repeated game trust model based on unknown node type. In *Proceedings of the IEEE International Conference on Computer Science & Service System* (pp. 655–658).

Gao, L., Yan, Z., & Yang, L.T. (2017, to appear). Game theoretical analysis on acceptance of a cloud data access control system based on reputation. *IEEE Transactions on Cloud Computing*.

Garmehi, M., & Analoui, M. (2016). Envy-free resource allocation and request routing in hybrid CDN–P2P networks. *Journal of Network and Systems Management, 24*(4), 884–915.

Goswami, A., Gupta, R., & Parashari, G.S. (2017). Reputation-based resource allocation in P2P systems: A game theoretic perspective. *IEEE Communications Letters, 21*(6), 1273–1276.

Guo, M., & Bhattacharya, P. (2016). Mechanism design for replica placement in peer-assisted content delivery networks with heterogeneous behavior models. In *Proceedings of the 40th IEEE Annual Computer Software and Applications Conference* (Vol. 1, pp. 500–501).

Hawlitschek, F., Teubner, T., Adam, M.T.P., Borchers, N.S., Moehlmann, M., & Weinhardt, C. (2016). Trust in the sharing economy: An experimental framework. In *Proceedings of the 37th International Conference on Information Systems*. Dublin, Ireland.

Hong, Y., Goel, S., & Liu, W.M. (2016). An efficient and privacy-preserving scheme for P2P energy exchange among smart microgrids. *International Journal of Energy Research, 40*(3), 313–331.

Hu, H., Wen, Y., & Niyato, D. (2017). Public cloud storage-assisted mobile social video sharing: A supermodular game approach. *IEEE Journal on Selected Areas in Communications, 35*(3), 545–556.

Jin, X., Li, M., Cui, G., Liu, J., Guo, C., Gao, Y., Wang, B., & Tan, X. (2015). RIMBED: Recommendation incentive mechanism based on evolutionary dynamics in P2P networks. In *Proceedings of the 24th International Conference on Computer Communication and Networks* (pp. 1–8).

Jin, R., He, X., & Dai, H. (2017). On the tradeoff between privacy and utility in collaborative intrusion detection systems-a game theoretical approach. In *Proceedings of the Hot Topics in Science of Security: Symposium and Bootcamp, HoTSoS* (pp. 45–51). New York: ACM.

Jung, K., Jo, S., & Park, S. (2015). A game theoretic approach for collaborative caching techniques in privacy preserving location-based services. In *Proceedings of the International Conference on Big Data and Smart Computing* (pp. 59–62).

Kang, X., & Wu, Y. (2015). Incentive mechanism design for heterogeneous peer-to-peer networks: A Stackelberg game approach. *IEEE Transactions on Mobile Computing, 14*(5), 1018–1030.

Kasthurirathna, D., Piraveenan, M., & Uddin, S. (2016). Modeling networked systems using the topologically distributed bounded rationality framework. *Complexity, 21*(S2), 123–137.

Khethavath, P., Thomas, J.P., & Chan-tin, E. (2017). Towards an efficient distributed cloud computing architecture. *Peer-to-Peer Networking and Applications, 10*(5), 1152–1168.

Koloniari, G., & Pitoura, E. (2012). A game-theoretic approach to the formation of clustered overlay networks. *IEEE Transactions on Parallel and Distributed Systems, 23*(4), 589–597.

Kurve, A., Griffin, C., Miller, D.J., & Kesidis, G. (2013). Optimizing cluster formation in super-peer networks via local incentive design. *Peer-to-Peer Networking and Applications, 8*, 1–21.

Laporte, G., Mesa, J.A., & Perea, F. (2010). A game theoretic framework for the robust railway transit network design problem. *Transportation Research Part B: Methodological, 44*(4), 447–459.

Lin, Y., & Shen, H. (2015). Autotune: game-based adaptive bitrate streaming in P2P-assisted cloud-based VoD systems. In *Proceedings of the IEEE International Conference on Peer-to-Peer Computing (P2P)* (pp. 1–10).

Liu, Z., Li, J., Esposito, C., Castiglione, A., & Palmieri, F. (2016). Optimal data replica placement in large-scale federated architectures. In G. Wang, I. Ray, J.M. Alcaraz Calero, & S.M. Thampi

(Eds.), *Proceedings of the International Conference on Security, Privacy and Anonymity in Computation, Communication and Storage* (pp. 257–267). Zhangjiajie: Springer.

Maani, E., Chen, Z., & Katsaggelos, A.K. (2012). A game theoretic approach to video streaming over peer-to-peer networks. *Signal Processing: Image Communication, 27*(5), 545–554.

Mahini, H., Dehghan, M., Navidi, H., & Masoud Rahmani, A. (2016). Game-plive: A new game theoretic mechanism for P2P live video streaming. *International Journal of Communication Systems, 29*(6), 1187–1203.

Mandapati, S., & Kishore, V.R. (2016). Improved file search and sharing mechanism in structured P2P systems. *International Journal of Research in Computer and Communication Technology, 5*(8), 421–424.

Mart-nez-Cnovas, G., Val, E.D., Botti, V., Hernndez, P., & Rebollo, M. (2016). A formal model based on game theory for the analysis of cooperation in distributed service discovery. *Information Sciences, 326*, 59–70.

Matsuda, Y., Sasabe, M., & Takine, T. (2010). Evolutionary game theory-based evaluation of P2P file-sharing systems in heterogeneous environments. *International Journal of Digital Multimedia Broadcasting, 2010*, 12.

Moscibroda, T., Schmid, S., & Wattenhofer, R. (2011). Topological implications of selfish neighbor selection in unstructured peer-to-peer networks. *Algorithmica, 61*(2), 419–446.

Mostafavi, S., & Dehghan, M. (2016). Game-theoretic auction design for bandwidth sharing in helper-assisted P2P streaming. *International Journal of Communication Systems, 29*(6), 1057–1072.

Namvar, N., Bahadori, N., & Afghah, F. (2015). Context-aware D2D peer selection for load distribution in LTE networks. In *Proceedings of the 49th Asilomar Conference on Signals, Systems and Computers* (pp. 464–468).

Narang, P., & Hota, C. (2015). Game-theoretic strategies for IDS deployment in peer-to-peer networks. *Information Systems Frontiers, 17*(5), 1017–1028.

Niyato, D., & Saad, W. (2011). *Game theory in wireless and communication networks: Theory, models, and applications*. Cambridge: Cambridge University Press.

Parag, P., Shakkottai, S., & Menache, I. (2012). Service routing in multi-ISP peer-to-peer content distribution: Local or remote? In *International Conference on Game Theory for Networks* (pp. 353–368).

Park, J., & van der Schaar, M. (2010). A game theoretic analysis of incentives in content production and sharing over peer-to-peer networks. *IEEE Journal of Selected Topics in Signal Processing, 4*(4), 704–717.

Pozo, M., Manuel, C., González-Arangüena, E., & Owen, G. (2011). Centrality in directed social networks. A game theoretic approach. *Social Networks, 33*(3), 191–200.

Psannis, K., Xinogalos, S., & Sifaleras, A. (2014). Convergence of internet of things and mobile cloud computing. *Systems Science & Control Engineering: An Open Access Journal, 2*(1), 476–483.

Rzadca, K., Datta, A., & Buchegger, S. (2010). Replica placement in p2p storage: Complexity and game theoretic analyses. In *Proceedings of the 30th IEEE International Conference on Distributed Computing Systems* (pp. 599–609).

Rzadca, K., Datta, A., Kreitz, G., & Buchegger, S. (2015). Game-theoretic mechanisms to increase data availability in decentralized storage systems. *ACM Transactions on Autonomous and Adaptive Systems, 10*(3), 14:1–14:32.

Sengupta, S., Chatterjee, M., & Kwiat, K.A. (2010). A game theoretic framework for power control in wireless sensor networks. *IEEE Transactions on Computers, 59*(2), 231–242.

Shah, I., Jan, S., Khan, I., & Qamar, S. (2012). An overview of game theory and its applications in communication networks. *International Journal of Multidisciplinary Sciences and Engineering 3*(4), 5–11.

Shi, H.Y., Wang, W.L., Kwok, N.M., & Chen, S.Y. (2012). Game theory for wireless sensor networks: A survey. *Sensors, 12*(7), 9055–9097.

Siwe, A.T., & Tembine, H. (2016). Network security as public good: A mean-field-type game theory approach. In *Proceedings of the 13th International Multi-Conference on Systems, Signals Devices* (pp. 601–606).

Sun, R., Li, W., Zhang, H., & Ren, Y. (2017). An incentive mechanism for P2P network using accumulated-payoff based snowdrift game model. In J. Cheng, E. Hossain, H. Zhang, W. Saad, & M. Chatterjee (Eds.), *Proceedings of the 6th International Conference on Game Theory for Networks* (pp. 122–132). Kelowna: Springer.

Tao, K., Zhang, W., Zhong, H., & Zhang, X. (2010). A fair allocation and sharing incentive approach in P2P network based on supervising game. In *Proceedings of the 3rd IET International Conference on Wireless, Mobile and Multimedia Networks* (pp. 339–343).

Thakur, P.K., Thomas, M.V., & Chandrasekaran, K. (2015). An efficient game-theoretic approach for resource management in cloud federation. In *Proceedings of the International Conference on Emerging Research in Electronics, Computer Science and Technology* (pp. 70–75).

Voulkidis, A.C., Anastasopoulos, M.P., & Cottis, P.G. (2013). Energy efficiency in wireless sensor networks: A game-theoretic approach based on coalition formation. *ACM Transactions on Sensor Networks, 9*(4), 43.

Wang, Z., & Cheung, S.-c.S. (2016). On privacy preference in collusion-deterrence games for secure multi-party computation. In *Proceedings of the IEEE International Conference on Acoustics, Speech and Signal Processing* (pp. 2044–2048).

Wang, C., Chen, L., Chen, H., & Zhou, K. (2010). Incentive mechanism based on game theory in P2P networks. In *Proceedings of the 2nd IEEE International Conference on Information Technology and Computer Science* (pp. 190–193).

Wang, T.M., Lee, W.T., Wu, T.Y., Wei, H.W., & Lin, Y.S. (2012). New P2P sharing incentive mechanism based on social network and game theory. In *Proceedings of the 26th IEEE International Conference on Advanced Information Networking and Applications Workshops* (pp. 915–919).

Wang, Y., Cai, Z., Yin, G., Gao, Y., & Pan, Q. (2015). A trust measurement in social networks based on game theory. In M.T. Thai, N.P. Nguyen, & H. Shen (Eds.), *Proceedings of the 4th International Conference on Computational Social Networks* (pp. 236–247). Beijing: Springer.

Wu, W., Lui, J.C., & Ma, R.T. (2013). On incentivizing upload capacity in P2P-VoD systems: Design, analysis and evaluation. *Computer Networks, 57*(7), 1674–1688.

Xiang, X.B., Zeng, G.S., & Xia, D.M. (2010). Game model for trust establishing and steady-state analysis in P2P file-sharing environments. *Application Research of Computers, 9*, 081.

Xinogalos, S., Psannis, K.E., & Sifaleras, A. (2012). Recent advances delivered by HTML 5 in mobile cloud computing applications: A survey. In *Proceedings of the ACM International Conference Proceeding Series* (pp. 199–204).

Yuan, X., Min, G., Yang, L.T., Ding, Y., & Fang, Q. (2017). A game theory-based dynamic resource allocation strategy in geo-distributed datacenter clouds. *Future Generation Computer Systems, 76*, 63–72.

Zhang, G.Y., Liu, Y., & He, J.Z. (2015). MP2P resource node selection strategy based on altruism and bayesian game. *Applied Mechanics and Materials: Sensors, Measurement, Intelligent Materials and Technologies III, 738*, 1160–1168, Zürich: Trans Tech Publications.

Zuo, F., & Zhang, W. (2012). A game theoretic schema for overcoming selfish allocation in P2P file application. In *Proceedings of the 12th IEEE International Conference on Computer and Information Technology* (pp. 541–548).

A Proactive Model for Joint Maintenance and Logistics Optimization in the Frame of Industrial Internet of Things

Alexandros Bousdekis and Gregoris Mentzas

Abstract Equipment failures in manufacturing processes concern industries because they can lead to severe issues regarding human safety, environmental impact, reliability, and production costs. The stochastic nature of equipment degradation and the uncertainty about future breakdowns affect significantly the maintenance and inventory decisions. Proactive event processing can facilitate this decision-making process in an Industrial Internet of Things (IIoT) environment, but real-time data processing poses several challenges in efficiency and scalability of the associated information systems. Therefore, appropriate real-time, event-driven algorithms and models are required for deciding on the basis of predictions, ahead of time. We propose a proactive event-driven model for joint maintenance and logistics optimization in a sensor-based, data-rich industrial environment. The proposed model is able to be embedded in a real-time, event-driven information system in order to be triggered by prediction events about the future equipment health state. Moreover, the proposed model handles multiple alternative (imperfect and perfect) maintenance actions and associated spare parts orders and facilitates proactive decision making in the context of Condition-Based Maintenance (CBM). The proposed proactive decision model was validated in real industrial environment and was further evaluated with a comparative and a sensitivity analysis.

Keywords Proactivity · Event processing · IIoT · Condition-Based Maintenance · Spare parts ordering · Decision making · Predictive maintenance

A. Bousdekis (✉) · G. Mentzas
Information Management Unit (IMU), Institute of Communication and Computer Systems (ICCS), National Technical University of Athens (NTUA), Athens, Greece
e-mail: albous@mail.ntua.gr

© Springer Nature Switzerland AG 2019
A. Sifaleras, K. Petridis (eds.), *Operational Research in the Digital Era – ICT Challenges*, Springer Proceedings in Business and Economics,
https://doi.org/10.1007/978-3-319-95666-4_3

1 Introduction

Equipment failures in manufacturing processes concern industries because they can lead to severe issues regarding human safety, environmental impact, reliability, and production costs. The stochastic nature of equipment degradation and the uncertainty about future breakdowns affect significantly the decision-making process of experts in the context of Condition-Based Maintenance (CBM) strategy (Elwany and Gebraeel 2008; Lorén and de Maré 2015). To this end, mathematical modelling methods can be embedded in information systems capable of processing and analyzing real-time big data with the aim to facilitate decision making ahead of time for optimizing the maintenance and spare parts inventory operations. These methods can contribute to the Decide phase of the "Detect-Predict-Decide-Act" proactive principle. The e-maintenance concept can significantly enhance proactive decision making in maintenance-driven operations management. However, despite the increasing capabilities of e-technologies, maximizing the e-maintenance benefits for the overall maintenance efficiency requires more than technology (Guillén et al. 2016). There is the need for models and methods capable of being embedded in real-time systems triggered by real-time prognostic information in an event processing, streaming computational environment. Maintenance and inventory management are strongly interconnected and should both be considered simultaneously when optimizing a company's operations (Van Horenbeek et al. 2013). The decision about proactive maintenance actions requires a balance between the cost due to premature action and the cost of unexpected breakdown, while the ordering time of spare parts and their stocking quantities need to be planned so that holding costs are minimized by avoiding, at the same time, stock-outs (Elwany and Gebraeel 2008; Bohlin and Wärja 2015).

Real-time data processing for proactive decision making poses several challenges in efficiency and scalability of the associated information systems. Currently, most of such models and methods can be run offline or on the basis of batches of data at specific sampling times. Although there are research works dealing with extracting insights about current and future situation of business processes, decision making on the basis of real-time, event-driven predictive analytics is still an unexplored area. More specifically, rarely joint maintenance and logistics decision models are real-time and event-driven, while they usually provide recommendations about a pre-defined maintenance action (assuming perfect maintenance) with its associated pre-defined order of spare parts.

We propose a proactive event-driven decision model for joint maintenance and logistics optimization in the frame of Industrial Internet of Things (IIoT). The proposed model is triggered by prognostic information in an event processing computational environment on the basis of sensor-generated real-time data. Unlike other approaches, the proposed model incorporates multiple alternative maintenance actions since the recommended proactive maintenance actions address perfect and various degrees of imperfect maintenance, while each one is mapped to the associated order of spare parts. The proposed decision model incorporates a

Markov Decision Process (MDP) model capable of being embedded in event-driven information systems for scalable proactive decision making regarding maintenance and logistics actions.

The rest of the paper is organized as follows. Section 2 presents a literature review about sensor-generated real-time data and proactive event-driven computing as well as joint optimization of maintenance and logistics. Section 3 describes the proposed proactive decision model for joint maintenance and logistics optimization in the frame of Industrial Internet of Things. Section 4 presents the deployment of an information system incorporating the aforementioned model, while Sect. 5 presents the evaluation results. Finally, Sect. 6 concludes the paper and discusses the future work.

2 Literature Review

2.1 Industrial Internet of Things and Proactive Event-Driven Computing in Manufacturing Enterprises

Sensors deployment for measuring temperature, vibration, pressure, etc., is continuously increasing in industries since it enhances their monitoring capabilities by integrating various devices equipped with sensing, identification, processing, communication, and networking capabilities (Bi et al. 2014). To this end, the Industrial Internet of Things (IIoT) paradigm has been evolved. IIoT requires the emergence of IT architectures and infrastructure in order to support the real-time, scalable handling, processing, and storage of increasingly growing amounts of sensor data gathered from various and heterogeneous sources (Bousdekis et al. 2015a). Sensing devices can detect state changes of objects or conditions (e.g., degradation of manufacturing equipment) and create events, which can then be processed by a system or service for providing meaningful insights. Consequently, the real-time, event-driven information systems have been facilitated by the development of sensor technology, the expansion of broadband connectivity and the emergence of predictive analytics (Lee et al. 2014) using a web-service communication paradigm (Theorin et al. 2016).

Event-driven architectures are able to close the business–ICT gap by delivering appropriate business functionality and enabling interconnectivity at an object level (Potocnik and Juric 2014; Zimmermann et al. 2015). Unlike previous paradigms which send requests and wait for responses (responsive computing) (Etzion and Niblett 2010) or others that require continuous update of all the system components each time a sensor measurement is gathered (near real-time computing) (Elwany and Gebraeel 2008), in event-driven systems, that are reactive in nature, processing is triggered on the basis of events for scalable and efficient real-time big data processing. The development of appropriate models and methodologies contributed significantly to the expansion of reactive event-driven systems. A similar contribution is necessary for the expansion of proactive computing. Proactivity refers to the ability to avoid or eliminate the impact of undesired future events, or to exploit future opportunities, by applying predictive models combined with real-time sensor data and automated decision-making technologies (Engel et al. 2012). A crucial concept in proactive computing is the proactive Event Processing Network, which consists of various types of processing elements called proactive Event Processing Agents, aiming to support processing of predicted events as well as actions and actuators as part of the model. Proactive event-driven computing indicates the use of event-driven applications for real-time predictions and decisions ahead of time, before a critical event occurs, according to the "Detect-Predict-Decide-Act" principle (Engel et al. 2012; Feldman et al. 2013; Sejdovic et al. 2016). Each phase is implemented as an Event Processing Agent. There is a large variety of methods, algorithms, and information systems dealing with the Detect and the Predict phase; however, the Decide and Act phases have not been extensively explored (Bousdekis et al. 2015b).

2.2 Joint Maintenance and Logistics Optimization

Companies keep inventories of spare parts in order to have availability in case of maintenance. The amount of spare parts in inventory depends on the demand, i.e., the corrective, preventive, and predictive maintenance actions requiring the associated spare parts. Therefore, maintenance and inventory management are strongly interconnected and should both be considered simultaneously when optimizing a company's operations (Van Horenbeek et al. 2013). For this reason, the field of joint maintenance and logistics optimization has gathered research interest with the aim to take into account the trade-off between CBM implementation and spare parts ordering policies (Van Horenbeek et al. 2013; Basten et al. 2015), although there are relatively few contributions until now (Keizer et al. 2017).

Since CBM is a proactive maintenance strategy, its implementation can take place according to the "Detect-Predict-Decide-Act" proactive principle for event-driven computing (Bousdekis et al. 2015b) through a digital transformation for adapting manufacturing operations driven by the maintenance function. To this end, the e-maintenance concept can exploit the IIoT paradigm in order to enable proactive decision making in the context of CBM. E-maintenance is referred to the emergence of technologies which are able to optimize maintenance-related workflows and the integration of business performance enabling openness and interoperation of e-maintenance with other components of e-enterprise (Guillén et al. 2016). However, apart from the e-technologies, there is the need for models and methods in order to make e-maintenance a key element to satisfy operational requirements, to improve production system performance and to support inventory and operation guidance, beyond simple notifications and warnings (Muller et al. 2008; Pistofidis et al. 2012; Bousdekis et al. 2015a; Guillén et al. 2016).

The problem of joint maintenance and logistics optimization has gathered a lot of interest from different perspectives. Several decision methods have been used and formulated according to the problem at hand. Several research works have made use of simulation models (e.g., Monte Carlo simulation and discrete event simulation) (Sarker and Haque 2000; Hu et al. 2008; Wang 2012), while multi-objective models have also been considered (Nosoohi and Hejazi 2011). In the last years, the use of condition monitoring has been widely investigated. Therefore, methods for continuous review (s, S) of ordering policies (Xie and Wang 2008; Wang et al. 2012; Keizer et al. 2017) as well as sensor-driven cost risk-based models (Wu et al. 2007; Elwany and Gebraeel 2008) have been developed. However, the decision models existing in the literature are subjected to the limitations presented in Sect. 2.3.

2.3 Existing Limitations and beyond the State of the Art

Existing research works in joint maintenance and logistics optimization use reliability distributions given by the manufacturer specification or derived from experimental setups or collected in real-time through sensors in laboratory environment. Moreover, almost all published papers on this domain consider the implementation of CBM by taking into account the current level of degradation, but not the prediction about the future degradation, the future failure or other prognostic information. So, joint maintenance and spare parts decision models have not been coupled with algorithms for real-time, event-driven prognostics, as a consequence of a general lack of methods for the Decide phase of the proactive principle. Such an approach could support manufacturing companies to minimize their major costs, since a decrease in spare parts inventory cost is among the most significant indirect benefits provided by CBM (Van Horenbeek et al. 2013). Therefore, due to the availability of real-time prognostics, CBM actions can be recommended and spare parts can be ordered Just-In-Time. On the other hand, the equipment downtime may be affected by logistics-related delays, while the time needed for finishing the implementation of the appropriate maintenance actions is rarely accurately known (Van Horenbeek et al. 2013). Finally, the vast majority of published papers assume that the parts of equipment are perfectly maintained after a pre-defined action implementation or do not mention any assumption regarding the degree of restoration (Van Horenbeek et al. 2013).

To overcome the aforementioned limitations, the proposed model is triggered by prognostic information in an event processing computational environment on the basis of sensor-generated real-time data. Unlike other approaches, it incorporates multiple alternative proactive (perfect and imperfect) maintenance actions and spare parts orders. Moreover, it incorporates an MDP model handling transition probabilities distribution functions of time, while, in the place of state rewards, there are costs as functions of action implementation time. Consequently, its output is an action-time policy instead of an action-state policy. Overall, the proposed model takes advantage of proactive event-driven computing and is capable of being embedded in event-driven information systems for scalable proactive decision making in terms of maintenance and logistics actions.

3 The Proposed Model

3.1 Overview

We contribute to the Decide phase of the proactive principle by proposing a proactive event-driven decision model for joint maintenance and logistics optimization supported by the IIoT technology. The proposed model can be embedded in a real-time, event processing information system in order to: (1) be configured (at design time) by the user with the aim to insert the required domain knowledge; and (2) be triggered (at runtime) by real-time prognostic information in the form of a prediction event. Its output is a set of recommendations about the optimal mitigating (perfect or imperfect) maintenance action (out of a list of alternative actions) along with its implementation time and the optimal order of spare parts that are related to this action along with the optimal ordering time.

At design time, the decision maker inserts domain knowledge with the aim to define and configure the various parameters of the proactive decision model. The domain knowledge is entered to the model through equipment instances, which are specific instances corresponding to a specific part of equipment to which the predicted failure corresponds. Domain knowledge entered by users corresponds to the proposed model's input parameters and includes the cost of the equipment failure (e.g., breakdown), the alternative actions along with their cost parameters, and the new lifetime after the action implementation (i.e., how much time each action prolongs the lifetime of the equipment) as well as the decision horizon (e.g., next planned maintenance). The latter is defined by the end of decision epoch, i.e., the time after which the effect of the predicted undesired event fades and the probability of its occurrence returns to normal (Engel et al. 2012). The action-related cost parameters deal with two factors: the cost of action implementation and the cost of action effect (after the action implementation). These two factors apply in both maintenance and inventory aspects and are expressed as a function of implementation time, because actions often affect operation until some specific future time (e.g., taking machinery down to maintenance and losing the rest of the working week). In this sense, the cost is a decreasing function in the activation time.

The real-time prognostic information is received in the form of a prediction event from the Predict phase and includes the probability distribution function (PDF) of the failure occurrence along with its associated parameters. The proposed decision model takes advantage of the basic model for proactive event-driven computing (Engel et al. 2012) and extends it in order to address the joint optimization of maintenance and spare parts ordering in a proactive way when there are multiple alternative maintenance actions and associated spare parts orders. To this end, an MDP model is used and is formulated accordingly.

3.2 The Mathematical Formulation for the Proposed Decision Model

The proposed proactive event-driven decision model for joint maintenance and logistics optimization is formulated according to the proactive approach (Engel et al. 2012). Therefore, the output of the MDP is not a policy consisting of an action-state pair, but a policy of an action-time pair, and therefore, the Bellman equation is structured accordingly. The proposed proactive decision model is able to provide recommendations about when to take which action provided that the cost of taking the action and/or the cost of the action effect changes over time. To do this, it incorporates the transition probability distributions as a function of implementation time. The state rewards of the MDP correspond to the costs as functions of implementation time. Consequently, the result is the action with the minimum expected loss (instead of the maximum utility) and the optimal time of applying it. The expected loss function of each action is estimated by using the backward induction algorithm for finite horizon problems (Watkins and Dayan 1992) and the Bellman equation is minimized with respect to time. The proactive formulation of the MDP model is solved for both maintenance and logistics so that the resulting expected loss functions are jointly optimized.

Figure 1 shows an example of the proactive MDP formulation for joint maintenance and logistics optimization for three alternative actions. On the basis of this formulation, for arbitrary number of actions, the equations of the joint decision model are derived, i.e., the maintenance equation (for each maintenance mitigating action) and the spare parts ordering equation (for each order associated with the respective maintenance mitigating action). Both of them are derived in relation to the predicted failure, but there are different transition probability functions and state rewards in the same formulation, depicted in Fig. 1. The state rewards correspond to the maintenance costs (i.e., cost of failure, cost of action implementation, and cost of action effect) for each alternative action and the inventory costs (i.e., shortage cost, holding cost) associated with each maintenance action along with their lead times. Table 1 shows the explanation of the proposed decision model's variables.

Maintenance Expected Loss Function

For the maintenance equation, based on the aforementioned MDP formulation, there is no cost (or benefit) of being at state S_n, hence $EL(S_n) = 0$. In state f, there is a penalty of C_f (i.e., the cost of failure), hence $EL(S_f) = C_f$. In state e_i we

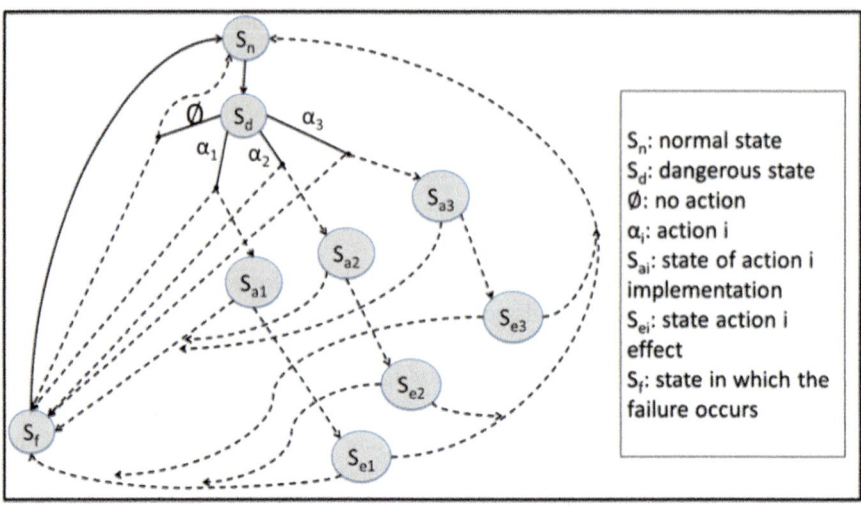

	S_n: normal state
	S_d: dangerous state
	$\emptyset$: no action
	α_i: action i
	S_{ai}: state of action i implementation
	S_{ei}: state action i effect
	S_f: state in which the failure occurs

Fig. 1 An example of the proactive MDP formulation for joint maintenance and logistics optimization

Table 1 Explanation of the proposed model's variables

Variable	Explanation
$P^f(t_1, t_2)$	Probability distribution function that the failure f occurs within the time interval (t_1, t_2) conditioned on not occurring until time t_1
$P_a^f(t_1, t_2)$	Probability distribution function that the failure f occurs within the time interval (t_1, t_2) conditioned on not occurring until time t_1 and assuming that the action a has been implemented exactly at time t_1
$EL^{a_i}(t)$	Expected loss function for maintenance action a_i
C_f	Cost of failure
$C_{e_i}(t)$	Cost function of the action effect
$C_{a_i}(t)$	Cost function of the action implementation
EL^{o_i}	Expected loss function for spare parts order o_i
C_{sp}	Cost of buying the spare parts
$C_s(t)$	Cost function of shortage inventory
L	Lead time between the time of placing the order up and the time of receiving the order
T	Decision horizon

incur penalty of $C_{e_i}\left(t_{e_i}\right)$ (i.e., the cost function of the action effect) and, given the probability to move to state f, the policy evaluation gives:

$$EL\left(S_{e_i}\right) = C_e\left(t_{e_i}\right) + P\left(S_{e_i}, S_f\right) * EL\left(S_f\right) = C_{e_i}\left(t_{e_i}\right) + P\left(S_{e_i}, S_f\right) * C_f$$

In state a_i, there is a penalty of $C_{a_i}\left(t_{a_i}\right)$ (i.e., the cost function of the action implementation) and given the probability to move to state f the policy evaluation gives:

$$EL\left(S_{a_i}\right) = C_{a_i}\left(t_{a_i}\right) + P\left(S_{a_i}, S_f\right) * EL\left(S_f\right) + P\left(S_{a_i}, S_{e_i}\right) * EL\left(S_{e_i}\right)$$
$$= C_{a_i}\left(t_{a_i}\right) + P\left(S_{a_i}, S_f\right) * C_f + P\left(S_{a_i}, S_{e_i}\right) * \left[C_{e_i}\left(t_{e_i}\right) + P\left(S_{e_i}, S_f\right) * C_f\right]$$

Finally, the state S_d has not any penalty itself. Therefore, the expected loss is computed as follows:

$$EL\left(S_d\right) = P\left(S_d, S_{a_i}\right) * EL\left(S_{a_i}\right) + P\left(S_d, S_f\right) * EL\left(S_f\right)$$
$$= P\left(S_d, S_{a_i}\right) * \left\{C_{a_i}\left(t_{a_i}\right) + P\left(S_{a_i}, S_f\right) * C_f + P\left(S_{a_i}, S_{e_i}\right) * \left[C_{e_i}\left(t_{e_i}\right)\right]\right\}$$
$$+P\left(S_{e_i}, S_f\right) * C_f\right]\right\} + P\left(S_d, S_f\right) * C_f$$

Consequently, the expected loss function for each mitigating maintenance action is derived from Eq. (1):

$$EL^{a_i} = P\left(S_d, S_{a_i}\right) * \left\{C_{a_i}\left(t_{a_i}\right) + P\left(S_{a_i}, S_f\right) * C_f + P\left(S_{a_i}, S_{e_i}\right) * \left[C_{e_i}\left(t_{e_i}\right)\right]\right\}$$
$$+P\left(S_{e_i}, S_f\right) * C_f\right]\right\} + P\left(S_d, S_f\right) * C_f \qquad (1)$$

Let EL^0 denote the expected loss of taking no action. Backward induction for this policy gives:
$$EL^0(S_d) = P(S_d, S_n) * EL^0(S_n) + P^0(S_d, S_f) * EL^0(S_f) = P^0(S_d, S_f) * C_f$$
The transition probabilities from S_d to S_f or S_{a_i} are:

$$P\left(S_d, S_f\right) = P^f\left(t_0, t_{a_i}\right)$$

$$P\left(S_d, S_{a_i}\right) = 1 - P^f\left(t_0, t_{a_i}\right)$$

To proceed from a_i to e_i, probabilities are given by:

$$P\left(S_{a_i}, S_f\right) = P^f\left(t_{a_i}, t_{e_i}\right)$$

$$P\left(S_{a_i}, S_{e_i}\right) = 1 - P^f\left(t_{a_i}, t_{e_i}\right)$$

that is, we move to S_{e_i} if f does not occur between the time the action is applied until the time it takes effect. The transition from S_{a_i} to S_f occurs with the complementary probability.

Finally, the distribution over the event occurrence in state ei is denoted by:

$$P\left(S_{e_i}, S_f\right) = P^f_{e_i}\left(t_{e_i}, T\right)$$

T indicates the decision horizon, i.e., the end of decision epoch. If no action is taken, the probability to go to state f is the probability of the event occurrence over the entire interval:

$$P^0\left(S_d, S_f\right) = P^f\left(t_0, T\right)$$

And $P^0(S_d, S_n)$ is the complementary probability.

Therefore, Eq. (1) is transformed to the expression of Eq. (2):

$$
EL^{a_i} = \left[1 - P^f\left(t_0, t_{a_i}\right)\right] * \left\{C_{a_i}\left(t_{a_i}\right)\right\}
$$

$$
+ P^f\left(t_{a_i}, t_{e_i}\right) * C_f + \left[1 - P^f\left(t_{a_i}, t_{e_i}\right)\right] * \left[C_{e_i}\left(t_{e_i}\right)\right]
$$

$$
+ P_{a_i}^f\left(t_{e_i}, T\right) * C_f\right\} + P^f\left(t_0, t_{a_i}\right) * C_f \tag{2}
$$

Equation (2) expresses the expected loss of each mitigating maintenance action. The minimization of the expected loss functions of all the alternative actions with respect to implementation time provides a recommendation about the optimal action (the action with the global minimum) and the optimal time for its implementation (the time when the expected loss has its global minimum). In Eq. (2), there is the cost function of the action implementation $C_{a_i}\left(t_{a_i}\right)$ (i.e., how much the process of action implementation costs—e.g., cost of spare parts, technician pay rate, etc.) and the cost function of the action effect $C_{e_i}\left(t_{e_i}\right)$ (i.e., how much the result of the action costs—e.g., cost of operating at reduced equipment load). Provided that an estimation of the duration of action implementation is known, $t_{a_i} = t$ and $t_{e_i} = t + \Delta t$, where t indicates the time of action implementation. The polynomial of the action cost function of implementation as well as the initial estimation of the duration of action implementation can be continuously updated through SEF, as we are explaining below. In addition, t_0 is considered equal to 0. Consequently, Eq. (2) is transformed to Eq. (3):

$$
EL^{a_i}(t) = \left[1 - P^f\left(t_0, t\right)\right] * \left\{C_{a_i}(t) + P^f\right\}
$$

$$
(t, t + \Delta t) * C_f + \left[1 - P^f\left(t, t + \Delta t\right)\right] * \left[C_{e_i}\left(t + \Delta t\right)\right]
$$

$$
+ P_{a_i}^f\left(t + \Delta t, T\right) * C_f\right\} + P^f\left(t_0, t\right) * C_f \tag{3}
$$

Considering a fixed cost function of action implementation and the time periods to which the cost function of action effect corresponds, Eq. (3) is transformed to:

$$
EL^{a_i}(t) = \left[1 - P^f\left(t_0, t\right)\right] * \left\{C_{a_i} + P^f\left(t, t + \Delta t\right) *
$$

$$C_f + \left[1 - P^f (t, t + \Delta t)\right] * \left[C_{e_i} (T - t - \Delta t)\right.$$

$$\left. + P^f_{a_i} (t + \Delta t, T) * C_f\right]\right\} + P^f (t_0, t) * C_f \qquad (4)$$

Logistics Expected Loss Function

Similarly to the previous calculations, the logistics-related equation (dealing with spare parts ordering) for each alternative maintenance action is derived from backwards induction algorithm on the basis of the same MDP formulation. In this case, there is a shortage inventory cost function $C_s(t)$ which is inserted in the following equations and a holding cost function which is taken into account indirectly due to the complementary probabilities. In addition, there is a cost of buying the spare parts C_{sp}. The state negative rewards represent the inventory-related costs and the action states represent the order of spare parts that is mapped to each action, as it has been defined at the configuration of the equipment instance. The ordering of spare parts business function is driven by maintenance, therefore, the MDP formulation remains the same, but each state has a different reward which corresponds to the spare parts ordering costs. So, backwards induction algorithm gives:

$$EL (S_n) = 0$$

$$EL (S_f) = C_s (t_f) = C_s (T - T) = 0$$

$$EL (S_{e_i}) = 0 + P (S_{e_i}, S_f) * EL (S'_f) = P (S_{e_i}, S_f) * C_s (t_{e_i})$$

$$EL (S_{a_i}) = C_{sp} + P (S_{a_i}, S_f) * EL (S'_f) + P (S_{a_i}, S_{e_i}) *$$
$$EL (S_{e_i}) = C_{sp} + P (S_{a_i}, S_f) * C_s (t_{a_i}) + P (S_{a_i}, S_{e_i}) *$$
$$P (S_{e_i}, S_f) * C_s (t_{e_i})$$

$$EL (S_d) = P (S_d, S_{a_i}) * EL (S_{a_i}) + P (S_d, S_f) * EL (S'_f)$$
$$= P (S_d, S_{a_i}) * \left[C_{sp} + P (S_{a_i}, S_f) * C_s (t_{a_i})\right.$$
$$+ P (S_{a_i}, S_{e_i}) * P (S_{e_i}, S_f) * C_s (t_{e_i})\right] + P (S_d, S_f) * C_s (t_d)$$

Therefore, the expected loss function for each action is given by:

$$EL^{o_i} = P\left(S_d, S_{a_i}\right) * \left[C_{sp} + P\left(S_{a_i}, S_f\right) * C_s\left(t_{a_i}\right)\right.$$
$$\left. + P\left(S_{a_i}, S_{e_i}\right) * P\left(S_{e_i}, S_f\right) * C_s\left(t_{e_i}\right)\right] + P\left(S_d, S_f\right) * C_s\left(t_d\right) \quad (5)$$

Let EL^0 denote the expected loss of taking no action. Backward induction for this policy gives:

$$EL^0\left(S_d\right) = P\left(S_d, S_n\right) * EL^0\left(S_n\right) + P^0\left(S_d, S_f\right) * EL^0\left(S_f\right) = P^0\left(S_d, S_f\right) * C_s\left(t_d\right)$$

Finally, the expected loss function of ordering the associated spare parts for each action is given by:

$$EL^{o_i}(t) = \left[1 - P^f\left(t_0, t_{a_i}\right)\right] * \left\{C_{sp} + P^f\left(t_{a_i}, t_{e_i}\right) * C_s\left(t_{a_i}\right)\right.$$
$$+ \left[1 - P^f\left(t_{a_i}, t_{e_i}\right)\right] * P_{a_i}^f\left(t_{e_i}, T\right) * C_s\left(t_{e_i}\right)\right\}$$
$$+ P^f\left(t_0, t_{a_i}\right) * C_s\left(t_d\right) \quad (6)$$

Taking into account the lead times of the spare parts orders, this equation can be transformed to:

$$EL^{o_i}(t) = \left[1 - P^f\left(t_0, t + L\right)\right] * \left\{C_{sp} + P^f\left(t + L, t + L + \Delta t\right) * C_s\left(t + L\right)\right.$$
$$+ \left[1 - P^f\left(t + L, t + L + \Delta t\right)\right] * P_{a_i}^f\left(t + L + \Delta t, T\right) * C_s\left(t + L + \Delta t\right)\right\}$$
$$+ P^f\left(t_0, t_{a_i}\right) * C_s(T) \quad (7)$$

Considering the time periods to which the shortage cost function corresponds, Eq. 7 is transformed to:

$$EL^{o_i}(t) = \left[1 - P^f\left(t_0, t + L\right)\right] * \left\{C_{sp} + P^f\left(t + L, t + L + \Delta t\right) * C_s\left(T - t - L\right)\right.$$
$$+ \left[1 - P^f\left(t + L, t + L + \Delta t\right)\right] * P_{a_i}^f\left(t + L + \Delta t, T\right) * C_s\left(T - t - L - \Delta t\right)\right\}$$
$$+ P^f\left(t_0, t + L\right) * C_s(T) \quad (8)$$

Joint Optimization of Maintenance and Logistics

Equations (3) and (7) constitute the generic proactive decision model for joint maintenance and logistics optimization that is triggered by a prediction event containing the PDF of the equipment under consideration failure. Since the PDF depends on the degradation modelling until the breakdown, it will usually follow distribution belonging to the exponential family (e.g., exponential, Weibull, and gamma) (Kapur and Pecht 2014), and therefore, it will fulfill the Markov property. Otherwise, it should be filtered and processed by other decision methods, e.g., Elwany and Gebraeel (2008). Before optimizing the equations of the proposed decision model, the PDFs should be calculated according to reliability theory, as shown in Eqs. (9) and (10).

$$P^f(t_1, t_2) = \frac{G^f(t_2) - G^f(t_1)}{1 - G^f(t_1)} \tag{9}$$

$$P_{a_i}^f(t_1, t_2) = \frac{G_{a_i}^f(t_2) - G_{a_i}^f(t_1)}{1 - G^f(t_1)} \tag{10}$$

$P^f(t_1, t_2)$ denotes the probability distribution function of the occurrence of the undesired event in the time interval (t_1, t_2), conditioned on not occurring until time t_1, while $P_{a_i}^f(t_1, t_2)$ denotes the probability distribution function of the occurrence of the undesired event in the time interval (t_1, t_2) conditioned on not occurring until time t_1 and assuming that the action a has been implemented exactly at time t_1. The event density function of u, denoted by $g^f(t)$, indicates the probability that f will occur at time t and the cumulative distribution function of g is denoted by $G^f(t)$. $G^f(t)$ indicates the probability that f will occur between time zero and time t, while $\overline{G}^f(t) = 1 - G^f(t)$ denotes the cumulative probability distribution function of the undesired event not occurring. When an action a is applied to reduce the probability of an undesired event, a is associated with a new event density function $g_a^f(t)$, which is the probability that f occurs at time t, although a has been applied before t. This happens because the implementation of action a does not prevent f with certainty. In Eq. (10), the conditioning (denominator) takes into account the fact that until the action occurrence at t_1, the distribution in place was G^f. The joint optimization of the maintenance and logistics equations is conducted by using the Brent's method which is root-finding algorithm combining the bisection method, the secant method and inverse quadratic interpolation (Brent 1971; Gegenfurtner 1992).

4 Information System Deployment in Industrial Environment

We validated our proposed approach in a real industrial environment in the area of oil and gas industry in the context. Although comparable industries such as automotive and aviation have recently started exploiting big data by analyzing them and processing them in suitable information systems, the oil drilling industry has not reached to that level yet. We embedded our approach in an event-driven information system and we integrated it with a system addressing the Detect phase (Riemer et al. 2015), one addressing the Predict phase (Stopar 2015) and one addressing the Act phase (Bousdekis et al. 2015a) of the proactive principle in a real-time event streaming computational environment. The oil drilling company aims to turn from time-based into CBM strategy by exploiting the IoT capabilities with the use of sensors and an event-driven infrastructure and by aligning its logistics operations. For the machine's gearbox equipment instance, the "Detect-Predict-Decide-Act" principle deals first with friction losses detection with the use of complex event patterns of lube oil temperature and RPM events characterized by an abnormal oil temperature rise measured over a percentage of the drilling period when drilling RPM exceeds a threshold (Detect). This pattern, learned at the offline phase, is an indication that the gearbox may be at a dangerous state. Therefore, a detection event is sent to the Predict phase where a prognostic model is developed for the estimation of the reliability distribution function of the gearbox. This prediction triggers Decide phase which provides a proactive recommendation about the optimal maintenance action and the optimal time of applying it as well as the optimal order of spare parts along with the optimal time for their ordering. Finally, the Act phase includes a Sensor-Enabled Feedback mechanism for supporting continuous monitoring.

At design time, the user interaction is realized with a GUI of the web-based application enabling the user to insert the required domain knowledge per equipment instance. In the current scenario, there are four alternative maintenance actions (lubrication of metal parts, operate at reduced equipment load, offshore maintenance, and full onshore maintenance) with different degrees of restoration and their associated orders of spare parts (lube oil, no ordering, gearbox, Derrick Drilling Machine—DDM), as shown in Table 2. The time-to-failure after the implementation of the maintenance action indicates the degree of restoration. The actions a1, a2, and a3 are implemented on the oil rig (offshore), while onshore maintenance, which corresponds to perfect ("good-as-new") maintenance, requires its movement onshore.

At some time, a prediction event about an exponential distribution function of the failure occurrence with a parameter $\lambda = 0.045$ triggers the decision algorithm. Eqs. (4) and (8) of the joint maintenance and logistics proactive decision model are formulated as shown below:

Table 2 The domain knowledge inserted during user configuration

Cost of failure (*Euro*)		350,000
Decision horizon (*h*)		240
Maintenance actions		
Time-to-failure after implementation (*h*)	a1: Lubrication of metal parts	1240
	a2: Operate at reduced equipment load	2050
	a3: Offshore maintenance	2960
	a4: Onshore Maintenance	3220
Spare parts orders		
Lead time (*h*)	o1: Lube oil	5
	o2: Swivel hook	8
	o3: Gearbox	24
	o4: DDM	48

$$
EL^{a_i}(t) = \left[1 - \left(1 - e^{-\lambda t}\right)\right] * \left\{ C_{a_i} + \left(1 - e^{-\lambda \Delta t}\right) * \right.
$$
$$
C_f + \left[1 - \left(1 - e^{-\lambda \Delta t}\right)\right]
$$
$$
* \left[C_{e_i}\left(T - t - \Delta t\right) \right.
$$
$$
+ \left(e^{(t + \Delta t)\left(\lambda - \lambda'\right)} - e^{-\lambda' T + \lambda(t + \Delta t)} \right) * C_f \left.\left.\right]\right\} + \left(1 - e^{-\lambda t}\right) * C_f
$$

$$
EL^{o_i}(t) = \left[1 - \left(1 - e^{-\lambda(t + L)}\right)\right] * \left\{ C_{sp} + \left(1 - e^{-\lambda \Delta t}\right) * C_s \left(T - t - L\right) \right.
$$
$$
+ \left[1 - \left(1 - e^{-\lambda \Delta t}\right)\right] * \left(e^{(t + L + \Delta t)\left(\lambda - \lambda'\right)} - e^{-\lambda' T + \lambda(t + L + \Delta t)} \right)
$$
$$
* C_s \left(T - t - L - \Delta t\right) \} + \left(1 - e^{-\lambda(t + L)}\right) * C_s(T)
$$

Although there is an indication of the most probable time-to-failure (parameter λ), the exponential degradation leads to high uncertainty in considering the deterministic value itself. Handling the PDF instead can lead to more accurate and reliable results. The expected loss functions are shown in Fig. 2 and their optimization results in the recommendation: Conduct offshore maintenance for gearbox replacement in 85.47 h and order the gearbox in 42.36 h. These recommendations are exposed to the user through the GUI.

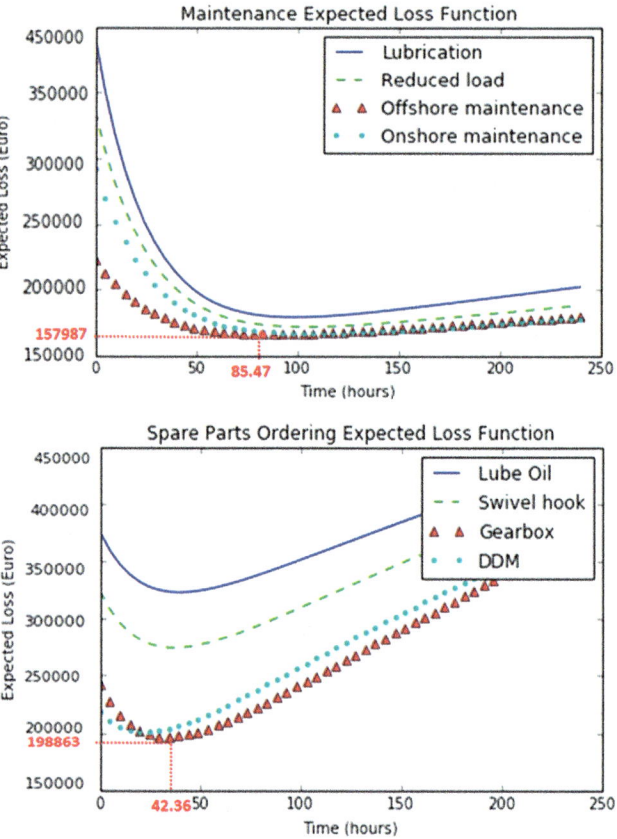

Fig. 2 The expected loss functions for (**a**) maintenance, and (**b**) logistics (ordering of spare parts)

5 Evaluation Results

5.1 Comparative Analysis

We compared the results of the proposed decision model for the aforementioned scenario with three cases: (1) the case of not having a prediction and therefore, of applying corrective maintenance and inventory-related actions (reactive approach), (2) the case of having a preventive policy with time-based maintenance and scheduled ordering, and (3) the case of having prediction but not proactive recommendations and therefore, of applying a preventive action immediately when the prediction is provided (myopic approach). In the first case, corrective maintenance actions last more than planned ones due to the lack of root causes knowledge, while emergency, unplanned ordering of spare parts requires a higher lead time along with a cost penalty due to the unplanned distribution. In the second case, there is the cost for time-based maintenance along with the risk of an unexpected failure between time intervals. In the third case, due to the failure prediction, immediate orders of spare parts are applied and preventive maintenance actions are implemented after the required lead time. However, there is the probability of a failure occurring before the spare parts arrived. The cost values for the comparative analysis have been derived from expert knowledge in combination with historical data analysis. The results are shown in Table 3.

Moreover, we conducted simulations of prediction events in the context of 5 real case studies, based on the configuration of 5 associated equipment instances by the users in the oil drilling company. For each scenario, we simulated 100 executions by sending prediction events. In all the scenarios, the expected loss of the proposed approach is significantly lower comparing to the reactive, preventive and the myopic approach leading to optimized business performance, as shown in Table 4. In the case of myopic policy, actions may be applied at some time according to domain knowledge, something which is not quantifiable and is constrained by the subjectivity of human decision-making process.

Table 3 Results of comparative analysis for the aforementioned scenario

Approach	Maintenance action	Logistics action	Total expected loss (maintenance and inventory)
Reactive	Onshore maintenance after oil rig moving	Immediate emergent ordering of DDM	1,492,000 Euro
Preventive	Onshore maintenance after oil rig moving	Scheduled ordering of DDM 48 h before maintenance action	1,021,430 Euro
Myopic	Operate at reduced equipment load when spare part arrives	Immediate ordering of swivel hook	825,000 Euro
Proactive	Offshore maintenance in 85.47 h	Ordering of gearbox in 42.36 h	356,850 Euro

Table 4 Results of comparative analysis for several executions in five scenarios

| Scenario | Total expected loss for each approach (*Euro*) | | | |
	Reactive	Preventive	Myopic	Proactive
1	1,491,360 ± 185,150	1,019,344 ± 143,229	827,635 ± 93,234	346,355 ± 71,566
2	874,362 ± 41,275	705,627 ± 39,631	596,122 ± 46,988	333,245 ± 37,461
3	122,644 ± 12,476	104,497 ± 9762	93,532 ± 11,855	50,769 ± 11,450
4	30,550 ± 3122	24,566 ± 3099	22,550 ± 3044	12,915 ± 2988
5	446,500 ± 23,110	411,433 ± 20,087	315,000 ± 19,750	191,235 ± 16,814

5.2   Sensitivity Analysis

Results of Sensitivity Analysis with Respect to the Prediction Events

In the context of the sensitivity analysis, we simulated several prediction events for investigating the resulting recommendations and the associated expected loss. Table 5 shows some indicative results of the sensitivity analysis. It should be noted that, since the decision horizon is in 240 h after the prediction event trigger, the recommended time of 240 means that the action should be performed as has been planned. According to the results, the recommendations can significantly change according to the prediction events. In addition, the earlier a failure is predicted and the proactive decision model is triggered, the less the expected loss is, while the decision maker has more time at their disposal to be prepared and align other manufacturing operations. This conclusion also means that there is a need for reliable and accurate predictive algorithms, with minimized false alarms (false positive and false negative) in order to early predict upcoming undesired events (e.g., equipment failures). In this way, proactive decision models will be able to provide recommendations that lead to a more optimized business performance.

Results of Sensitivity Analysis with Respect to the Costs

In order to conduct sensitivity analysis of the proactive decision model for joint maintenance and logistics optimization, we simulated four scenarios of cost structures between the action cost and the failure cost as well as between the shortage cost and the spare parts costs given a specific prediction. Figures 3 and 4 show two indicative plots for the maintenance and logistics expected loss functions, respectively (for one maintenance action and one spare parts order), while Tables 6 and 7 present the resulting optimal expected loss and the optimal implementation time for the specific action. Similarly to other proactive decision algorithms (Engel et al. 2012), the proposed proactive decision model is sensitive to its cost-related input parameters, since the expected loss functions are changed and they can lead to different recommendations.

6   Conclusions and Future Work

We presented a proactive event-driven decision model for joint maintenance and logistics optimization in an IIoT-based industrial environment. The proposed model addresses the Decide phase of the "Detect-Predict-Decide-Act" proactive principle. Unlike previous approaches, our proposed model is able to be embedded in an EDA in a scalable and efficient way. Moreover, it is able to provide recommendations of action-time pairs, when there are multiple alternative (imperfect and perfect) maintenance and logistical actions. Our approach was tested in a real industrial

Table 5 Results of sensitivity analysis with respect to the prediction events

Parameter	Maintenance			Spare parts ordering		
Predicted time-to-failure	Recommended action	Recommended time	Resulting expected loss	Recommended order	Recommended time	Resulting expected loss
10	a1	2.03	335,434.84	o1	0.00	205,031.98
20	a3	36.87	312,544.27	o3	15.12	199,433.39
50	a3	77.92	234,124.91	o3	39.82	174,861.74
100	a3	104.32	198,063.57	o3	87.87	126,523.99
150	a2	135.22	181,133.28	o2	118.11	120,475.45
200	a4	240.00	169,045.21	o4	189.34	101,366.56
240	a4	240.00	156,217.91	o4	193.21	96,661.94

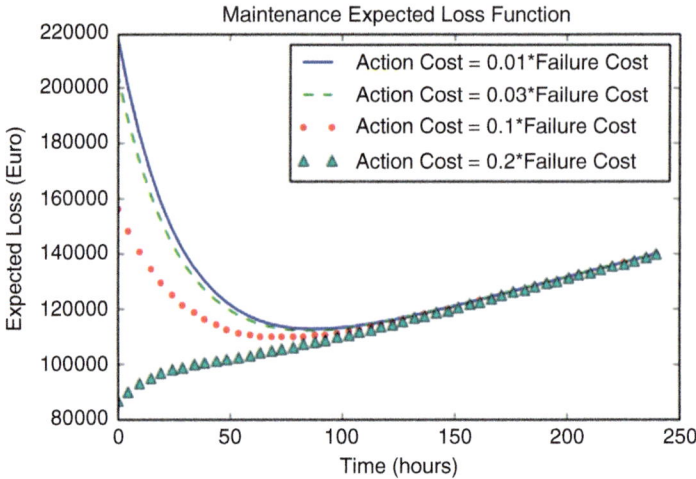

Fig. 3 Four cost structures for the maintenance expected loss function

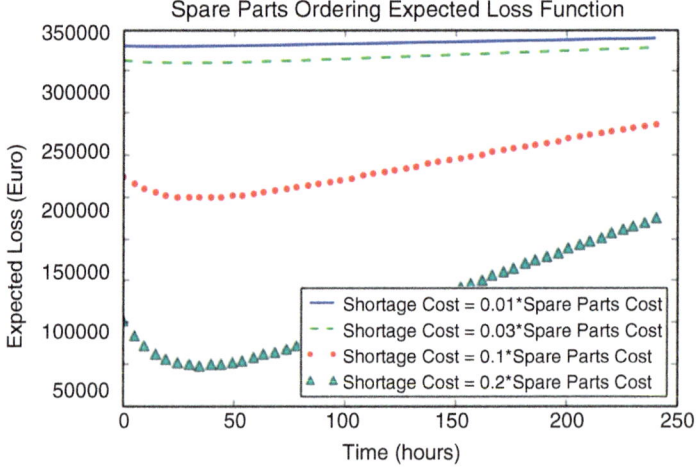

Fig. 4 Four cost structures for the spare parts ordering expected loss function

environment, in the area of oil and gas industry, while it was further evaluated through comparative and sensitivity analyses. The results showed that the proposed model can lead to a significant reduction of the expected losses caused by maintenance and logistical actions. Moreover, the time that a prediction event is received and the accuracy in cost-related input are crucial for the reliability and the business added value of the recommendations. Regarding our future work, we will develop a context-aware model for considering the context affecting the proactive decision model (i.e., its input parameters and thus, the recommendations themselves). Moreover, we aim to integrate the proposed decision model with a

Table 6 Results of the cost structures for the maintenance expected loss function

Action cost	Action expected loss (*Euro*)	Optimal action implementation time (*h*)
0.01 × Failure cost	117,211.42	87.78
0.03 × Failure cost	117,032.12	85.28
0.1 × Failure cost	115,146.47	73.65
0.2 × Failure cost	88,654.72	0

Table 7 Results of the cost structures for the spare parts ordering expected loss function

Shortage cost	Action expected loss (*Euro*)	Optimal action implementation time (*h*)
0.01 × Spare parts cost	345,871.02	18.21
0.03 × Spare parts cost	331,124.39	29.06
0.1 × Spare parts cost	200,009.99	34.97
0.2 × Spare parts cost	50,004.86	35.61

Sensor-Enabled Feedback mechanism and a portfolio optimization approach for supplier selection, since prices may be subjected to fluctuations.

Acknowledgments This work is partly funded by the European Commission projects: FP7 ProaSense—"The Proactive Sensing Enterprise" (612329) and H2020 UPTIME "Unified Predictive Maintenance System" (768634).

References

Basten, R. J., Van der Heijden, M. C., Schutten, J. M. J., & Kutanoglu, E. (2015). An approximate approach for the joint problem of level of repair analysis and spare parts stocking. *Annals of Operations Research, 224*(1), 121–145.

Bi, Z., Da Xu, L., & Wang, C. (2014). Internet of things for enterprise systems of modern manufacturing. *IEEE Transactions on Industrial Informatics, 10*(2), 1537–1546.

Bohlin, M., & Wärja, M. (2015). Maintenance optimization with duration-dependent costs. *Annals of Operations Research, 224*(1), 1–23.

Bousdekis, A., Magoutas, B., Apostolou, D., & Mentzas, G. (2015a). Review, analysis and synthesis of prognostic-based decision support methods for condition based maintenance. *Journal of Intelligent Manufacturing, 29*(6), 1–14.

Bousdekis, A., Papageorgiou, N., Magoutas, B., Apostolou, D., & Mentzas, G. (2015b). A real-time architecture for proactive decision making in manufacturing enterprises. In *OTM confederated international conferences "on the move to meaningful internet systems"* (pp. 137–146). New York: Springer International Publishing.

Brent, R. P. (1971). An algorithm with guaranteed convergence for finding a zero of a function. *The Computer Journal, 14*(4), 422–425.

Elwany, A. H., & Gebraeel, N. Z. (2008). Sensor-driven prognostic models for equipment replacement and spare parts inventory. *IIE Transactions, 40*(7), 629–639.

Engel, Y., Etzion, O., & Feldman, Z. (2012). A basic model for proactive event-driven computing. In: *Proceedings of the 6th ACM International Conference on Distributed Event-Based Systems* (pp. 107–118). ACM.

Etzion, O., & Niblett, P. (2010). *Event processing in action*. New York: Manning Publications Co.

Feldman, Z., Fournier, F., Franklin, R., & Metzger, A. (2013). Proactive event processing in action: A case study on the proactive management of transport processes (industry article). In: *Proceedings of the 7th ACM International Conference on Distributed Event-Based Systems* (pp. 97–106). ACM.

Gegenfurtner, K. R. (1992). PRAXIS: Brent's algorithm for function minimization. *Behavior Research Methods, Instruments, & Computers, 24*(4), 560–564.

Guillén, A. J., Crespo, A., Gómez, J. F., & Sanz, M. D. (2016). A framework for effective management of condition based maintenance programs in the context of industrial development of E-maintenance strategies. *Computers in Industry, 82*, 170–185.

Hu, R., Yue, C., & Xie, J. (2008). Joint optimization of age replacement and spare ordering policy based on generic algorithm. In: *Proceedings of 2008 International Conference on Computational Intelligence And Security* (pp. 156–161).

Kapur, K. C., & Pecht, M. (2014). *Reliability engineering*. Hoboken: John Wiley & Sons.

Keizer, M. C. O., Teunter, R. H., & Veldman, J. (2017). Joint condition-based maintenance and inventory optimization for systems with multiple components. *European Journal of Operational Research, 257*(1), 209–222.

Lee, J., Kao, H. A., & Yang, S. (2014). Service innovation and smart analytics for industry 4.0 and big data environment. *Procedia CIRP, 16*, 3–8.

Lorén, S., & de Maré, J. (2015). Maintenance for reliability—A case study. *Annals of Operations Research, 224*(1), 111–119.

Nosoohi, I., & Hejazi, S. R. (2011). A multi-objective approach to simultaneous determination of spare part numbers and preventive replacement times. *Applied Mathematical Modelling, 35*(3), 1157–1166.

Muller, A., Suhner, M. C., & Iung, B. (2008). Formalisation of a new prognosis model for supporting proactive maintenance implementation on industrial system. *Reliability Engineering & System Safety, 93*(2), 234–253.

Pistofidis, P., Emmanouilidis, C., Koulamas, C., Karampatzakis, D., & Papathanassiou, N. (2012). A layered e-maintenance architecture powered by smart wireless monitoring components. In: *2012 IEEE International Conference on Industrial Technology (ICIT)* (pp. 390–395). IEEE.

Potocnik, M., & Juric, M. B. (2014). Towards complex event aware services as part of SOA. *IEEE Transactions on Services Computing, 7*(3), 486–500.

Riemer, D., Kaulfersch, F., Hutmacher, R., & Stojanovic, L. (2015). StreamPipes: Solving the challenge with semantic stream processing pipelines. In: *Proceedings of the 9th ACM International Conference on Distributed Event-Based Systems* (pp. 330–331). ACM.

Sarker, R., & Haque, A. (2000). Optimization of maintenance and spare provisioning policy using simulation. *Applied Mathematical Modelling, 24*(10), 751–760.

Sejdovic, S., Hegenbarth, Y., Ristow, G. H., & Schmidt, R. (2016). Proactive disruption management system: How not to be surprised by upcoming situations. In: *Proceedings of the 10th ACM International Conference on Distributed and Event-based Systems* (pp. 281–288). ACM.

Stopar, L. (2015). A Multi-Scale methodology for explaining data streams. *Conference on Data Mining and Data Warehouses (SiKDD 2015) held at the 18th International Multiconference on Information Society IS-2015. October 5th, 2015, Ljubljana, Slovenia.*

Theorin, A., Bengtsson, K., Provost, J., Lieder, M., Johnsson, C., Lundholm, T., & Lennartson, B. (2016). An event-driven manufacturing information system architecture for industry 4.0. *International Journal of Production Research, 55*(5), 1–15.

Van Horenbeek, A., Buré, J., Cattrysse, D., Pintelon, L., & Vansteenwegen, P. (2013). Joint maintenance and inventory optimization systems: A review. *International Journal of Production Economics, 143*(2), 499–508.

Wang, W. (2012). A stochastic model for joint spare parts inventory and planned maintenance optimization. *European Journal of Operational Research, 216*(1), 127–139.

Wang, W., Pecht, M. G., & Liu, Y. (2012). Cost optimization for canary-equipped electronic systems in terms of inventory control and maintenance decisions. *IEEE Transactions on Reliability, 61*(2), 466–478.

Watkins, C. J., & Dayan, P. (1992). Q-learning. *Machine Learning, 8*(3–4), 279–292.

Wu, S. J., Gebraeel, N., Lawley, M. A., & Yih, Y. (2007). A neural network integrated decision support system for condition-based optimal predictive maintenance policy. *IEEE Transactions on Systems, Man, and Cybernetics-Part A: Systems and Humans, 37*(2), 226–236.

Xie, J., & Wang, H. (2008). Joint optimization of condition-based preventive maintenance and spare ordering policy. In: *Proceedings of 4th international conference on wireless communications networking and mobile computing, (WiCOM 08)* (pp. 1–5).

Zimmermann, A., Schmidt, R., Sandkuhl, K., Wißotzki, M., Jugel, D., & Möhring, M. (2015, September). Digital enterprise architecture-transformation for the internet of things. In: *Enterprise Distributed Object Computing Workshop (EDOCW), 2015 IEEE 19th International* (pp. 130–138). IEEE.

Adoption of Digital Currencies: The Companies' Perspective

Ioanna Roussou and Emmanouil Stiakakis

Abstract In recent years, digital currency was launched and spread due to technological developments, economic changes, monetary and political conditions in a steadily rising rate. This paper aims to provide the findings of an academic research about the actual use of digital currency by companies and freelancers. The research was based on the Diffusion of Innovations Theory and the Technology Acceptance Model. The goal of the survey was to investigate the actual use of digital currency, as a means of transaction by companies and how it is affected by the constructs of Perceived Ease of Use, Perceived Usefulness, and Perceived Security directly and other constructs indirectly, according to the research model. Based on the responses provided by 254 companies and freelancers the findings exhibit that the penetration of digital currency usage is in increasing progress. This survey's findings are significant for businessmen, banks, financial institutions, digital currency's users and experts, scientists and policy makers.

Keywords Digital currency · Companies · DOI · TAM · Bitcoin

1 Introduction

Nowadays, scientists and businesses consider digital currency as a technologically pioneering innovation, although sometimes financially disruptive. Bitcoin and altcoins shape a new system with a steady pace by changing the today's financial structure, networks and markets. Blockchain, the underlying technology of Bitcoin, is the major innovation and Bitcoin as a currency system is the initial application of blockchain (Antonopoulos 2014). Digital currency, starring Bitcoin, combines and evolves previous technological innovations (*Internet, Mobile technology, Open*

I. Roussou (✉) · E. Stiakakis
Department of Applied Informatics, University of Macedonia, Thessaloniki, Greece

© Springer Nature Switzerland AG 2019
A. Sifaleras, K. Petridis (eds.), *Operational Research in the Digital Era – ICT Challenges*, Springer Proceedings in Business and Economics,
https://doi.org/10.1007/978-3-319-95666-4_4

47

Source code, Asymmetric Cryptography, Hash Function, Proof of Work concept, Peer to Peer networks, etc.) (Psannis et al. 2014).

Technological developments, economic changes, monetary and political conditions in recent years conduced to the gradual spread of the adoption and the use of digital currency. Although Bitcoin was an American innovation and its price is affected mainly by American economic variables (Wijk 2013), the European economic crisis has contributed to the widespread dissemination of digital currency (Saito 2013).

In literature, there is a scientific and research gap about the acceptance, adoption and the use of digital currency by companies. Until now, surveys aimed to the knowledge, acceptance and the use of digital currency by individuals. Furthermore, there is not adequate academic research about the adoption of digital currency as a means of transaction.

According to Metcalfe's law (Gilder 1993), networks provide a competitive advantage to the diffusion of innovations. In the same vein, companies will provide a competitive advantage to the diffusion of digital currency for transactions globally. According to Tasca (2016), Western Union is the most similar payment network to Bitcoin, instead of VISA, MasterCard or Discover, because they are both used for remittances and relatively big money transfers between individuals, rather than for shopping. The adoption of digital currency by companies as an alternative way of payment would be an additional advantage; however, businesses should pay attention to pros and cons.

2   Choice and Combination of Theory Models

The two keywords of the notion of digital currency that match with the combined application of IDPM and TAM are «innovation» and «technological». In literature, previous integration of the two theories conduced to significant findings and more completed responses (Sigala et al. 2000; Chen et al. 2002; Wu and Wang 2005). Previous studies also have proven that there are many complementary characteristics between the two theory models and are used in the adoption of Information Systems and Information Technology (Chen et al. 2002; Lee et al. 2011). The two basic factors of TAM, Perceived Usefulness and Perceived Ease of Use are considered that are included in the five Perceived characteristics of the innovation in IDPM by many researchers. Three of these characteristics were proved to have a constant affection to the adoption of an innovation: Relative Advantage, Compatibility and Complexity (Tornatzky and Klein 1982; Agarwal and Prasad 1998; Kolodinsky et al. 2004) and influence more the decisions for continuance of adoption (Moore and Benbasat 1991). Additionally, the characteristics of IDPM, Relative Advantage and Complexity are acknowledged to be complementary with the factors of TAM, Perceived Usefulness and Perceived Ease of Use (Moore and Benbasat 1991). In many studies, the conceptual terms of Relative Advantage and Perceived Usefulness are used alternatively and are measured by similar items, although there are some differences in their notion (Wang et al. 2011). The use of Relative Advantage is more appropriate in case of comparison among different technologies, in order to make clear which technology has the competitive advantage for prospective users. The use of the construct of Perceived Usefulness is more appropriate for the current proposed research model, as this study does not compare digital currencies between themselves, in order to examine the adoption of digital currency by companies. Subsequently, the characteristic of Compatibility is the only one that is not taken into account in TAM and is proposed to be examined as a distinct construct in the research model of this study. The factors of Perceived Usefulness and Perceived Ease of Use mediate the influence of Compatibility to the Intended Use of the customers (Oh et al. 2003) and prospective users who feel familiar with a technology can estimate better the usefulness and ease of use of this technology. Finally, the combined use of IDPM and TAM is reflected also in the research tool of this study. TAM is addressed mainly to individuals, while IDPM is addressed not only to individuals but also to structures like organizations, companies, social groups and countries. The questionnaire of this survey is constituted by four sections, the first two of which are addressed to companies' representatives and the last two ask for the personal views of the respondents.

2.1 Diffusion of Innovation Theory (DOI) and Innovation Decision Process Model (IDPM)

DOI explains the way of acceptance and diffusion of an innovation within a social system and was developed by Rogers in 1962. According to DOI, diffusion is defined as the process by which an innovation is spread through certain channels over time to the members of a social system. Innovation is defined as an idea, practice or phenomenon that is considered as new by a person or other unit of adoption. The main elements in the diffusion of new ideas are four: Innovation, Communication channels, Time and Social system. DOI classifies adopters in five categories according to their different rate of innovativeness: (1) Innovators, (2) Early Adopters, (3) Early Majority, (4) Late Majority and (5) Laggards. Innovativeness is the grade at which a person or another unit of adoption is relatively previous in the adoption of new ideas than other members of the social system (Rogers 1962; Rogers 1995).

The IDPM, which is based on DOI, demonstrates five characteristics that conduce to the diffusion of innovation: Relative advantage, Compatibility with existing values and practices, Complexity, Trialability and Observability. The innovations that have the above five perceived characteristics have more probabilities to be successful and adopted. DOI bases the decision of adoption of a new technology mainly on the perceptions about this technology within the decision-making unit (DMU) (Rogers 1995; Tatnall and Burgess 2004). The Innovation Decision Process is described as a process through which an individual or another DMU passes from

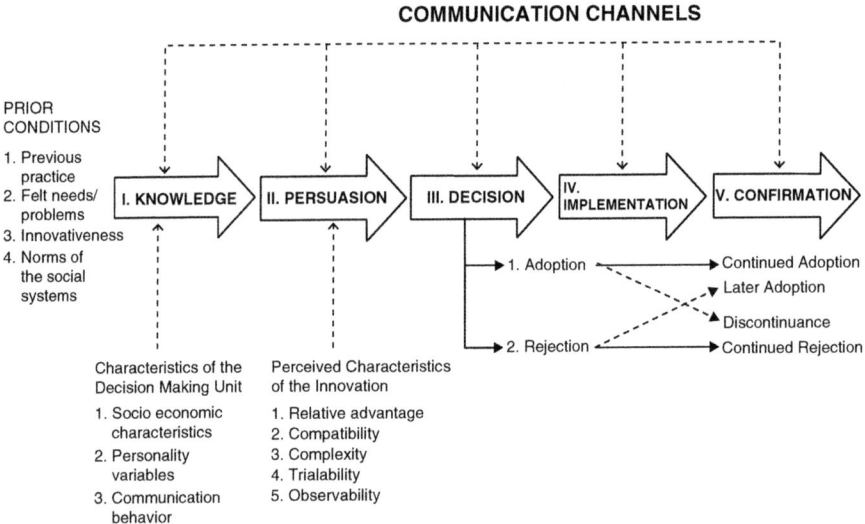

Fig. 1 IDPM (Source: Rogers (1995). Diffusion of innovations (fourth ed.))

the following five stages: (1) knowledge, (2) persuasion, (3) decision of adoption or rejection, (4) implementation and (5) confirmation. The IDPM is based on the theory of communication, where a new idea is communicated through channels to the audience (potential adopters) and has been used to study the adoption of Information Technology (Fig. 1).

2.2   Technology Acceptance Model (TAM)

Technology Acceptance Model (TAM) explains the users' behaviour about adopting technology and aims to predict the IT adoption by them. TAM proposed by Davis in 1989 and is based on the Theory of Reasoned Action (TRA) (Fishbein and Ajzen 1975; Ajzen and Fishbein 1980). TAM is primarily recognized in behavioural technology adoption. The basic factors of TAM are two: 1) Perceived Usefulness, i.e. the grade at which the user believes that the adoption of technology will enhance his job performance and 2) Perceived Ease of Use, i.e. the grade at which the user considers that the use of a system requires zero effort (Fig. 2).

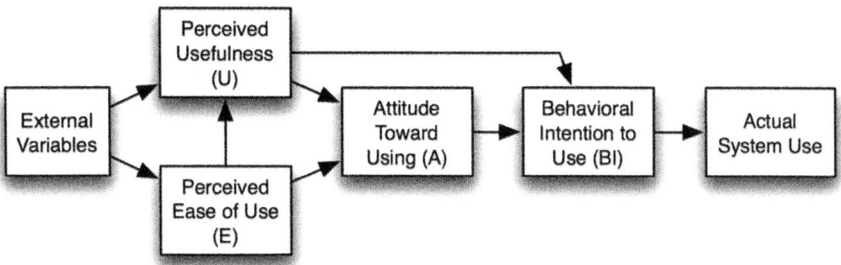

Fig. 2 TAM (Source: Davis et al. (1989) "User Acceptance of Computer Technology: A Comparison of Two Theoretical Models")

2.3 Digital Currency

Wagner (2014) defines digital currency as the currency that is saved and transmitted in an electronic way. There is often a misunderstanding and mistaken use of the terms digital currency, virtual currency and e-money. The term of digital currency has a broad meaning, in which virtual currencies and cryptocurrencies are included. Today, the majority of transactions with state currencies are executed electronically, and due to the digital nature of these transactions, often traditional currencies are assumed to be digital. In addition, innovation and technology in Informational Systems have been used for a long time ago to help move from a global economy relied on cash in a cashless economy (Wonglimpiyarat 2015). At the beginning, virtual currencies were used only in computer games and social networks and gradually their use expanded in other aspects of everyday life. The developments in the field of cryptography conduced to the creation of cryptocurrencies, as means of transactions that provide more security and control of the generation of other units. Bitcoin is a pioneering system, which relies in cryptography and its main feature is the decentralized nature (Nakamoto 2008). Since 2009, when the first transaction with bitcoins took place, a host of altcoins appeared, the majority of which, relies on the infrastructure of Bitcoin.

In addition to technical approaches, there is also adequate literature about socioeconomic aspects of digital currency. According to Smyth (2013) the basic reasons that drove people to adopt Bitcoin are political, curiosity and challenge. The morality of paper, plastic or payments with bitcoins was also discussed, and the conclusion of the study was that the use of a payment system is the one that characterizes the system as good or "evil" (Krugman 2013; Angel and McCabe 2015). Bitcoin relies solely on the supply and demand of the markets (Saito 2013), and in general, digital currency shows network effects: as the adoption of digital currency increased, its value becomes higher. As users of digital currency are increased, more companies are persuaded to adopt digital currency and vice versa.

According to Metcalfe's law, the value of a network is proportional to the square of the number of nodes, and is applied in the case of digital currency. This is the "internet consistency" that leads to increased returns in a networked economy. The investigation of the competition of digital currency against traditional currencies or their coexistence is proposed by researchers (Gans and Halaburda 2013; Balestrieri and Huberman 2014). In the next years, other popular models, like Bitcoin, will appear and policy makers need to boost their beneficial uses while minimizing their negative effects (Chowdhury and Mendelson 2013).

3 Proposed Research Model

In this section the proposed research model and constructs are introduced and analysed. Based on the combination of the two theories and acknowledging digital currency as an innovation of technology, seven constructs are proposed to constitute the research model, as follows: Characteristics of DMU, Previous Practices, Compatibility, Perceived Usefulness, Perceived Ease of Use and Perceived Security and Actual Use of digital currency.

The construct of Actual digital currency Use is the dependent variable and all the rest are the direct or indirect independent variables. The proposed research model derives from the combination of the theory models of IDPM and TAM, and the analysis that follows starts with the constructs that have an indirect effect and continue with the constructs that have a direct effect on the Actual Use of digital currency. The indirect constructs derive from IDPM and the direct constructs derive from TAM. The direct effect of Perceived Security is also examined. Figure 3 depicts the proposed research model below.

3.1 Indirect Effect

According to IDPM, the Characteristics of the DMU include socioeconomic characteristics, personality variables and communication behaviour. For the purpose of the survey as DMU is considered the company that participates in the survey. The characteristics that are taken into account as items and are related to the formulation of this construct are: the business sector, size, annual turnover, foundation year, headquarters location, export activity of the company, the way the revenues in digital currency are made in case the company has adopted the digital currency as a means of transaction (socioeconomic and company's personality variables) and the means by which the company is aware about the digital currency (communication behaviour). It is pointed out that headquarters location is a particular item because every country in the European Union treats digital currency in a different legal and fiscal way. Some countries *(i.e. Isle of Man (UK), Slovenia, Finland, Ireland and the Netherlands constitute the top five most popular European countries for*

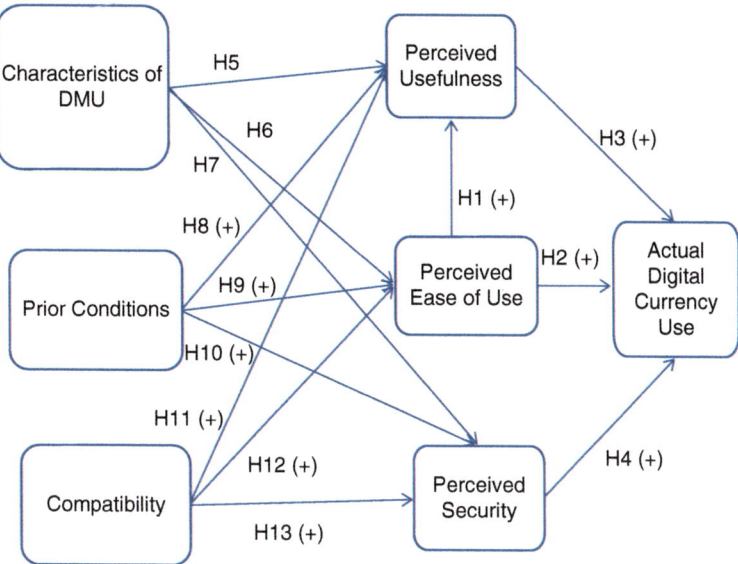

Fig. 3 Proposed research model

bitcoin, ranked by the number of bitcoin ATMs per capita) (Coindesk 2014) are more familiar with the use of digital currency while others are not so much. According to IDPM the Characteristics of DMU influence the knowledge (first) stage. Thus, the items aforementioned regarded as an integrated construct are expected to affect indirectly the Actual Use, but directly the Perceived Ease of Use, Perceived Usefulness and Perceived Security of digital currency in a positive or negative way, that is a result that will come out from the survey.

Furthermore, according to IDPM prior conditions precede the first stage of knowledge. Prior conditions are mentioned as previous practice, felt needs/problems, innovativeness and the norms of the social systems. The items of the questionnaire that affect this construct are: the types of e-payments that the company use and their percentage of the total annual turnover, the business software and Web Services of the company, the main reasons for adoption of digital currency and the rate that the company embrace technological innovations. The construct of Prior Conditions is considered that affects Perceived Ease of Use, Perceived Usefulness and Perceived Security directly, and the Actual Use of digital currency indirectly.

Finally, previous studies' findings (Agarwal and Prasad 1998; Kolodinsky et al. 2004) show that the characteristic of Compatibility is included in the three characteristics of innovation of IDPM, which are related to the adoption of an innovation steadily, as aforementioned. The other two characteristics are Relative Advantage and Complexity, and are considered as complementary to Perceived Usefulness and Perceived Ease of Use, the two main factors of TAM (Moore and

Benbasat 1991). It is deduced that Compatibility is not taken into account in TAM and is examined as a distinct construct in the proposed research model. When a new technology is perceived as accordant with the existing working ideas, values and practices provides a notion of familiarity to the potential users and is more probable to be adopted faster than other technologies that do not seem compatible with previous values and practices (Chen et al. 2002). Perceived Compatibility influences the intention of the user towards Bitcoin (Kumpajaya and Dhewanto 2015) and Perceived Usefulness and Perceived Ease of Use act as moderators to the influence of Compatibility to the Intended Use of the customers (Oh et al. 2003). Usefulness and Ease of Use of a technology are estimated better by potential users who feel familiar with this technology; nevertheless, a new idea would not be adopted only because is perceived as compatible. Perceived Usefulness and Perceived Ease of Use of e-commerce are affected positively by Perceived Compatibility (Crespo et al. 2013). Finally, Compatibility is considered that decreases incertitude (Rogers 1995), thus it is deduced that Compatibility affects Perceived Security. So, in the proposed research model, the indirect effect of Compatibility to Actual Use of digital currency and its direct effect on Perceived Usefulness, Perceived Ease of Use and Perceived Security are examined.

3.2   Direct Effect

When individuals perceive ICT as useful, they have also intention to use them (Wang et al. 2011). In the same vein, when the use of digital currency is easy, it is more probable for potential users to transact within this system (Kumpajaya and Dhewanto 2015). As mentioned above TAM is based on TRA, thus Perceived Ease of Use and Perceived Usefulness influence Attitude towards use and Behavioural Intention to use and consequently the Actual System Use. In IDPM, the Perceived Characteristics of Innovation influence the second stage of Persuasion. The stage of Decision is the third stage, thus it is deduced that potential users of a new technology have to be persuaded first for its usefulness and ease of use and then to decide whether to adopt or reject it. However, the target group of this study is the company, which as DMU as mentioned in IDPM, decides about the adoption or not of an innovation and the individuals that work in the company have to comply with this decision, thus the Attitude towards using or the Behavioural Intention to use do not play an important role in this case. For these reasons, the immediate effect of Perceived Ease of Use and Perceived Usefulness towards the Actual digital currency Use is investigated in the current study. Eventually, the examination of the effect that Perceived Ease of Use has on Perceived Usefulness, according to TAM, as far as digital currency is concerned, is also included in the proposed research model.

Finally, the construct of Perceived Security (Perceived Security) is examined as an additional construct in the proposed research model. Perceived Security was found to have an effect on Behavioural Intention, when examined as an additional distinct belief (Cheng et al. 2006). For the reasons mentioned above, Behavioural

Intention is not examined in this study, thus the direct influence of Perceived Security towards the Actual Use of digital currency is proposed to be tested. The concept of Security is complex and has many definitions. Digital currency is considered to have many risks, due to exchange rates instability and web nature. Some risks that derive from the use of the system could be loss of funds, loss of digital wallet, cyberattacks and so on. The use of digital currency as a means of transactions integrates digital currency in e-payments, and in order to increase the attraction and preserve users, Perceived Security has to be increased (Chellappa and Pavlou 2002; Stroborn et al. 2004; Tsiakis and Sthephanides 2005; Linck et al. 2006; Kousaridas et al. 2008).

3.3 Research Hypotheses

According to the above analysis, the research hypotheses are described as follows:

H1: Perceived Ease of Use of digital currency affects Perceived Usefulness of digital currency.
H2: Perceived Ease of Use of digital currency affects Actual Use of digital currency.
H3: Perceived Usefulness of digital currency affects Actual Use of digital currency.
H4: Perceived Security of digital currency affects Actual Use of digital currency.
H5: Characteristics of the DMU affect Perceived Usefulness of digital currency.
H6: Characteristics of the DMU affect Perceived Ease of Use of digital currency.
H7: Characteristics of the DMU affect Perceived Security of digital currency.
H8: Prior Conditions affect Perceived Usefulness of digital currency.
H9: Prior Conditions affect Perceived Ease of Use of digital currency.
H10: Prior Conditions affect Perceived Security of digital currency.
H11: Compatibility affects Perceived Usefulness of digital currency.
H12: Compatibility affects Perceived Ease of Use of digital currency.
H13: Compatibility affects Perceived Security of digital currency.

4 Methodology

4.1 Sample and Data Collection

The collected sample was 254 responses from companies and freelancers. The survey was launched on April 2016 and closed in January 2017. Initially, the questionnaire was sent in European companies and gradually worldwide.

Companies' mailing lists were gathered by Internet, Chambers and Associations. The questionnaire was made in Google Forms, was sent online through various platforms and was circulated in various Social Media and forums, either by link or qr-code. Follow-ups and reposting were made several times.

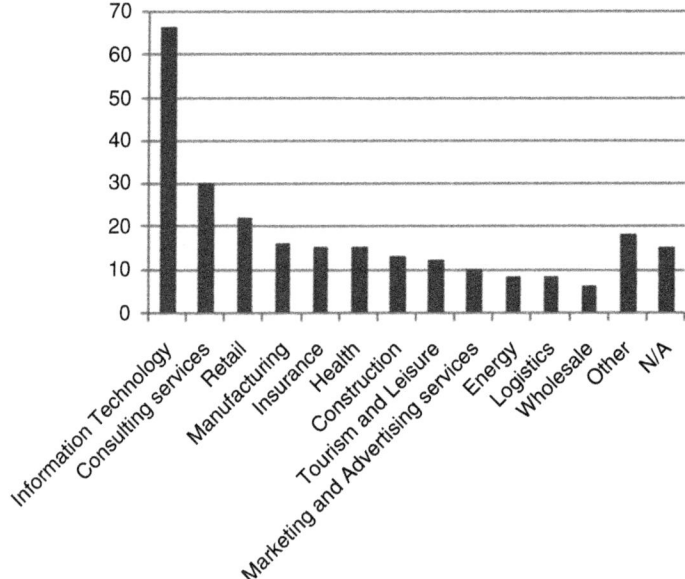

Fig. 4 Sector

The questionnaire was structured, anonymous and not limited to be answered by only one person from each company. It was composed by 31 questions, divided into 4 sections and 2 subsections: the first section was entitled "Background Information about the company, the second was entitled "The company's views on digital currency" and divided into two subsections according to the adoption or not of digital currency by the company, the third section was entitled "Personal Views about Digital currency" and the last one, the fourth section was entitled "Personal Views about prospects of digital currency".

5 Characteristics of the Sample and Results

The identity and findings of the research are depicted subsequently.

In the total sample of 254 responses, 66 companies activate in Information Technology, 30 in Consulting Services, 22 in Retail, 16 in Manufacturing, 15 in Insurance, 15 in Health, 13 in Construction, 12 in Tourism and Leisure, 10 in Marketing and Advertising services, 8 in Energy, 8 in Logistics, 6 in Wholesale, 18 in other sectors and 15 did not reply in this question, as depicted in Fig. 4.

In the total sample of 254 responses, 56 companies operate since 10–25 years, 55 operate since 5–10 years, 53 have been founded the last 2 years, 51 operate since 2–5 years and 39 operate more than 25 years, as depicted in Fig. 5.

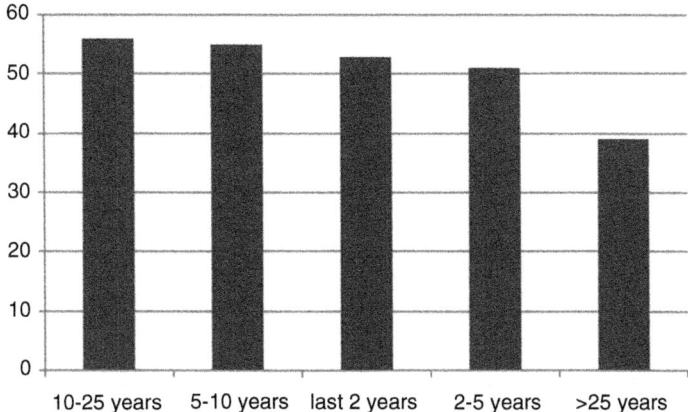

Fig. 5 Years of foundation

Fig. 6 Headquarters
inside/outside EU

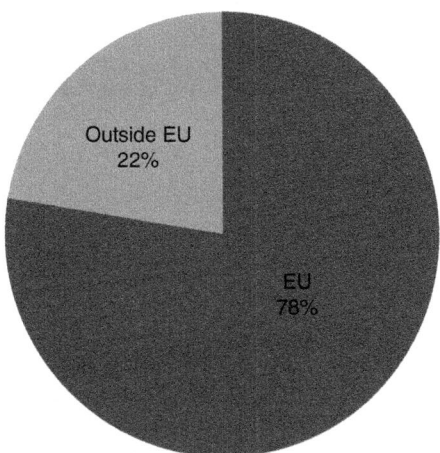

Figure 6 indicates that the headquarters of 78% of companies are located in the European Union, while 22% outside the European Union.

Figure 7 depicts that 109 of the companies have adopted the digital currency as a means of transaction, while 145 have not adopted it.

Figure 8 depicts the main reasons for adoption of the digital currency by the respondent companies as follows: freedom in payments (17%), ease of use (12%), low cost of transactions (12%), keeping up with the technological developments (10%), approach of new customers seeking transactions in digital currency (9%), gaining a competitive advantage (9%), speed of transactions (7%), company customers' requests (5%), improvement of the company's image (5%), increasing sales turnover (3%), control avoidance by central organizations (3%), transparency of transaction and rules (3%), adoption of digital currency by competitors (2%),

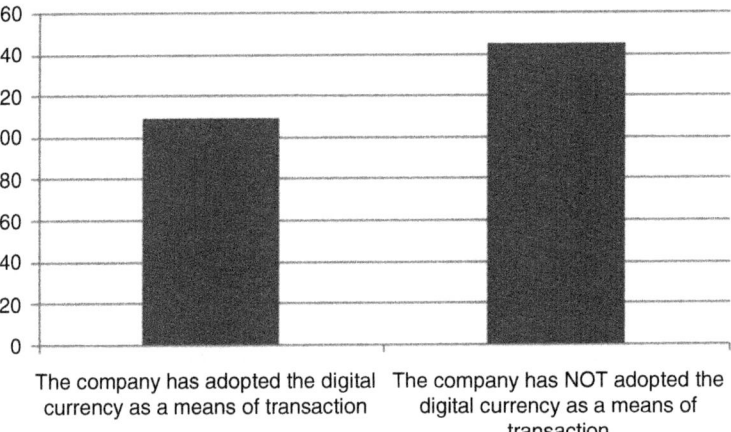

Fig. 7 Company's adoption of DC

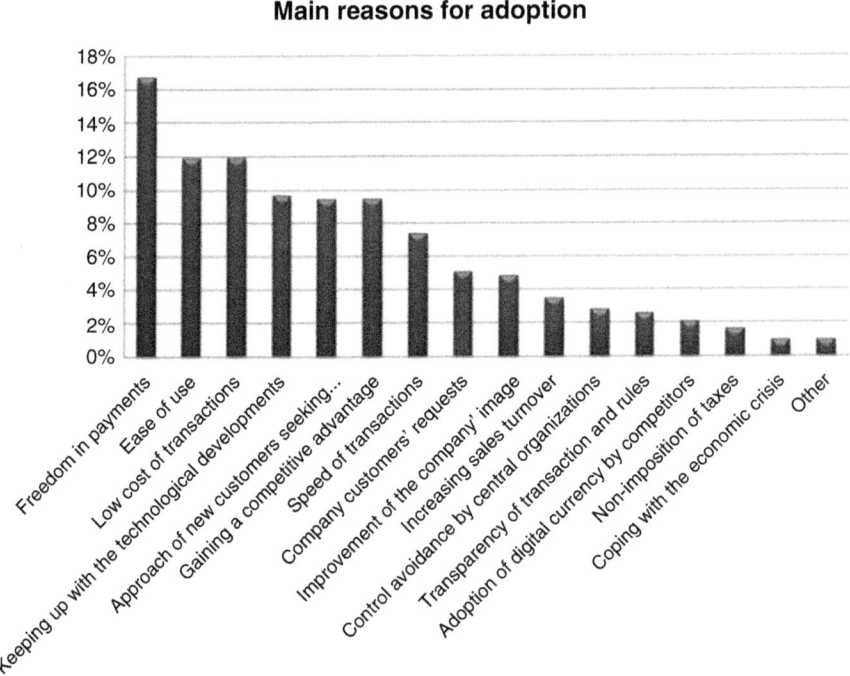

Fig. 8 Main reasons for adoption

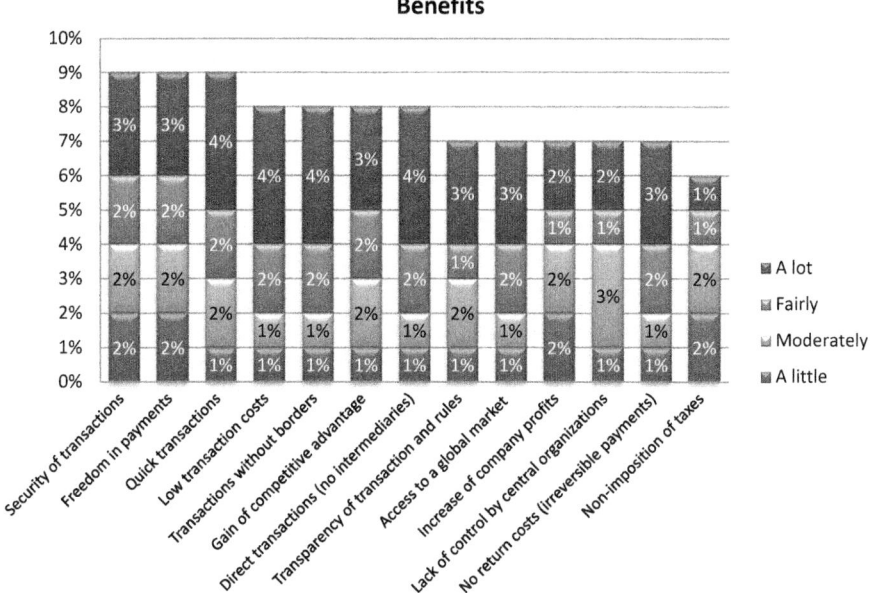

Fig. 9 Benefits of the adoption of the digital currency as a means of transaction

non-imposition of taxes (2%), coping with the economic crisis (1%) and other reasons (1%).

Figure 9 depicts the benefits that the respondent companies considered that derived by the adoption of the digital currency as a means of transaction as follows: security of transactions (9%), freedom in payments (9%), quick transactions (9%), low transaction costs (8%), transactions without borders (8%), gain of competitive advantage (8%), direct transactions (no intermediaries) (8%), transparency of transaction and rules (7%), access to a global market (7%), increase of company profits (7%), lack of control by central organizations (7%), no return costs (irreversible payments) (7%) and non-imposition of taxes (6%).

Figure 10 depicts the internal reasons of the respondent companies for non-adoption of the digital currency as a means of transaction as follows: lack of motivation to use the digital currency (15%), lack of adequate information about its functioning (13%), incompatibility with other company's systems (12%), ignorance about its further utilization (11%), unavailability of suitable software (11%), lack of suitable infrastructure (11%), lack of experience/difficulty in managing e-transactions (10%), non-acceptance of innovations by the company (10%) and lack of familiarity with technology (7%).

Figure 11 depicts the external reasons of the respondent companies for non-adoption of the digital currency as a means of transaction as follows: not widespread to the general public (14%), high volatility in exchange rate (12%), lack of legislative /institutional framework (12%), governmental restrictions (12%), security

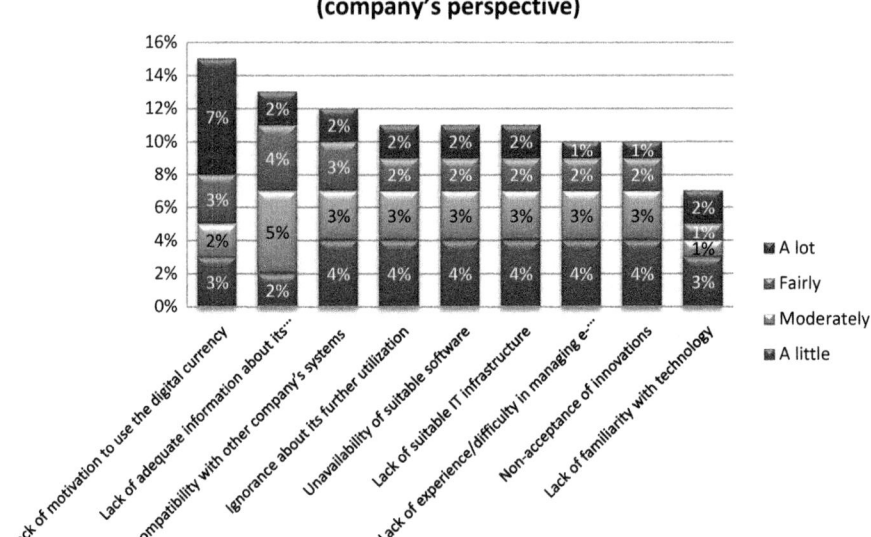

Fig. 10 Internal reasons for non-adoption

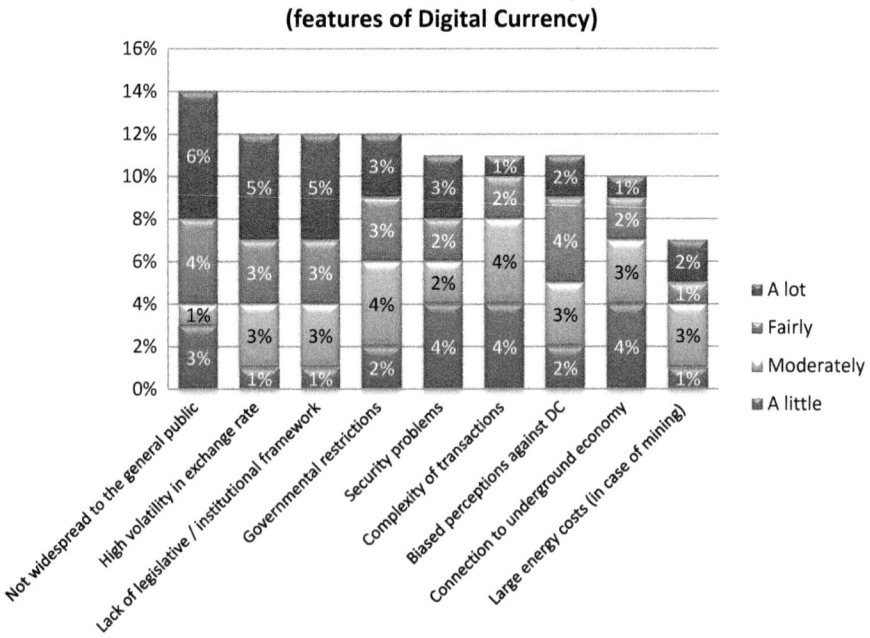

Fig. 11 External reasons for non-adoption

Fig. 12 Perceived Ease of
Use

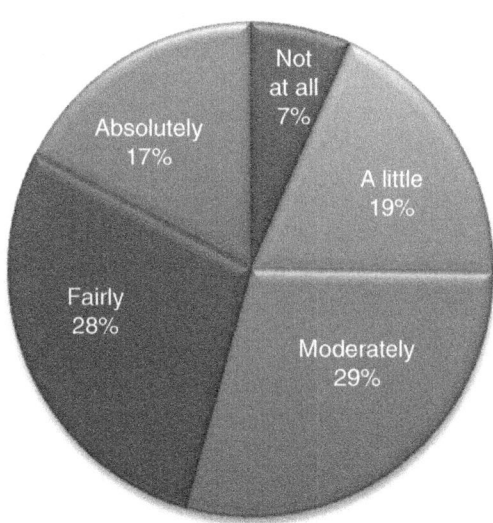

Perceived Ease of Use

problems (11%), complexity of transactions (11%), biased perceptions against digital currency (11%), connection to underground economy (10%) and large energy costs (in case of mining) (7%).

Figure 12 illustrates that the majority of the respondents (29%) think that the use of the digital currency is easy moderately, followed by 28% who consider its use easy fairly, while 19% find its use easy a little, 17% absolutely and 7% not at all.

Figure 13 illustrates that the majority of the respondents (39%) believe that digital currency will be used in conjunction with traditional currencies, followed by 28% who believe that it will be used more than nowadays; 19% believe that it will dominate the e-payment methods, while 6% believe it will disappear.

6   Conclusions

The main three factors that conduce to the adoption of digital currency are: (1) freedom in payments, (2) ease of use and (3) low cost of transactions. On the contrary, the main factors for non-adoption of digital currency are: (1) by the company's point of view: lack of motivation to use digital currency and lack of adequate information about its functioning and (2) concerning the digital currency itself: that it is not widespread to the general public and high volatility in exchange rates. The pace of adoption of digital currency reminds of other technologies, like Internet or email. Digital currency is still very new and thus it is very early to make any predictions.

Fig. 13 Future means of transaction

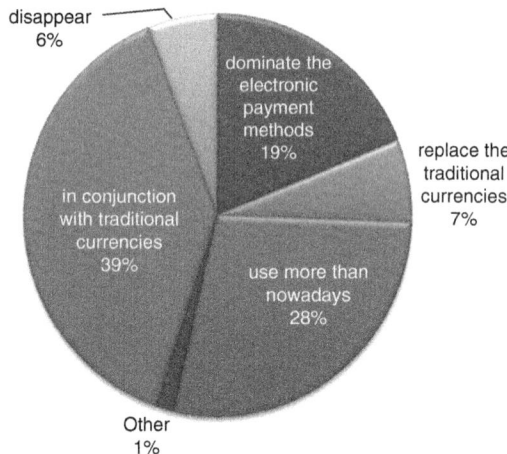

Future of DC as a means of transaction

disappear 6%

dominate the electronic payment methods 19%

replace the traditional currencies 7%

in conjunction with traditional currencies 39%

use more than nowadays 28%

Other 1%

7   Limitations

The limitations of this survey are summarized as follows: (1) as aforementioned the survey was circulated on the Web, thus a different method for gathering data, such as post, phone calls or interview with a company's representative could give different conclusions, (2) the questionnaire didn't take into consideration the job title of the participant, thus it cannot be concluded whether the responses reflect the official and point of view of the company, (3) the accuracy of the answers was relied on the integrity of each participant and (4) the survey tool was in English, many terms were technological and the theme was specialized, thus some of the companies may were restrained from answering, as their home language would be more preferable to them or they mistook digital currency with e-payments with fiat money.

8   Future Research

Research concerning the adoption of digital currency in a particular business sector or a country exclusively would be very interesting. Different research tools could make easier the collection of the data. Future studies in digital currency could be based in other theories and concern various themes, i.e. legislative and fiscal regimes, ethics and socioeconomic issues. Furthermore, blockchain applications are also a very interesting field of research. Finally, extension of this research and statistical analysis by Structural Equation Modeling (SEM) is proposed.

References

Agarwal, R., & Prasad, J. (1998). A conceptual and operational definition of personal innovativeness in the domain of information technology. *Information Systems Research, 9*, 204–215.

Ajzen, I., Fishbein, M. (1980). *Understanding attitudes and predicting social behaviour.*

Angel, J. J., & McCabe, D. (2015). The ethics of payments: Paper, plastic, or bitcoin? *Journal of Business Ethics, 132*, 603–611.

Antonopoulos, A. M. (2014). *Mastering bitcoin: Unlocking digital cryptocurrencies.* Newton: O'Reilly Media.

Balestrieri, F., Huberman, B. (2014). *Bitcoin as a monetary issue.*

Chellappa, R., & Pavlou, P. (2002). Perceived information security, financial liability and consumer trust in electronic commerce transactions. *Logistics Information Management, 15*, 358–368.

Cheng, T.C.E., Lam, D.Y.C., & Yeung, A.C.L. (2006). Adoption of internet banking: An empirical study in Hong Kong. *Decision Support Systems, 42*, 1558–1572.

Chen, L., Gillenson, M. L., & Sherrell, D. L. (2002). Enticing online consumers: An extended technology acceptance perspective. *Information Management, 39*, 705–719.

Chowdhury, A., Mendelson, B. (2013). *Virtual currency and the financial system: The case of bitcoin.*

CoinDesk (2014). *State-of-bitcoin. Report analysis, emerging trends.*

Crespo, A. H., de los Salmones Sanchez, M. M. G., & del Bosque, I. R. (2013). Influence of users' perceived compatibility and their prior experience on B2C e-commerce acceptance. In *Electronic business and marketing.* Berlin: Springer.

Davis, F. D., Bagozzi, R. P., & Warshaw, P. R. (1989). User acceptance of computer technology: A comparison of two theoretical models. *Management Science, 35*, 982–1003.

Fishbein, M., & Ajzen, I. (1975). *Belief, attitude, intention and behavior: An introduction to theory and research.* Boston: Addison-Wesle, Reading.

Gans, J.S., Halaburda, H. (2013). *Some economics of private digital currency.* SSRN Electron.

Gilder, G. (1993). Metcalfe's law and legacy. *Forbes ASAP: A Technology Supplement, 152*, 158–159.

Kolodinsky, J., Hogarth, J., & Hilgert, M. (2004). The adoption of electronic banking technologies by US consumers. *International Journal of Bank Marketing, 22*, 238–259.

Kousaridas, A., Parissis, G., & Apostolopoulos, T. (2008). An open financial services architecture based on the use of intelligent mobile devices. *Electronic Commerce Research and Applications, 7*, 232–246.

Krugman P (2013) Bitcoin is evil. The conscience of a liberal. *The New York Times.*

Kumpajaya, A., & Dhewanto, W. (2015). The acceptance of bitcoin in Indonesia. *Journal of Basic Microbiology, 4*, 28–38.

Lee, Y. H., Hsieh, Y. C., & Hsu, C. N. (2011). Adding innovation diffusion theory to the technology acceptance model: Supporting employees' intentions to use e-learning systems. *Educational Technology & Society, 14*, 124–137.

Linck, K., Pousttchi, K., Wiedemann, D.G. (2006). Security issues in mobile payment from the customer viewpoint. In: *Proceedings of the 14th European Conference on Information Systems (ECIS 2006)*, Goteborg.

Moore, G. C., & Benbasat, I. (1991). Development of an instrument to measure the perceptions of adopting an information technology innovation. *Information Systems Research, 2*, 192–221.

Nakamoto, S. (2008). *Bitcoin: A peer-to-peer electronic cash system.* White paper.

Oh, S., Ahn, J., & Kim, B. (2003). Adoption of broadband Internet in Korea: the role of experience in building attitudes. *Journal of Information Technology, 18*, 267–280.

Psannis, K. E., Xinogalos, S., & Sifaleras, A. (2014). Convergence of internet of things and mobile cloud computing. *Systems Science & Control Engineering, 2*, 476–483.

Rogers, E. M. (1995). *Diffusion of innovations* (4th ed.). New York: Free Press.

Rogers, E. M. (1962). *Diffusion of innovations* (1st ed.). New York: Free Press.

Saito, T. (2013). Bitcoin: A search-theoretic approach. *International Journal of Innovation in the Digital Economy, 6*, 52–71.

Sigala, M., Airey, D., Jones, P., & Lockwood, A. (2000). The diffusion and application of multimedia technologies in the tourism and hospitality industries. In D. Fesenmaier et al. (Eds.), *Information and communication technologies in tourism*. Wien: Springer.

Smyth, L. (2013). *Overview of Bitcoin Community*. Survey FEB - MAR 2013. https://spacedruiddotcom.wordpress.com/2013/04/13/overview-of-bitcoin-community-survey-feb-mar-2013/. Accessed 18 Sep 2014.

Stroborn, K., Heitmann, A., Leibold, K., & Frank, G. (2004). Internet payments in Germany: A classificatory framework and empirical evidence. *Journal of Business Research, 57*, 1431–1437.

Tasca, P. (2016). The dual nature of bitcoin as payment network and money. In: C. Beer, E. Gnan, & U. W. Birchler (Eds.), *Cash on Trial, Proceedings of the SUERF Conference*.

Tatnall, A., & Burgess, S. (2004). Using actor-network theory to identify factors affecting the adoption of e-commerce in SMEs. In *E-business innovation and change management*. Hershey: IGI Global.

Tornatzky, L., & Klein, R. (1982). Innovation characteristics and innovation adoption-implementation: A meta-analysis of findings. *IEEE Transactions on Engineering Management, 29*, 28–45.

Tsiakis, T., & Sthephanides, G. (2005). The concept of security and trust in electronic payments. *Computers & Security, 24*, 10–15.

D. van Wijk (2013). *What can be expected from the Bitcoin?* Thesis, Erasmus Universiteit Rotterdam.

Wagner, A. (2014). Digital vs. virtual currencies. *Bitcoin Magazine 22*.

Wang, Y., Meister, D., & Wang, Y. (2011). Reexamining relative advantage and perceived usefulness. *International Journal of Information and Communication Technology Education, 7*, 46–59.

Wonglimpiyarat, J. (2015). Bitcoin: The revolution of the payment system? *Journal of Population and Social Studies, 9*, 230–240.

Wu, J. H., & Wang, S. C. (2005). What drives mobile commerce? An empirical evaluation of the revised technology acceptance model. *Information and Management, 42*, 719–729.

Unemployment Prediction in UK by Using a Feedforward Multilayer Perceptron

Georgios N. Kouziokas

Abstract Artificial intelligence has been applied in many scientific fields the last years with the development of new neural network technologies and machine learning techniques. In this research, artificial neural networks are implemented for developing prediction models in order to forecast unemployment. A Feedforward Neural Network architecture was applied, since it is considered as the most suitable in times series predictions. The best artificial neural network forecasting model was evaluated by testing different network topologies regarding the number of the neurons, the number of the hidden layers, and also the nature of the transfer functions in the hidden layers. Several socioeconomic factors were investigated in order to be taken into consideration so as to construct the optimal neural network based forecasting model. The results have shown a very good prediction accuracy regarding the unemployment. The proposed methodology can be very helpful to the authorities in adopting proactive measures for preventing further increase of unemployment which would cause a negative impact on the society.

Keywords Artificial intelligence · Economic development · Neural networks · Public administration · Unemployment

1 Introduction

The rapid growth of information and communication technology has affected thoroughly public administration practices in the direction of adopting sustainable urban development and management strategies. The increased amount of information in public management, the latest years, has led the public stakeholders to the adoption of new technologies and information systems in order to deal with public

G. N. Kouziokas (✉)
Department of Planning and Regional Development, School of Engineering,
University of Thessaly, Volos, Greece
e-mail: gekouzio@uth.gr

© Springer Nature Switzerland AG 2019
A. Sifaleras, K. Petridis (eds.), *Operational Research in the Digital Era – ICT Challenges*, Springer Proceedings in Business and Economics,
https://doi.org/10.1007/978-3-319-95666-4_5

management issues and problems in a more computerized way. Several studies have shown the increased need for reforming public administration by implementing practices based on Information and Communication Technology (ICT) in order to promote advanced reformation in public sector (Dunleavy et al. 2006; Kouziokas 2016b, c, 2017a, b).

The development of new artificial intelligence techniques has increased the adoption artificial intelligence in many scientific sectors. Neural networks have been implemented by several researchers as an advanced prediction tool in several public management issues such as environmental management (Kouziokas et al. 2016, 2017; Kouziokas 2017a, b), public transportation (Kouziokas 2016a, 2017c), knowledge management (Wiig 2002), and decision making (Cortès et al. 2000; Kouziokas and Perakis 2017; Metaxiotis et al. 2003).

The application of several prediction techniques such as artificial neural networks in forecasting unemployment rates has been studied by several researchers (Chen 2008; Franses et al. 2004; Karathanasopoulos et al. 2015; Olmedo 2014).

Chen (2008) has studied the implementation of the nonlinear grey Bernoulli model in order to forecast the unemployment rates in ten countries. The results showed that they can help governments to develop economic and labor strategies. Franses et al. (2004) have used autoregressive time series model with by taking into consideration several factors in order to forecast the unemployment rates in three countries. The results have shown that the proposed technique yields good prediction results. Olmedo (2014) has applied nearest neighbor analysis and artificial neural networks so as to forecast the unemployment rates. The results have shown a very good prediction accuracy. Karathanasopoulos et al. (2015) have studied the prediction of unemployment in the USA by combining radial basis neural networks and support vector regressions. The results have shown that this methodology provides results with increased accuracy.

In this research, artificial neural network models were applied in order to forecast the unemployment rates in United Kingdom. This research has taken into consideration several factors that influence the unemployment rates, so as to feed the neural network models. Also, multiple network architectures were tested regarding the type of the transfer functions and the number of the hidden layer neurons in order to find the optimal forecasting model. In the next sections, the methodology of the research, the theoretical framework, and also the results are presented and discussed.

2 Theoretical Background

2.1 Artificial Neural Networks

Artificial neural networks (ANNs) are computing systems that can simulate the structure of the human brain system. In an artificial neural network the input data are processed in order to produce the output values. The advantage of neural networks is that they can model relationships of nonlinear nature. The information traverses through the network connections in order to produce an output according to the input (Basheer and Hajmeer 2000). Artificial neural networks are utilized in this study to predict unemployment rates by taking into consideration several socioeconomic factors that affect the unemployment rates according to the literature.

2.2 Multilayer Perceptron

A feedforward multilayer perceptron (FFMLP) was used in this study, as many researchers have shown that it is the most appropriate for time series forecasting problems (Hornik 1991). The characteristic of a feedforward multilayer neural network is that all neurons are connected only in a forward direction, between the layers (Svozil et al. 1997). A typical structure of a feedforward multilayer neural network is composed of an input layer, an output layer, and one or more hidden layers. Each layer is composed with a number of neurons (Koskela et al. 1996). The architecture of a typical feedforward neural network is illustrated in Fig. 1.

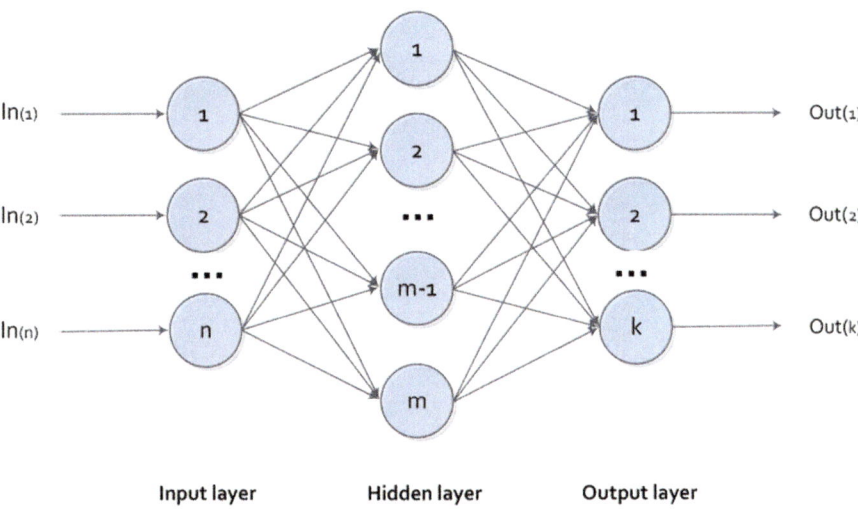

Fig. 1 The topology of a feedforward neural network, where *n* is the number of the neurons in the input layer, m is the number of the neurons in the hidden layer, and *k* is the number of the neurons in the output layer

2.3   Levenberg–Marquardt Training Algorithm

The Levenberg–Marquardt algorithm is usually used as a technique to solve nonlinear problems and also time series problems. Furthermore, another reason for selecting the Levenberg–Marquardt algorithm as the learning algorithm for training the feedforward multilayer neural network is that it is considered as one of the fastest training algorithms compared to other algorithms. The Levenberg–Marquardt algorithm is an iterative optimization method and combines the minimization advantages of the two algorithms, the Gauss-Newton algorithm and also the steepest descent algorithm used for solving nonlinear least-squares problems (Marquardt 1963).

2.4   Unemployment

According to the International Labor Organization[1], the unemployment rate is the proportion of the population who is economically active (those who work and also the population that is seeking and is available to work) which are unemployed. Figure 2 shows the unemployment rates in Europe from 2004 to 2015.

	2004	2005	2006	2007	2008	2009	2010	2011	2012	2013	2014	2015
EU-28	9.3	9.0	8.2	7.2	7.0	9.0	9.6	9.7	10.5	10.9	10.2	9.4
Euro area	9.3	9.1	8.4	7.5	7.6	9.6	10.2	10.2	11.4	12.0	11.6	10.9
Belgium	8.4	8.5	8.3	7.5	7.0	7.9	8.3	7.2	7.6	8.4	8.5	8.5
Bulgaria	12.1	10.1	9.0	6.9	5.6	6.8	10.3	11.3	12.3	13.0	11.4	9.2
Czech Republic	8.3	7.9	7.1	5.3	4.4	6.7	7.3	6.7	7.0	7.0	6.1	5.1
Denmark	5.5	4.8	3.9	3.8	3.4	6.0	7.5	7.6	7.5	7.0	6.6	6.2
Germany	10.4	11.2	10.1	8.5	7.4	7.6	7.0	5.8	5.4	5.2	5.0	4.6
Estonia	10.1	8.0	5.9	4.6	5.5	13.5	16.7	12.3	10.0	8.6	7.4	6.2
Ireland	4.5	4.4	4.5	4.7	6.4	12.0	13.9	14.7	14.7	13.1	11.3	9.4
Greece	10.6	10.0	9.0	8.4	7.8	9.6	12.7	17.9	24.5	27.5	26.5	24.9
Spain	11.0	9.2	8.5	8.2	11.3	17.9	19.9	21.4	24.8	26.1	24.5	22.1
France	8.9	8.9	8.8	8.0	7.4	9.1	9.3	9.2	9.8	10.3	10.3	10.4
Croatia	13.9	13.0	11.6	9.9	8.6	9.2	11.7	13.7	16.0	17.3	17.3	16.3
Italy	8.0	7.7	6.8	6.1	6.7	7.7	8.4	8.4	10.7	12.1	12.7	11.9
Cyprus	4.6	5.3	4.6	3.9	3.7	5.4	6.3	7.9	11.9	15.9	16.1	15.0
Latvia	11.7	10.0	7.0	6.1	7.7	17.5	19.5	16.2	15.0	11.9	10.8	9.9
Lithuania	10.9	8.3	5.8	4.3	5.8	13.8	17.8	15.4	13.4	11.8	10.7	9.1
Luxembourg	5.0	4.6	4.6	4.2	4.9	5.1	4.6	4.8	5.1	5.9	6.0	6.4
Hungary	6.1	7.2	7.5	7.4	7.8	10.0	11.2	11.0	11.0	10.2	7.7	6.8
Malta	7.2	6.9	6.8	6.5	6.0	6.9	6.9	6.4	6.3	6.4	5.8	5.4
Netherlands	5.7	5.9	5.0	4.2	3.7	4.4	5.0	5.0	5.8	7.3	7.4	6.9
Austria	5.5	5.6	5.3	4.9	4.1	5.3	4.8	4.6	4.9	5.4	5.6	5.7
Poland	19.1	17.9	13.9	9.6	7.1	8.1	9.7	9.7	10.1	10.3	9.0	7.5
Portugal	7.8	8.8	8.9	9.1	8.8	10.7	12.0	12.9	15.8	16.4	14.1	12.6
Romania	8.0	7.1	7.2	6.4	5.6	6.5	7.0	7.2	6.8	7.1	6.8	6.8
Slovenia	6.3	6.5	6.0	4.9	4.4	5.9	7.3	8.2	8.9	10.1	9.7	9.0
Slovakia	18.4	16.4	13.5	11.2	9.6	12.1	14.5	13.7	14.0	14.2	13.2	11.5
Finland	8.8	8.4	7.7	6.9	6.4	8.2	8.4	7.8	7.7	8.2	8.7	9.4
Sweden	7.4	7.7	7.1	6.1	6.2	8.3	8.6	7.8	8.0	8.0	7.9	7.4
United Kingdom	4.7	4.8	5.4	5.3	5.6	7.6	7.8	8.1	7.9	7.6	6.1	5.3

Fig. 2 Unemployment in Europe from 2004 to 2015. Source: Eurostat: http://ec.europa.eu/eurostat/statistics-explained/index.php/Unemployment_statistics)

---

[1]http://www.ilo.org.

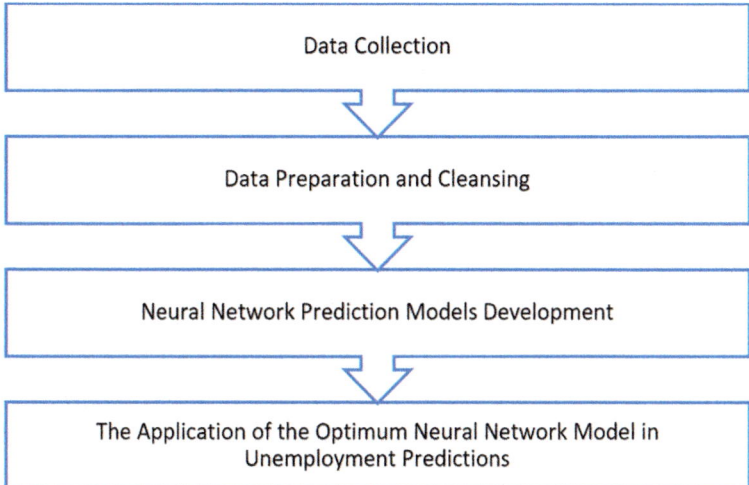

Fig. 3 Overview of the followed methodology

3   Research Methodology

The research methodology is divided into four stages: data collection, data cleansing and preparation, artificial neural network forecasting model development, and at last the implementation of the optimal neural network model in order to forecast the unemployment rates in United Kingdom. In the first stage, the data were collected regarding the unemployment rates and also data regarding socioeconomic factors that influence the unemployment rates such as GDP growth, exports of goods, and services were collected. In the second stage, the data were checked for possible gaps and were prepared in order to feed the artificial neural network forecasting models. In the third phase, several network topologies were tested in order to develop the optimal network forecasting model. In the last stage, the optimal neural network model was implemented so as to forecast the unemployment rates in UK. An overview of the research methodology is illustrated in Fig. 3.

4   Results

4.1   Data Collection and Preparation

The data about the socioeconomic factors such as the annual GDP (Growth Domestic Product) growth and the exports of goods and services (annual % growth) were collected from the official website of the UK Office for National Statistics (ONS). Furthermore, the data about the unemployment rates were collected also

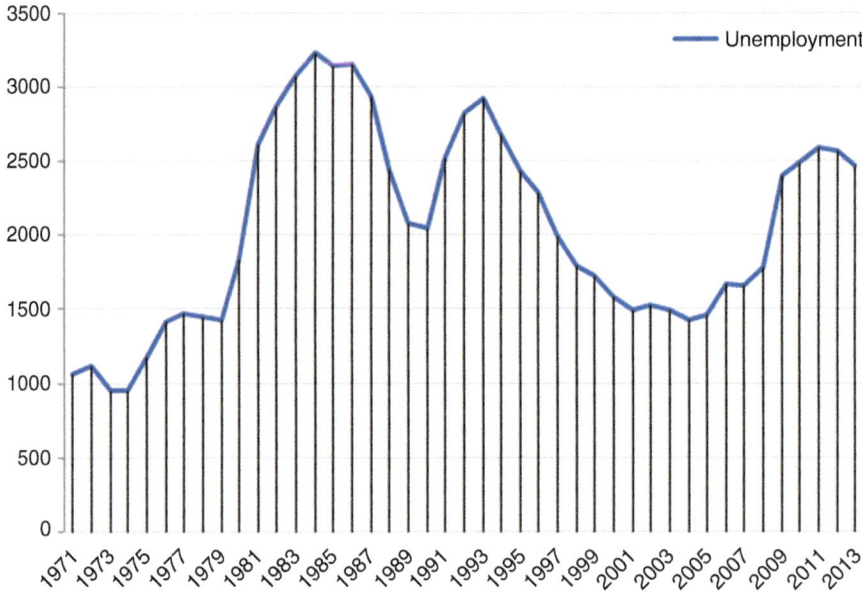

Fig. 4 The unemployment (thousands) in UK from 1971 to 2013

from the official website of the United Kingdom Office for National Statistics (ONS).

The collected data cover the time period from 1971 to 2013 for the United Kingdom. The data were preprocessed and prepared to be used to feed the Artificial Neural Network Models. Also, the data were checked for gaps, incoherences, and duplicates. Figure 4 shows the unemployment (thousands) in UK from 1971 to 2013.

4.2   Artificial Neural Network Models

Firstly, the literature was investigated in order to find the parameters that affect the unemployment rates to be used as input variables in the constructed neural network models. According to the literature several socioeconomic factors influence the levels of unemployment rates. The most important factors are: the GDP growth and the growth of exports of goods and services (Bayar 2014; Ozughalu and Ogwumike 2013). The neural network models were developed and tested by using the above-mentioned socioeconomic factors as input variables that influence the levels of the unemployment rates and also the historical values of the unemployment rates.

The data were separated into three different parts. Sixty percent of the primary data was used as the training set, 20% for the validation set, and the 20% for the test set. The training data set was used in order to train the neural network models by using collected data. The validation set was used in order to evaluate the artificial neural network modes. The Levenberg–Marquardt Algorithm was used as the learning algorithm as it is considered as one of the fastest training algorithms compared to other learning algorithms (Lourakis 2005).

4.3   Optimal Forecasting Model

In order to find the optimal neural network model multiple tests were performed. Firstly, the performance of every neural network developed model was tested by using different neural network architectures. The testing parameters of the neural network structures were the number of the hidden layers and the transfer functions in the hidden layers. Architectures with one and two hidden layers were investigated, and the optimal topology that produced the best prediction results was the one with two hidden layers in this case study.

The most common transfer functions were investigated: Log-Sigmoid Transfer Function (LSTF), Positive Linear Transfer Function (PLTF), Tanh-Sigmoid Transfer Function (TSTF), Elliot Sigmoid Transfer Function (ESTF), and Linear Transfer Function (LTF). The optimal network architecture was found to be the one with 14 neurons and Linear Transfer Function (LTF) as the transfer function in the first hidden layer and nine neurons and Tanh-Sigmoid Transfer Function (TSTF) in the second hidden layer as the transfer function.

The optimal model was evaluated according to the minimum Mean Squared Error (MSE) among all the other constructed neural network prediction models. The Mean Squared Error (MSE) was calculated by using the following equation:

$$MSE = \frac{\sum_{i=1}^{N} \left(y_{pi} - y_{r_i} \right)^2}{N} \tag{1}$$

where y_{pi} represents the predicted value, y_{r_i} represents the real value, and N is the number of the output values.

The Mean Squared Error (MSE) of the optimal model was found to be 0.2457 at epoch 8 and the Root Mean Squared Error (RMSE) was 0.4957. The results have shown a very good prediction accuracy. In Fig. 5 the neural network topology of the optimal model is illustrated.

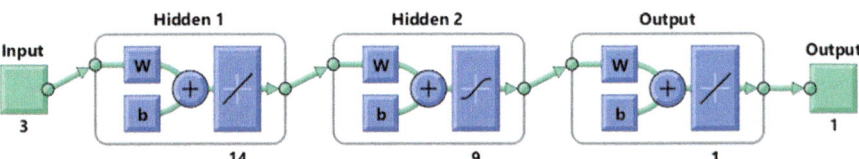

Fig. 5 The topology of the produced optimal artificial neural network model

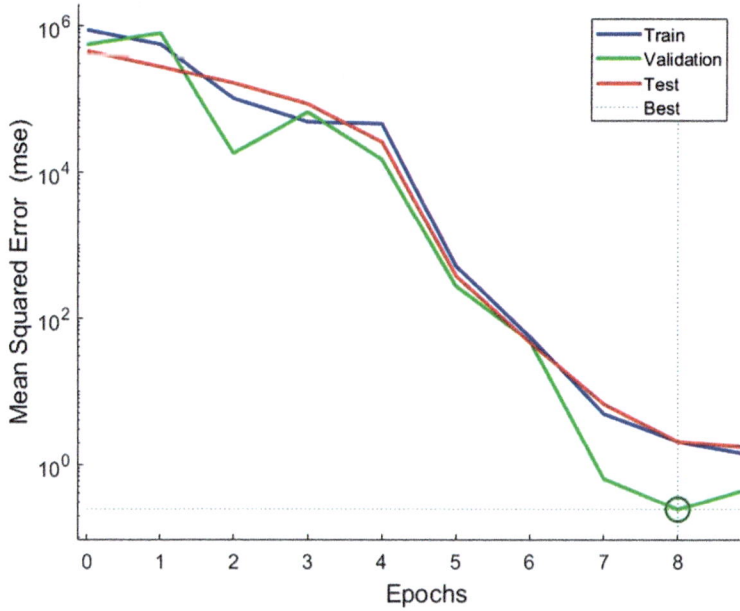

Fig. 6 The performance plot of the test, validation, and training set by using the optimal neural network model according to the minimum Mean Squared Error (MSE)

Figure 6 shows performance plot of the test, validation, and training set by using the optimal neural network model according to the minimum Mean Squared Error (MSE).

5   Conclusions and Discussion

Adopting artificial intelligence in public management can be very valuable for the authorities especially when they are dealing with problems related to proactive management which requires the adoption of prediction techniques. The application of neural networks in many scientific fields has been highly increased the last decades with the development of new neural network technologies and machine learning techniques.

In this research, artificial intelligence was utilized in order to develop neural network models for forecasting the levels of unemployment. A feedforward neural network architecture was implemented since it is considered as the most suitable in times series predictions. Several socioeconomic factors that affect the unemployment levels were taken into consideration so as to develop the neural network based forecasting models, such as GDP growth, growth of exports of goods and services, since these factors influence the levels of unemployment according to the literature (Bayar 2014; Ozughalu and Ogwumike 2013).

The final results have shown a very good forecasting accuracy of the levels of unemployment in the United Kingdom. The optimal artificial neural network model was developed by testing different neural network architectures. The proposed methodology has shown better forecasting results compared to other researches (Franses et al. 2004; Olmedo 2014). These results can be very promising for the public administrators and stakeholders in adopting proactive measures for preventing further increase of unemployment which would have a negative impact on the society and on the quality of life of the citizens.

Acknowledgments The UK Department for Business, Energy and Industrial Strategy and the UK Office for National Statistics websites for retrieving the data.

References

Basheer, I., & Hajmeer, M. (2000). Artificial neural networks: Fundamentals, computing, design, and application. *Journal of Microbiological Methods, 43*(1), 3–31.

Bayar, Y. (2014). Effects of economic growth, export and foreign direct investment inflows on unemployment in Turkey. *Investment Management and Financial Innovations, 11*(2), 20–27.

Chen, C.-I. (2008). Application of the novel nonlinear grey Bernoulli model for forecasting unemployment rate. *Chaos, Solitons & Fractals, 37*(1), 278–287.

Cortès, U., Sànchez-Marrè, M., Ceccaroni, L., R-Roda, I., & Poch, M. (2000). Artificial intelligence and environmental decision support systems. *Applied Intelligence, 13*(1), 77–91.

Dunleavy, P., Margetts, H., Bastow, S., & Tinkler, J. (2006). New public management is dead—Long live digital-era governance. *Journal of Public Administration Research and Theory, 16*(3), 467–494.

Franses, P. H., Paap, R., & Vroomen, B. (2004). Forecasting unemployment using an autoregression with censored latent effects parameters. *International Journal of Forecasting, 20*(2), 255–271.

Hornik, K. (1991). Approximation capabilities of multilayer feedforward networks. *Neural Networks, 4*(2), 251–257.

Karathanasopoulos, A., Sermpinis, G., Stasinakis, C., & Theofilatos, K. (2015). Forecasting US unemployment with radial basis neural networks, Kalman filters and support vector regressions. *Computational Economics, 47*, 1–19.

Koskela, T., Lehtokangas, M., Saarinen, J., & Kaski, K. (1996). Time series prediction with multilayer perceptron, FIR and Elman neural networks. In *Proceedings of the World Congress on Neural Networks* (pp. 491–496). Citeseer.

Kouziokas, G. N. (2016a). Artificial intelligence and crime prediction in public management of transportation safety in urban environment. In *Proceedings of the 3rd Conference on Sustainable Urban Mobility* (pp. 534–539). Volos: University of Thessaly.

Kouziokas, G. N. (2016b). Geospatial based information system development in public administration for sustainable development and planning in urban environment. *European Journal of Sustainable Development, 5*(4), 347–352. https://doi.org/10.14207/ejsd.2016.v5n4p347.

Kouziokas, G. N. (2016c). Technology-based management of environmental organizations using an environmental management information system (EMIS): Design and development. *Environmental Technology & Innovation, 5*, 106–116. https://doi.org/10.1016/j.eti.2016.01.006.

Kouziokas, G. N. (2017a). An information system for judicial and public administration using artificial intelligence and geospatial data. In *Proceedings of the 21st Pan-Hellenic Conference on Informatics* (pp. 1–2). Larissa: ACM, 3139402. https://doi.org/10.1145/3139367.3139402.

Kouziokas, G. N. (2017b). Machine learning technique in time series prediction of gross domestic product. In *Proceedings of the 21st Pan-Hellenic Conference on Informatics* (pp. 1–2). Larissa: ACM, 3139443. https://doi.org/10.1145/3139367.3139443.

Kouziokas, G. N. (2017c). The application of artificial intelligence in public administration for forecasting high crime risk transportation areas in urban environment. *Transportation Research Procedia, 24*, 467–473. https://doi.org/10.1016/j.trpro.2017.05.083.

Kouziokas, G. N., & Perakis, K. (2017). Decision support system based on artificial intelligence, GIS and remote sensing for sustainable public and judicial management. *European Journal of Sustainable Development, 6*(3), 397–404. https://doi.org/10.14207/ejsd.2017.v6n3p397.

Kouziokas, G. N., Chatzigeorgiou, A., & Perakis, K. (2016). Predicting environmental data in public management by using artificial intelligence. In *Proceedings of the 11th International Scientific Conference eRA-11* (pp. 39–46). Piraeus: Piraeus University of Applied Sciences.

Kouziokas, G. N., Chatzigeorgiou, A., & Perakis, K. (2017). Artificial intelligence and regression in predicting ground water levels in public administration. *European Water, 57*, 361–366.

Lourakis, M. I. A. (2005). A brief description of the Levenberg-Marquardt algorithm implemented by levmar. *Foundation of Research and Technology, 4*, 1–6.

Marquardt, D. W. (1963). An algorithm for least-squares estimation of nonlinear parameters. *Journal of the Society for Industrial and Applied Mathematics, 11*(2), 431–441.

Metaxiotis, K., Ergazakis, K., Samouilidis, E., & Psarras, J. (2003). Decision support through knowledge management: The role of the artificial intelligence. *Information Management & Computer Security, 11*(5), 216–221.

Olmedo, E. (2014). Forecasting spanish unemployment using near neighbour and neural net techniques. *Computational Economics, 43*(2), 183–197.

Ozughalu, U. M., & Ogwumike, F. O. (2013). Can economic growth, foreign direct investment and exports provide the desired panacea to the problem of unemployment in Nigeria. *Journal of Economics and Sustainable Development, 4*(1), 36–51.

Svozil, D., Kvasnicka, V., & Pospichal, J. (1997). Introduction to multi-layer feed-forward neural networks. *Chemometrics and Intelligent Laboratory Systems, 39*(1), 43–62.

Wiig, K. M. (2002). Knowledge management in public administration. *Journal of Knowledge Management, 6*(3), 224–239.

Performance Evaluation of Routing Protocols for BIG Data Application

Evangelos Balasas, Kostas E. Psannis, and Manos Roumeliotis

Abstract In the last years, the rapid growth in network communications necessitates the deep knowledge of the process called routing. To be more specific, routes of information (packets) are held on the device called router, which is responsible for the optimal transmission of pieces of data (packets) from the source to the destination by using the routing protocols and routing algorithms, which cooperate for the search and the selection of the best path. There are two different types of routing process: static routing, which is done manually by the administrator of the network and dynamic routing, which is done automatically through the usage of routing protocols. Static routing protocol is used when the network architecture is simple, while dynamic routing protocols are used when the architecture complexity increases. There are various types of dynamic routing protocols being widely used. The three categories of dynamic routing protocols are the distance-vector protocols like RIP, which uses the Bellman-Ford algorithm, the link-state routing protocols like OSPF, which uses the Dijkstra algorithm, and a hybrid type of routing protocol like EIGRP, which uses an algorithm called Dual. In this paper, we will not only illustrate a comparative analysis of the characteristics and the metrics of dynamic routing protocols, but we will also compare the performance of different Interior Gateway routing protocols, like EIGRP, OSPF, and RIP, in real-time applications big data, video conferencing, and VoIP, based on end-to-end packet delay, network convergence duration, packet delay variation, and Jitter of VoIP by using Riverbed Modeller simulator. Our aim is to show how dynamic routing protocols perform in real-time applications, while some failures happen on different network links.

Keywords EIGRP · OSPF · RIP · QoS · Big data

E. Balasas (✉) · K. E. Psannis · M. Roumeliotis
Department of Applied Informatics, University of Macedonia, Thessaloniki, Greece
e-mail: mis1424@uom.edu.gr

© Springer Nature Switzerland AG 2019
A. Sifaleras, K. Petridis (eds.), *Operational Research in the Digital Era – ICT Challenges*, Springer Proceedings in Business and Economics,
https://doi.org/10.1007/978-3-319-95666-4_6

75

1   Introduction

The process of sending packets from the source to the destination using the best path which is based on routing algorithms is called routing. Every routing algorithm uses some metrics, such as delay, bandwidth, cost, and hop count in order to calculate and find the best route. After finding the best route, routing algorithms send an update to inform the routing tables in all network routers. Every router stores only the information that is related to the network directly (not immediately) connected to it. The above information is shared to neighbor routers only, and then it is shared throughout the whole network through routing protocols. Routing protocols determine the way of interaction among network routers and select the best routes between two nodes by distributing information. In this way, routers are informed about the whole topology of the network. There are two main categories of Interior Gateway routing protocols:

- Distance-vector protocols (RIP)
- Link-state protocols (OSPF)

Moreover, there is one enhanced distance-vector protocol, called EIGRP, which defers from the other protocols of its category in the usage of algorithm (it uses Dual algorithm) and the metrics it uses to calculate and select the best path.

RIP (Routing Information Protocol) is a distance-vector routing protocol which makes use of Bellman-Ford algorithm. In addition, it uses hop count as a metric to find the best route. This protocol is mainly used in small networks due to the small number of hops (only 15) that it can count. It supports VLSM (Variable Length Subnet Masking) (only the RIPv2) and it has two versions, RIPv1 and RIPv2 (Balasas 2017).

OSPF (Open Shortest Path First) is a link-state routing protocol which uses the Dijkstra algorithm and cost as a metric in order to find and select the best path. Moreover, OSPF has no limitations in hop count and it supports VLSM. So, it can be a good choice in large networks.

EIGRP (Enhanced Interior Gateway Routing Protocol) is an enhanced distance-vector protocol which makes use of DUAL (Diffusing Update Algorithm) algorithm and composite metrics, delay and bandwidth to name but a few, to choose the best route. It supports VLSM and can count up to 255 hops (www.cisco.com).

Nowadays, the need of using big data in networks has become a necessity, and the proper selection of the right routing protocol for better transmission of big data on the network is of vital importance (Psannis 2015; Christos and Psannis 2017; Gupta et al. 2018) (Fig. 1).

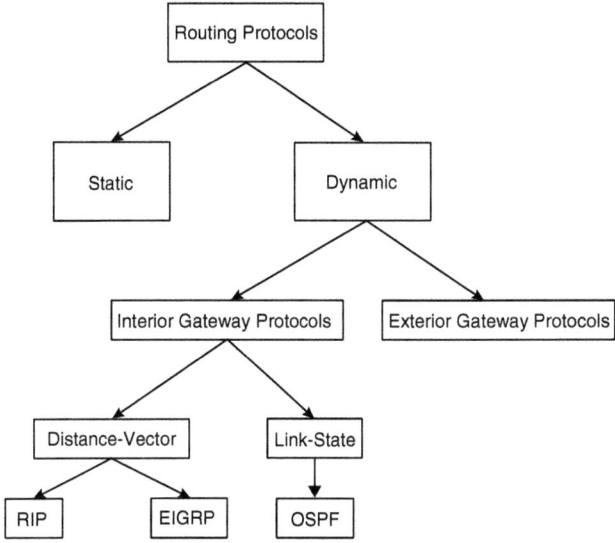

Fig. 1 Types of routing protocols

2 Related Research Review

Many researches, which investigate the performance of the routing protocols in different network topologies, have been done in the field of the process of routing. In the first research, the authors evaluated the performance of OSPF, RIP, IGRP, and EIGRP in real-time applications, based on convergence, queuing delay, utilization, and end-to-end delay with the usage of the OPNET simulator. They concluded that EIGRP performed better than the others routing protocols (Jalali et al. 2014). The authors of the second research illustrated a comparative performance analysis of three (OSPF, RIP, and EIGRP) Interior Getaway Protocols in the terms of HTTP page response, e-mail upload response time and network convergence, queuing delay, utilization, and throughout. They ended up to the conclusion that EIGRP outperforms OSPF and RIP in their study (Kaur and Mir 2014). Abdulkadhim simulated EIGRP, OSPF, and RIP in OPNET simulator. He analyzed the protocols performance based on network convergence and convergence activity, and he concluded that OSPF has much more convergence activity than RIP, while it has faster convergence time. Moreover, he showed that OSPF performs better than the other routing protocols while some link failures take place on the network (Abdulkadhim 2015). Ashoor analyzed the performance of link-state and distance-vector algorithms in a mesh network and presented an analysis of dynamic routing protocols (Ashoor 2015). The authors of the next research presented a comparative performance analysis of OSPF and EIGRP based on Cisco Packet Tracer 6.0.1 simulator. They concluded that EIGRP performs better than OSPF in terms of convergence time and delay (Mardedi and Rosidi 2015). Dey et al. illustrated a performance analysis and redistribution of OSPF, EIGRP, and RIPv2 based on Cisco Packet Tracer simulator (Dey et al. 2015). Another research done by Shewaye Sirika and Smita Mahajine presented in detail the characteristics of RIP, EIGRP, and OSPF and simulated these routing protocols on two different simulators in order to compare their performance, OPNET and Cisco Packet Tracer. They decided that EIGRP is the best for fast convergence, while RIPv2 is suitable for small networks, while OSPF is suitable for very large networks (Sirika and Mahajine 2016). The authors of the next research presented a comparative analysis of EIGRP, OSPF, and their combination for real-time application on the OPNET simulator. They concluded that the combination of EIGRP and OSPF has a better performance than OSPF and EIGRP. Moreover, the research presented that the combination of EIGRP and OSPF perform better in terms of packet loss, end-to-end delay, and packet delay variation than both EIGRP and OSPF (Kodzo et al. 2016).

2.1   Comparison of Dynamic Routing Protocols

Table 1 presents a comparative analysis of the features of RIP, OSPF, and EIGRP routing protocols.

2.2   Simulation Scenario

In order to compare the evaluation performance of routing protocols (RIP, OSPF, and EIGRP) for big data application, we create and implement one case with

Table 1 Comparison of dynamic routing protocols

Features	Routing protocols		
	RIPv2	OSPF	EIGRP
Interior/exterior?	Interior	Interior	Interior
Type	Distance-vector	Link-state	Hybrid
Administrative distance	120	110	90 (internal)/170 (external)
Hop count limit	15	No limit	255
Convergence	Slow	Fast	Very fast
Update timers	30 s	Only when change occurs	Only when change occurs
Updates	Full table	Only changes	Only changes
Classful/classless	Classless	Classless	Classless
Algorithm	Bellman-Ford	Dijkstra	DUAL
Supports VLSM	Yes	Yes	Yes
Default metric	Hop count	Bandwidth/delay	Cost

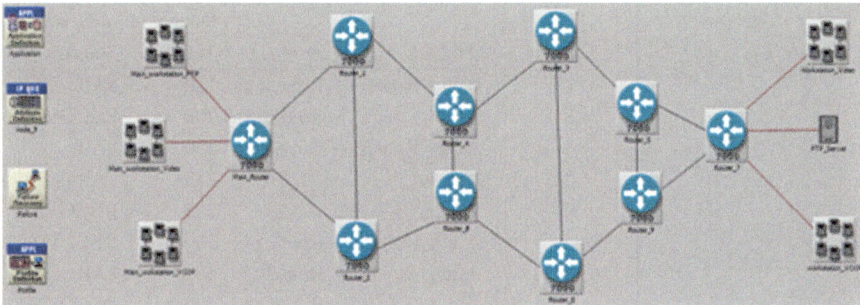

Fig. 2 Network topology using Riverbed Modeller simulator

three scenarios in the same network topology. Moreover, the comparison is based on convergence duration, video conferencing packet end-to-end delay, jitter of voice, and voice packet end-to-end delay. The network composed of the following configuration services and network devices (Fig. 2):

- Application configuration.
- Profile configuration.
- Failure—Recovery configuration.
- QoS Attribute configuration.
- Cisco 7000 Routers.
- PPP_DS3 Duplex Links.
- Ethernet 1000 BaseT Duplex Links.
- Application Server.
- Ethernet workstations.

The Application definition object is set to support FTP big data, video conferencing (High Resolution Video), and voice conferencing (PCM Quality Speech). Also, the Profile definition object is set to support and define the applications (FTP, video conferencing, and VoIP) and the Failure–Recovery object is set to define the failure and recovery time.

In order to compare to a greater extent the three routing protocols in real-time application we use one case in three scenarios configured with RIP, OSPF, and EIGRP, respectively. The simulation run time was set to 1200 s (20 min) and two situations were set in Failure–Recovery object to illustrate the performance of those routing protocols. In our case two links failure took place at the same time (Table 2).

Table 2 Double failure case

| | Double failure case | |
Link	Time (s)	Status
Main_Router → Router_1	150	FAIL
Main_Router → Router_1	200	RECOVER
Main_Router → Router_1	250	FAIL
Router_7 → Router_9	255	FAIL
Router_7 → Router_9	295	RECOVER
Main_Router → Router_1	300	RECOVER
Main_Router → Router_1	400	FAIL
Main_Router → Router_1	500	RECOVER

Results

Network Convergence Duration

As convergence duration is defined as the time needed for routers to have the same routing table or to be in the same state. According to the simulation result, EIGRP showed the best performance due to its fast convergence feature. Although the RIP routing protocol had been showing the worst performance in the beginning of the simulation, finally it improved its performance in the second half of the simulation time.

In addition, although OSPF had been presenting the best performance in the beginning of the simulation, finally, after the two links failure that had taken place, it showed the worst performance in our case study (Fig. 3).

Video Conferencing Packet Delay Variation

Video conferencing packet delay variation refers to the difference among end-to-end delay for video packets in a one-way flow, with any lost packet being ignored.

What we can conclude from the simulation result is that EIGRP and OSPF routing protocols performed better than RIP (Fig. 4).

Video Conferencing Packet End-to-End Delay

Video conferencing packet end-to-end delay refers to the time needed for a video packet to be transmitted across the network from source to the destination. According to the figure, OSPF showed the worst performance and this result mainly stemmed from the second link failure that had happened in the network. The EIGRP routing protocol showed the second better performance, while RIP displayed the better and most stable performance in the duration of simulation (Fig. 5).

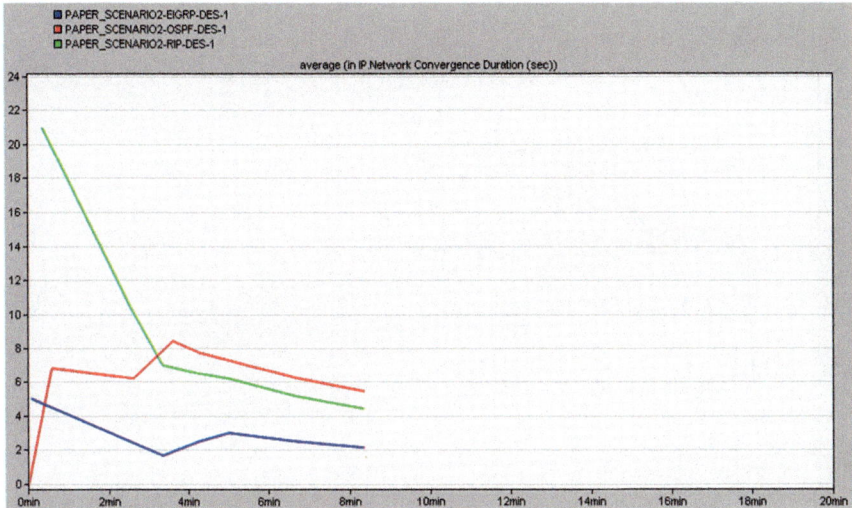

Fig. 3 Network convergence duration

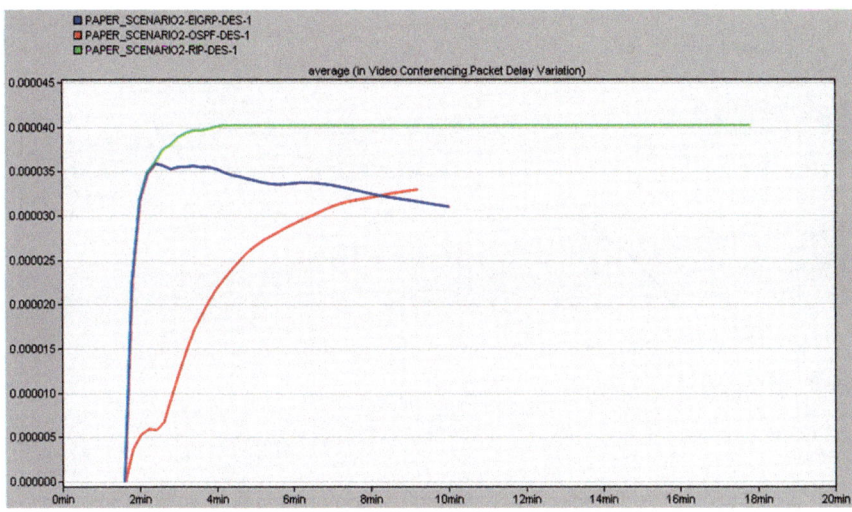

Fig. 4 Video conferencing packet delay variation

Video Conferencing Traffic Sent

Video conferencing traffic sent refers to the amount of video conferencing data sent during data transmission. From the simulation result we can conclude that all three routing protocols sent the same amount of video data (Fig. 6).

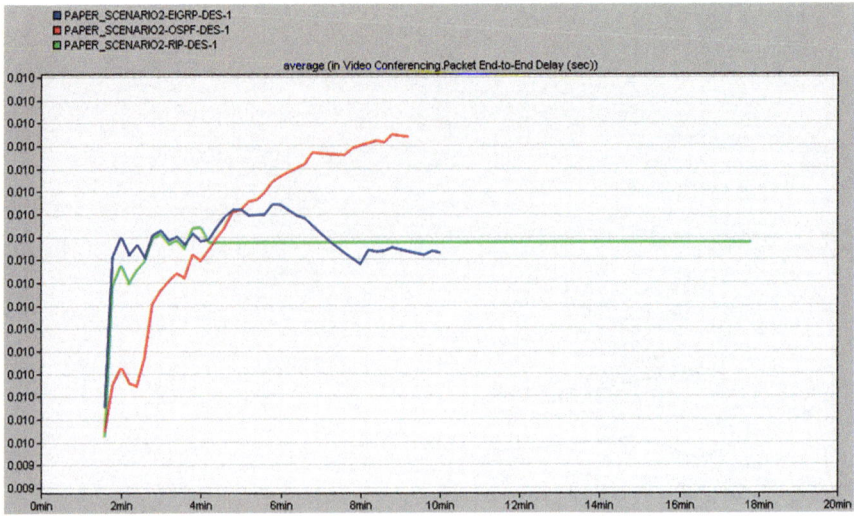

Fig. 5 Video packet end-to-end delay

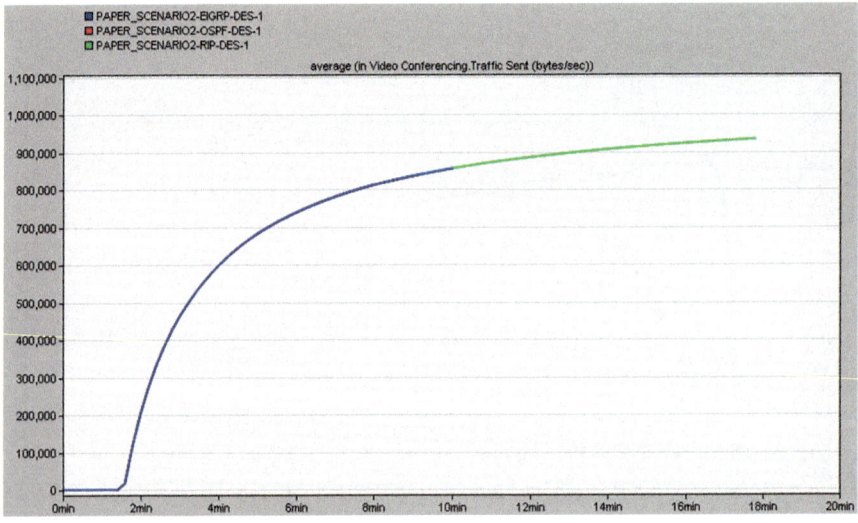

Fig. 6 Video conferencing traffic sent

Video Conferencing Traffic Received

Video conferencing traffic received refers to the amount of video conferencing data received during data transmission. From the simulation result we can conclude that EIGRP and OSFP routing protocols achieved to receive the whole amount of video data, while RIP routing protocol received only the half amount of video conferencing data (Fig. 7).

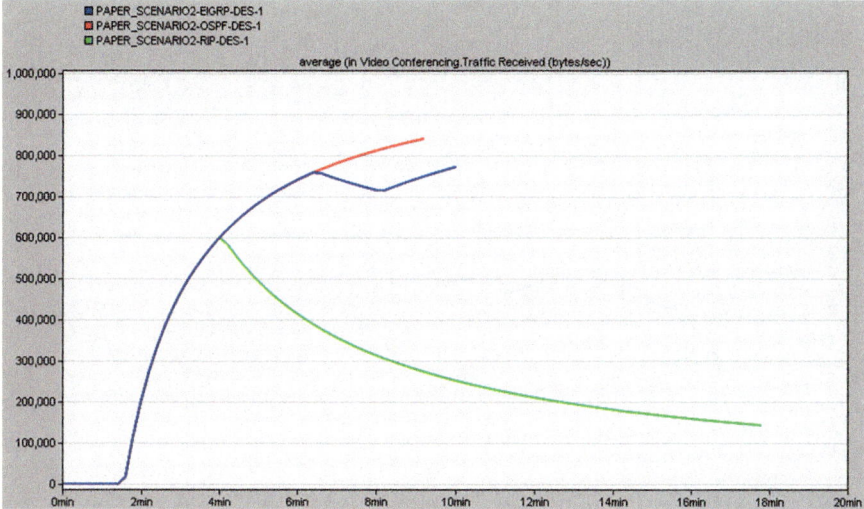

Fig. 7 Video conferencing traffic received

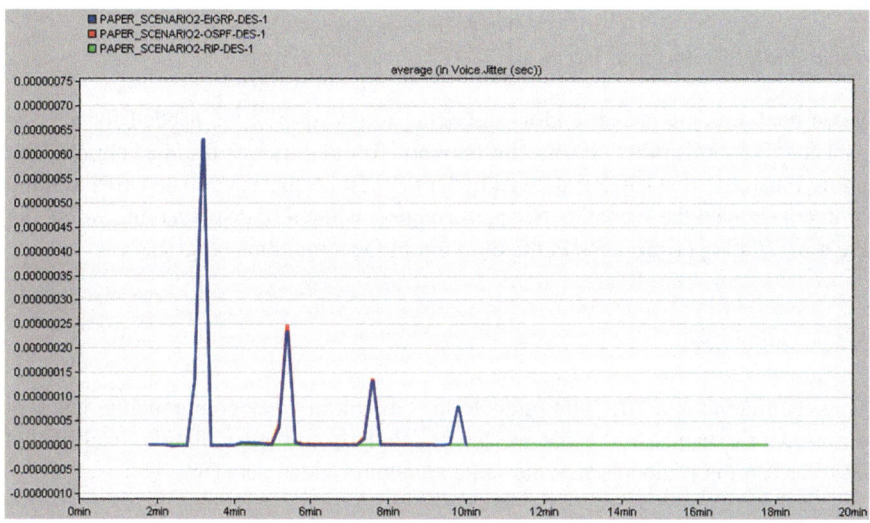

Fig. 8 Jitter of VoIP

Jitter of VoIP

Jitter of VoIP refers to a delay in receiving a voice data packet. This delay usually affects the transmission of voice data and the quality of voice. What we can conclude from the simulation result is that OSPF and EIGRP showed the same delay in receiving a voice packet (Fig. 8).

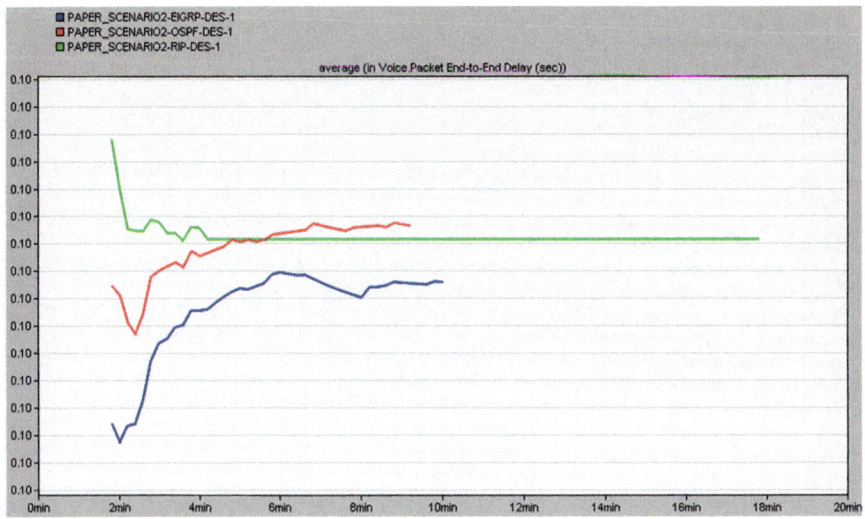

Fig. 9 Voice packet end-to-end delay

Voice Packet End-to-End Delay

Voice conferencing packet end-to-end delay refers to the time needed for a voice packet to be transmitted across the network from source to the destination. The figure illustrates that EIGRP showed by far the best performance. The OSPF routing protocol showed the second better performance, while RIP displayed the worst, but the most stable performance in the duration of the simulation (Fig. 9).

Voice Traffic Sent

Voice conferencing traffic sent refers to the amount of voice conferencing data sent during data transmission. What we can conclude from the simulation result is that all three routing protocols sent the same amount of video data (Fig. 10).

Voice Traffic Received

Voice conferencing traffic received refers to the amount of voice conferencing data received during data transmission. According to the simulation result, EIGRP and OSFP routing protocols achieved to receive the whole amount of video data, while RIP routing protocol received only the half amount of video conferencing data (Fig. 11).

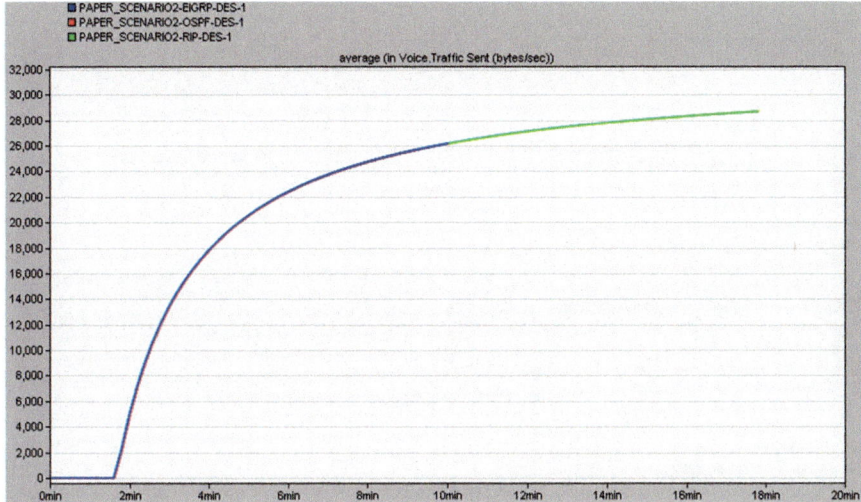

Fig. 10 Voice traffic sent

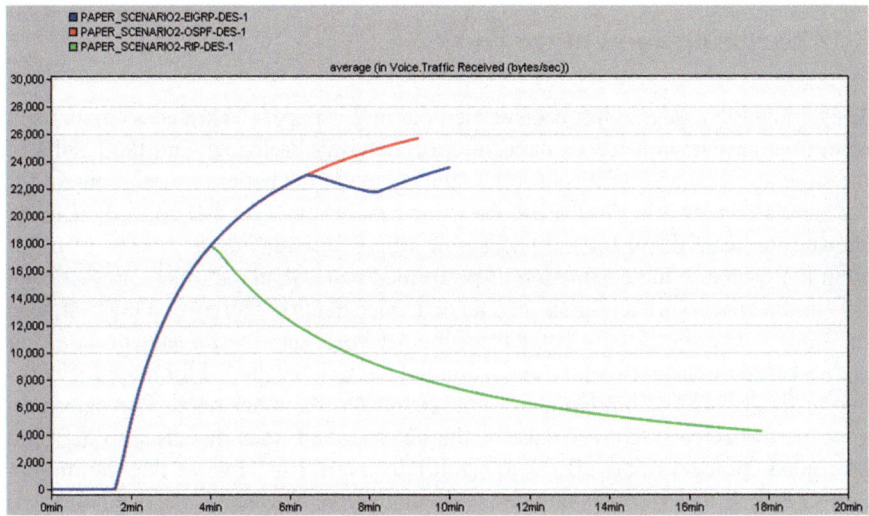

Fig. 11 Voice traffic received

MOS of Voice

MOS (Mean Opinion Score) of voice is a value that represents the quality of voice. The result of the simulation shows that all three protocols presented a good voice quality (Fig. 12).

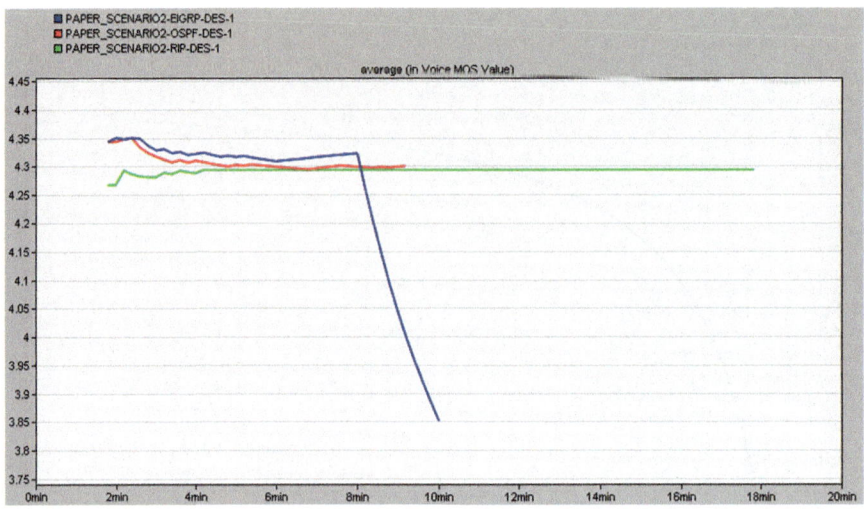

Fig. 12 MOS of voice

3 Conclusion and Future Work

The simulation case that has been carried out in this paper illustrated a comparison of evaluation performance of three Interior Getaway Protocols, and the results of the simulation play a significant role in the choice of the better routing protocol for the simulated network. Firstly, EIGRP is the best protocol for fast convergence and showed the least delay for the packets of video conferencing and voice to travel from the source to the destination. It performed better than the others protocols on the simulated network and presented a good voice quality. Moreover, OSPF showed the same performance with EIGRP in jitter of voice and the amount of data sent and received on the network. Thus, it would be a suitable choice for huge networks due to its absence of limitations in hop count. On the other hand, RIP showed a good performance in convergence of the network and jitter of voice, so it would be a good choice for networks with small hop count. It is obvious that the routing protocols have a vital role in network communication. Nowadays, the need of use of big and different data, such as multimedia and haptic data, in networks has become a necessity. It will be significant in the future to carry out a comparative study for routing protocols with the usage of big haptic and multimedia data applications in order to test the network performance, while some failure happen on network links. The future research would be of great use to Cloud networks so as to transmit faster and safer big data in long-distance networks.

References

Abdulkadhim, M. (2015). Routing protocols convergence activity and protocols related traffic simulation with it's impact on the network. *International Journal of Computer Science Engineering and Technology, 5*(3), 40–43.

Ashoor, A. S. (2015). Performance analysis between distance vector algorithm (DVA) & link state algorithm (LSA) for routing network. *International Journal of Scientific & Technology Research, 4*(2), 101–105.

Evangelos Balasas. (2017, March). *Optimization in Packet Management on a Router Network* (pp. 11–27). Master Thesis in MIS, University of Macedonia.

Christos, S., & Psannis, K. E. (2017). Efficient and secure big data delivery in cloud computing. *Multimedia Tools and Applications, 76*, 22803. https://doi.org/10.1007/s11042-017-4590-4.

Dey, G.K., Ahmed, M.M., & Ahmmed, K.T. (2015). Performance analysis and redistribution among RIPv2, EIGRP & OSPF routing protocol. In: *International Conference on Computer and Information Engineering, Rajshahi* (pp. 21–24).

Gupta, B. B., Yamagushi, S., Zhang, Z., & Psannis, K. E. (2018). Security and privacy of multimedia big data in the critical infrastructure. *Multimedia Tools and Applications, 77*, 10995.

Jalali, S. Y., Wani, S., & Derwesh, M. (2014). Qualitative analysis and performance evaluation of RIP, IGRP, OSPF and EGRP using OPNET™. *Advance in Electronic and Electric Engineering, 4*(4), 389–396.

Kaur, S., & Mir, R. N. (2014). Performance analysis of interior gateway protocols. *Advanced Research in Electrical and Electronic Engineering, 1*(5), 59–63.

Kodzo, A. B. S., Mohammed, M. A., Degadzor, A. F., & Asante, D. M. (2016). Routing protocol (EIGRP) over open shortest path first (OSPF) protocol with Opnet. *International Journal of Advanced Computer Science and Applications, 7*(5), 77–82.

Mardedi, L. Z. A., & Rosidi, A. (2015). Developing computer network based on EIGRP performance comparison and OSPF. *International Journal of Advanced Computer Science and Applications, 6*(9), 80–86.

Kostas E. Psannis. (2015, June). Toward convergence of information theory for efficient data collection. *Policy-making in the BIG DATA ERA: Opportunities and challenges organized by Computer Laboratory, University of Cambridge.*

Sirika, S., & Mahajine, S. (2016). Performance evaluation of dynamic routing protocols for real time application. *International Journal of Engineering Trends and Technology, 32*(7), 328–337.

Vehicle Routing Problem for Urban Freight Transportation: A Review of the Recent Literature

Sotiris P. Gayialis, Grigorios D. Konstantakopoulos, and Ilias P. Tatsiopoulos

Abstract This paper presents a literature review of the Vehicle Routing Problem (VRP) for urban freight transportation. After introducing the methodological approach followed for the review, the analysis of the latest bibliography is presented. The fact that the variants of the VRP have grown and similarly have their practices and applications made the VRP popular in the academic literature. Hence, the number of articles published is constantly increasing, and it is difficult to monitor the developments of the research field. In this paper, after considering existing research papers, a review from Scopus scientific database is presented. The taxonomy of the last decade's literature of the VRP for urban freight transportation is given and critical insights are discussed. After the categorization of the articles, the trends of the VRP for urban freight transportation are featured and analyzed. This analysis and the knowledge gained will be used in a forthcoming research project in order to support the application of VRP algorithms in the functionality of a vehicle routing and scheduling information system. This review is a useful tool for academia's and practitioners who study the adoption of VRP algorithms in IT solutions in order to effectively schedule deliveries and routes in city logistics environment.

Keywords Vehicle Routing Problem · Scheduling · Urban Freight Transportation · City logistics · Algorithms · Literature review

1 Introduction

Freight transportation is the delivery of products from distribution centers to several drop points. The scheduling of deliveries and the routing of vehicles in urban areas is affected by traffic conditions which have a significant impact on travel time and

S. P. Gayialis (✉) · G. D. Konstantakopoulos · I. P. Tatsiopoulos
National Technical University of Athens, School of Mechanical Engineering, Sector of Industrial Management and Operational Research, Zografos, Athens, Greece
e-mail: sotga@central.ntua.gr

© Springer Nature Switzerland AG 2019   89
A. Sifaleras, K. Petridis (eds.), *Operational Research in the Digital Era – ICT Challenges*, Springer Proceedings in Business and Economics,
https://doi.org/10.1007/978-3-319-95666-4_7

consequently on delivery efficiency and customer service. Planners have to assign many orders to many vehicles and, for each vehicle, assign a delivery sequence, trying to provide a balance between supplying first class service to customers at an acceptable cost. In doing so, there are a number of additional constraints that must be considered, such as the weight or volume capacity of the vehicle, the total daily time available, loading and unloading times, drivers working hours, different vehicle speeds, traffic congestion, access restrictions, and environmental constraints. Decision making for urban freight transportation involves VRP theory and algorithms in order to model and solve real-life problems in city logistics (Gonzalez-Feliu and Salanova-Grau 2015).

Logistic managers have faced the Vehicle Routing Problem (VRP) in practice, ever since multi-drop freight transportation vehicles were introduced. First attempts to the solution to the VRP have been addressed by various software tools since the 1980s. These attempts have been significantly enhanced by the development of Geographical Information Systems (GIS) and Advanced Planning and Scheduling Systems in the 2000s (Gayialis and Tatsiopoulos 2004). Various software products have been developed to solve the VRP variants, based on the research that has been done. Theoretical research in the field of vehicle routing started with the "Truck Dispatching Problem" posed by Dantzig and Ramser (1959), who used a linear programming formulation in order to produce a near optimal solution with four routes to a problem of 12 drop points. Clarke and Wright (1964) generalized the Truck Dispatching Problem, which was introduced by Dantzig and Ramser (1959), to the Vehicle Routing Problem. It is now more than 50 years since the publication of these seminal works and the research in the field has an explosive growth. Relevant research has led to the development of new theories in VRP and other areas of combinatorial optimization. Ball et al. (1983), Christofides (1985), Golden and Assad (1986, 1988), and Ball (1995) presented distinguished research work for the VRP. Laporte and Osman (1995) have published a bibliography since 1995, containing over 500 articles on vehicle routing. The VRP, however, focuses on specific constraints imposed either by the customer or by the resources used to affect the delivery. When academic operations researchers address the complex Vehicle Routing Problem for scheduling the deliveries, they tend to fragment the various issues and tackle only a single issue in order to minimize the number of variables under consideration at any one time.

It is still encountered in our days, mainly in the domain of logistics and transport, and it is one of the most widely studied topics in the field of Operational Research. In the VRP, m vehicles, with identical capacities (Q), initially located at a central depot, are to deliver discrete quantities of goods to n customers, which are geographically diffused around the central depot. Concurrently, the aim of the VRP, beyond serving customers, is to minimize the travelled distance.

Due to the difficulty the VRP presents and because of its practical applications, many models have been created for solving the problem and many variants of the basic VRP have been compiled, with different parameters, leading to a different structure of the basic VRP. Firstly, the classical VRP is equivalent to the Capacitated

VRP (CVRP) in which, the capacity of the vehicle must not be exceeded (Lysgaard et al. 2004). However, there is another possibility that the vehicles do not have the same capacities which leads to the Heterogeneous Fleet VRP (HVRP).

Another important variant which was created a decade after the classical VRP was the Multi-Depot VRP (MDVRP) in which, the company has several depots from which it can serve its customers, while the objective is still to service all customers and minimize the number of vehicles and distance travelled (Montoya-Torres et al. 2015). At the same period, the Stochastic VRP (SVRP) was created, where, the customers, the demand of each customer or service and travel times are random.

In addition, in the VRP with Pick-up and Delivering (VRPPD), goods are transported, not only from the central depot to customers, but in the opposite direction too. Hence, in VRPPD it is necessary to take into account that the total delivery load and the total pickup load should both fit into the vehicle (Wassan and Nagy 2014). Furthermore, due to the need for specific arrival time information and for better customer services, an extra restriction to the VRP was added, time windows. The VRP with Time Windows (VRPTW) is the same with the classical VRP, but constrained by a time interval within which the customers have to be supplied (Beheshti et al. 2015).

Another variant worth mentioning is the Dynamic VRP (DVRP) in which customer requests, that are trips from an origin to a destination, appear dynamically (Pillac et al. 2013) or when data and information regarding to the VRP such as travel time, change dynamically. Another significant variant which takes into account time is the Time Dependent VRP (TDVRP) in which travel times change as time passes. The reason why this happens is due to traffic congestion. The factors which affect travel times are: (1) the location, and (2) the time of the day (Huang et al. 2017).

During the last decade, many researchers have tried, while solving the VRP, to minimize carbon (or fuel emissions) as carbon dioxide (CO_2) emitted by trucks is the main greenhouse gas. In addition, the Green VRP has been strengthened due to the technical developments and the road traffic information which allows planning vehicle routes and schedules and taking time-varying speeds into account (Teng and Zhang 2016; Qian and Eglese 2016). In the same field belongs the Hybrid VRP where vehicles can work both electrically and with petroleum-based fuel (Mancini 2017).

VRP has numerous practical applications in the industry. Solving the Vehicle Routing Problem can assist companies in reducing their costs, as a big part of a product's price originates from transportation. Companies are trying to adopt VRP software solutions with appropriate algorithms in order to reduce transportation costs, mileages, and time spent while increasing customer services. Maybe the most challenging issue for companies is urban transportation, as traffic congestion often hinders the delivery of products on time.

The scope of the paper is to review and categorize research papers in the field of VRP for urban freight transportation and to provide a methodology for the analysis of the VRP research field and the categorization of the research papers. The results and methodology of the review can assist researchers in studying the research field, as well as practitioners in understanding the various aspects of the VRP in order to support the design of software solutions.

In the next sections of this paper, we first record the papers which are related to the VRP for urban freight transportation through a specific research process in Sect. 2. Section 3 introduces the research methodology followed and presents the survey's main topics and some numerical results. In Sect. 4, we feature the trends of the VRP since the present paper will be used as an analysis for a research project of a Vehicle Routing and Scheduling Information System.

2   Literature Review Research Approach

The current paper followed a systematic literature review adopted from the work (Alexander et al. 2014; Eksioglu et al. 2009; Braekers et al. 2016). After the need for a review is identified, a research protocol is appointed, selection and de-selection criteria defined, and then papers assessed and outcomes composed. It aims at an efficient and well-recorded coverage which includes only necessary variants and may lead to potential developments and applications.

The Scopus database was used for an advanced search in accordance with Table 1. The aim of the present paper is to identify papers relevant to the VRP for urban freight transportation which are analyzed for featuring the last decade's trends. Every paper was studied thoroughly in order to achieve the right categorization which leads to an established statistical analysis.

The full list of papers extracted from the Scopus database, applying the search terms of Table 1 can be found in the following link (178 papers): https://goo.gl/1eRBfw.

Following the described process, including the application of deselection criteria of Table 1, 111 documents were selected and categorized according to the methodology proposed in the next section. This methodology produced a credible and essential data to an upcoming research project about VRP systems for urban freight transportation.

The final list of papers presented in this literature review after the application of deselection criteria of Table 1 can be found in the following link (111 papers): https://goo.gl/yoVrKQ.

Figure 1 shows the distribution of reviewed papers by journal. It is worth noting that the first journal is European Journal of Operational Research which accounts 13 papers. 17 journals account more than one paper (2–13 papers) and in total 65 papers which means 60% of the reviewed publications. All other 46 journals published 1 paper in the last decade according to the implemented research protocol of Table 1.

Figure 2 shows the distribution by publication year of the 111 reviewed papers as well as all the articles that fell under our search criteria in Scopus database (Table 1). Year 2017 on this diagram includes papers published during the first quarter of the year. According to this graphic, it is obvious that there is an increasing trend, demonstrating the increasing interest in "urban freight transportation" research area.

Table 1 Research Protocol

Research protocol	Title: Set of "Vehicle Routing Problem" or "VRP"
Research variable:	Description
Databases:	Scopus: This is an international database, covering a wide range of peer-reviewed academic publications, estimated at 20.000
Publication type:	Peer-reviewed papers only: These represent work at a final stage of completion
Language:	English-only: This provides wide coverage, and there was no translation capability
Data range:	The limits were set from 2006 till the first quarter of 2017, in order to include papers published at least in the last decade
Search fields:	Search terms were applied to titles, abstracts, and keywords only
Search terms:	(TITLE-ABS-KEY("Vehicle Routing Problem" or "VRP" or "Vehicle Routing") AND PUBYEAR >2006) AND ("urban freight transport*" OR "urban freight" OR "goods movement" OR "urban logistics" OR "city Logistics") AND (LIMIT-TO (SRCTYPE,"j") OR LIMIT-TO (SRCTYPE,"k") OR LIMIT-TO (SRCTYPE,"b")) AND (LIMIT-TO (DOCTYPE,"ar") OR LIMIT-TO (DOCTYPE,"ch") OR LIMIT-TO (DOCTYPE,"re") OR LIMIT-TO (DOCTYPE,"bk")) AND (LIMIT-TO (SUBJAREA,"COMP") OR LIMIT-TO (SUBJAREA,"ENGI") OR LIMIT-TO (SUBJAREA,"DECI") OR LIMIT-TO (SUBJAREA,"BUSI")) AND (LIMIT-TO (LANGUAGE,"English")) The primary search terms are the phrases "Vehicle Routing Problem," "VRP," and "Vehicle Routing." After the first phase, the terms "urban freight transport," "goods movement," "urban logistics," "urban freight," and "city logistics" are added, and the papers are limited to those whose subject area is Computer Science, Engineering, Decision Sciences, or Business Management, excluding Mathematics as the paper is focused in information systems and not to mathematical formulations. The former queries are applied to acclaimed document sources such as Article, Book Chapter, or Review and their Source type limited to Journal, Book Series, or Books
Deselection criteria: Relevance to the research problem:	The deselection criterion is relevant to the research scope: To explore applied solutions of the various VRP variants for urban freight transportation. Some papers are clearly irrelevant based on the title or the abstract while others are also deemed irrelevant after a more thorough review, as they refer to waste collection, cash in transit, truck and trailer, battery swap stations, location routing, food distribution, and parcels and documents. For the remaining papers, the full text was reviewed in order to achieve a detailed categorization

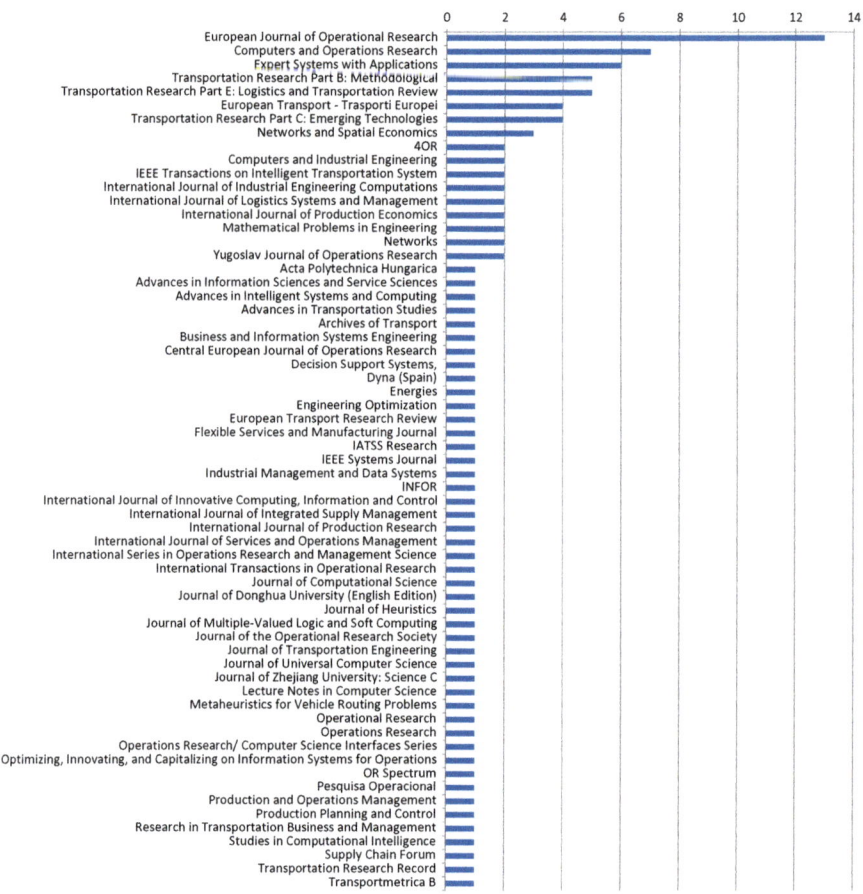

Fig. 1 Distribution of reviewed papers by journal

3   Methodology and Results

3.1   The Methodology for Analysis and Taxonomy of the Papers

The VRP is an extensively analyzed problem, which finds significant application in urban freight transportation. The delivery of products from distribution centers to several drop points within the cities faces difficulties such as traffic congestion, which lead to delays in the scheduled routes of vehicles. Hence, companies are seeking for software and systems which can reduce or ideally eliminate the obstacles, and schedule reliable routes, taking simultaneously more than one parameters of the classical VRP into account. Besides software solutions, mainly research papers propose and develop algorithms for solving specific variants of the VRP, without

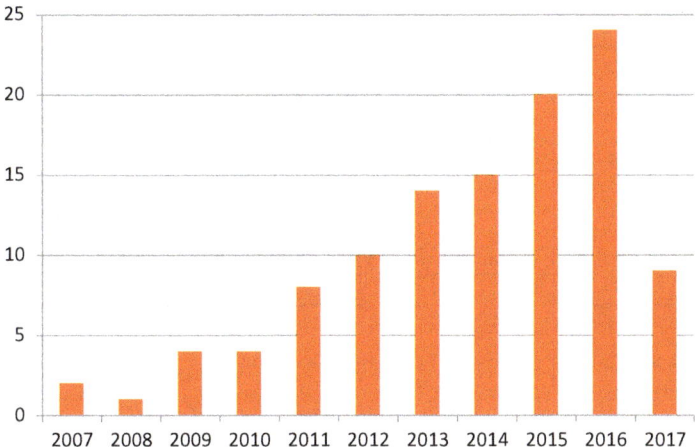

Fig. 2 Distribution of reviewed papers by year

offering complex solutions. The evaluation, primarily of software and secondarily of individual algorithms, is important to be implemented through case studies as they help in understanding real systems and taking reliable outcomes.

Consequently, the conducted survey is exhibited in three dimensions. The first dimension includes the different variants of the VRP, the second dimension consists of the algorithms used for the solution of these variants of the VRP, and the third dimension, the paper type.

Figure 3 depicts the methodology followed for the analysis of the finally selected 111 papers, including the three dimensions. These dimensions are appropriate for a systematic analysis of the research field of the VRP, in cases of applied projects for the design of specifications of VRP software, its development and implementation. Software solutions for VRP usually need adaptation and additional development in order to meet a specific company's needs. The proposed methodological approach and the research results can assist such projects in defining the VRP, selecting appropriate algorithms, and assessing the suitability of applied methods in similar cases. The three dimensions of the methodological approach are described in the following sections.

Dimension 1: VRP Variants

The most common variants of VRP include the Capacitated VRP (CVRP), the VRP with Time Windows (VRPTW), the Time Dependent VRP (TDVRP), the Green VRP, the Multi-Depot VRP (MDVRP), and the Multi-Echelon VRP (MEVRP). Besides these most common VRP variants, which are presented in the introduction, there are few more that have not yet been presented. The Two-Echelon VRP, originating from the Multi-Echelon VRP, involves two levels of routing problems,

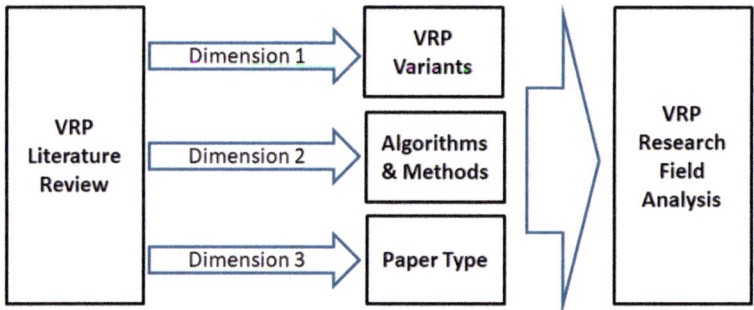

Fig. 3 Methodology for the analysis of the VRP research field

as satellites are supplied from the depot and the customer demands are transported from satellites (Baldacci et al. 2013). In the VRP with Satellite Facilities (VRPSF), satellites are used to replenish vehicle during a route, giving the opportunity to drivers making deliveries until the end of their shift, without necessarily returning to the central depot (Bard et al. 1998). A VRP which is similar to the VRPSF and gathers interest especially for city logistics is the Multi-Trip (MTVRP), where each vehicle can go back to the depot, be reloaded, and commence another trip, making several trips during the working day (Cattaruzza et al. 2014). As regards to the Multi-Depot VRP, every customer is visited exactly once by a vehicle based at one of several depots and each route must start and end at the same depot (Crevier et al. 2007; Renaud et al. 1996).

A very important variant which is close to the TDVRP is the Real-Time VRP where a re-optimization procedure runs in order for new routes to be identified, every time, travel time between a pair of nodes is updated (Okhrin and Richter 2008). Furthermore, Real-Time Traffic Data can be used to develop routing strategies that tend to minimize the time spent due to traffic congestion and consequently costs, while maximizing customer services (Kim and Lewis 2004).

In the Periodic VRP (PVRP) a set of customers has to be visited on a given time horizon, once or several times (Angelelli and Speranza 2002). In the Split Delivery VRP (SDVRP), the assumption that a customer must be visited by one vehicle only is relaxed and the objective is still to find the routes which minimize the cost (Archetti and Speranza 2012). Finally, the Open VRP differs from the classical VRP, as vehicles are not required to return to the depot after the end of the route (Sariklis and Powell 2000).

Dimension 2: Algorithms and Methods

In spite of the extensive research of the Vehicle Routing Problem, there is no single algorithm that optimally solves every problem, even no single algorithm for a specific VRP variant. Algorithms and methods have been developed for optimally solving certain classes of vehicle routing and scheduling problems, tackling only a single issue in order to minimize the number of variables under consideration at any one time. Practical real-life applications of Vehicle Routing Problems offer heuristic or metaheuristic algorithms as solutions while there are some exact approaches in the literature.

Many researchers have faced most of the presented VRP variants in search of a solution. The methods they propose are Heuristic, Metaheuristic, Exact, and Simulation. Exact optimization methods may guarantee finding an optimal solution but due to the fact that the VRP is an NP Hard Problem only a few problems can be solved. On the contrary, heuristic and metaheuristic optimization methods may not guarantee that an optimal solution is found, but they provide an adequate solution that guides the search for the immediate goals, in less time (Rothlauf 2011). Simulation methods apply what-if analyses, for generating multiple scenarios, selecting the best one and using these in the main algorithms (Alexander et al. 2014).

Dimension 3: Paper Type

Besides the VRP variants and the kind of methods researchers present, it is important to estimate the number of papers (1) conducting a literature review or survey which means broader theoretical knowledge, (2) the papers proposing and developing algorithms or even these which describe or present another existing algorithm or any other solution, (3) the papers which have computational results and test data, and (4) the papers which present works on software and systems development which is a focal point in our research. This categorization of the papers is useful in order to distinguish the papers that are useful for assisting practical applications of the VRP algorithms, especially in freight transportation in cities.

3.2 Research Results

According to the categorization of 111 papers, the CVRP proves to be the most common variant of the VRP in urban freight transportation, followed by the VRPTW (Table 2). Many of the other VRP variants have lately been studied such as the Green and Hybrid VRP due to the need for minimization of carbon and fuel emissions or the TDVRP, the DVRP and the Real Time VRP, where new technologies offer better feasible solutions. In the research of Braekers et al. (2016), conducted for articles published till the middle of 2015, it is crucial to stress that the MEVRP and the VRPSF were not included, but have since attracted research interest. Other VRP variants such as the VRPTW, the MDVRP, the SVRP, and HVRP are producing similar results.

Table 2 lists all the VRP variants identified in the analyzed papers. As presented in this table, about 40% of the papers dealing with urban freight transportation examine Capacitated VRP and VRP with Time Windows. Many of the papers

Table 2 VRP variant

Variant	Number of articles (total = 111)	Relative percentage
Capacitated VRP	47	42.24%
VRP with Time Windows	42	37.84%
Green and Hybrid VRP	27	24.32%
Time Dependent VRP	21	18.92%
Multi-Echelon VRP and VRP with Satellite Facilities	15	13.51%
Multi-Depot VRP	11	9.91%
Stochastic VRP	10	9.01%
Dynamic VRP	9	8.11%
VRP with Heterogeneous Fleet	9	8.11%
Multi-trip VRP	8	7.21%
Real-Time VRP and VRP with Real-Time Data	8	7.21%
Pickup and Delivery VRP and VRP with Backhauls	7	6.31%
Periodic VRP	3	2.70%
Split Delivery VRP	2	1.80%
Open VRP	1	0.90%

examined deal with more than one VRP variants in order to solve real-life problems. That is the reason why in Table 2, the sum of the number of articles is more than 111. For example, 21 papers examine Time Depended VRP and Stochastic VRP, in parallel. Time Depended VRP is the problem which is combined with 15 other variants. Table 3 analytically presents how the variants of VRP are combined. Capacitated VRP (nr. 7 variant) is the most examined problem, and it is combined with all other variants (in 85 papers). VRP with Time Windows (nr. 4 variant) is combined with all the other variants in 63 papers totally. Dynamic VRP (nr. 1 variant) is combined with just 4 other variants in 7 papers totally.

In Table 4, the methods for solving VRP are presented, indicating that Heuristic and Metaheuristic algorithms are used more often to find solutions of the problem. Exact methods are developed less often due to their computational complexity while simulation methods are also less common in the literature. It is a logical outcome that heuristic and metaheuristic methods are used more often than the rest of the methods, mainly because the VRP is an NP Hard Problem. It should be noted the sum of Relative Percentages does not equal 100% due to the fact that many of the examined papers do not propose any solution but conduct a review or a survey.

In Table 5, the correlation between VRP variants and solution methods is presented. It is obvious that the two most common VRP variants, CVRP and VRPTW, are solved primarily with heuristic methods and secondarily with metaheuristic methods. On the other hand, the TDVRP and the Green and Hybrid VRP, which have been studied mostly over the last decade, are more often solved with metaheuristic approaches. This means that a trend seems to be developing for the application of

Table 3 Combinations of VRP variants (number of papers)

Variant	1	2	3	4	5	6	7	8	9	10	11	12	13	14	15
1	x			1			3				2				1
2		x		8	1	2	10	1	1	1	2	2	1		5
3			x	4	1		10					1	1	1	3
4				x	3	5	21	4	2	1	4	6	2	1	1
5					x	1	6		1		1		2		
6						x	3	1	1	1	1	1			
7							x	4	2	2	7	5	10		2
8								x	1	1		1			
9									x	1	1	1			
10										x		1			
11											x		1		
12												x			
13													x		
14														x	
15															x

Table appendix: VRP variants

1	Dynamic VRP
2	Time Dependent VRP
3	Green and Hybrid VRP
4	VRP with Time Windows
5	Multi-trip VRP and VRP with Satellite Facilities
6	Multi-Depot VRP
7	Capacitated VRP
8	Pickup and Delivery VRP and VRP with Backhauls
9	Split Delivery VRP
10	Periodic VRP
11	Stochastic VRP
12	VRP with Heterogeneous Fleet
13	Multi Echelon VRP
14	Open VRP
15	Real-Time VRP and VRP with Real-Time Data

metaheuristic methods in solving the VRP. In regard to the simulation method, it is used mainly in the calculation of travel times, which is an important parameter for solving most of the VRP variants.

Most papers deal with more than one variants of the VRP each time. Hence, when the author of each paper solves a specific VRP with multiple variants, we consider that the method applied solves all these variants. That is the reason why in Table 5, the sum of each method differs from the data in Table 4.

Figure 4 depicts this relation between methods used in the literature and the VRP variant they deal with. Capacitated VRP, VRP with Time Windows, Time dependent

Table 4 Applied methods

Applied method	Number of articles (total = 111)	Relative percentage
Heuristic	41	36.94%
Metaheuristic	30	27.03%
Exact	5	4.50%
Simulation	5	4.50%

Table 5 Methods per VRP variant

Variant	Heuristic	Metaheuristic	Exact	Simulation
Capacitated VRP	20	12	3	2
VRP with Time Windows	20	11	1	3
Green and Hybrid VRP	5	8	0	1
Time Dependent VRP	5	6	0	0
Two Echelon VRP and VRP with Satellite Facilities	8	4	2	1
Multi-Depot VRP	4	4	0	1
Stochastic VRP	3	1	0	2
Dynamic VRP	3	0	0	0
VRP with Heterogeneous Fleet	3	4	0	0
Multi-trip VRP	4	2	1	1
VRP with Real-Time Traffic Data	2	0	0	0
Pickup and Delivery VRP and VRP with Backhauls	3	3	0	0
Periodic VRP	2	1	1	0
Split Delivery VRP	2	1	o	1
Open VRP	0	1	0	0

VRP and VRP with Real-Time Traffic Data are the most relevant variants for urban freight transportation problems and in Fig. 4 is obvious that the most commonly used methods for such problems are heuristics and metaheuristics.

Table 6 indicates that most papers present Computational Results or Test Data due to the fact that a significant percentage of papers are relevant to Algorithms (whether they Propose/Develop or Present/Describe Algorithms), Case Studies, and Real-World Industrial Examples. Many Algorithms, and especially those who are proposed and developed, find application and tested in case studies, in order to be evaluated and draw conclusions from real problems. Furthermore, in many papers, time and traffic data of cities are received and are used in companies, in order to test and decide if the software and algorithm solutions they use are trustworthy. Literature Reviews or Surveys follow, as many researchers approach the VRP through a theoretical viewpoint. Finally, Software or Systems are rare, as few researches lead to such applications.

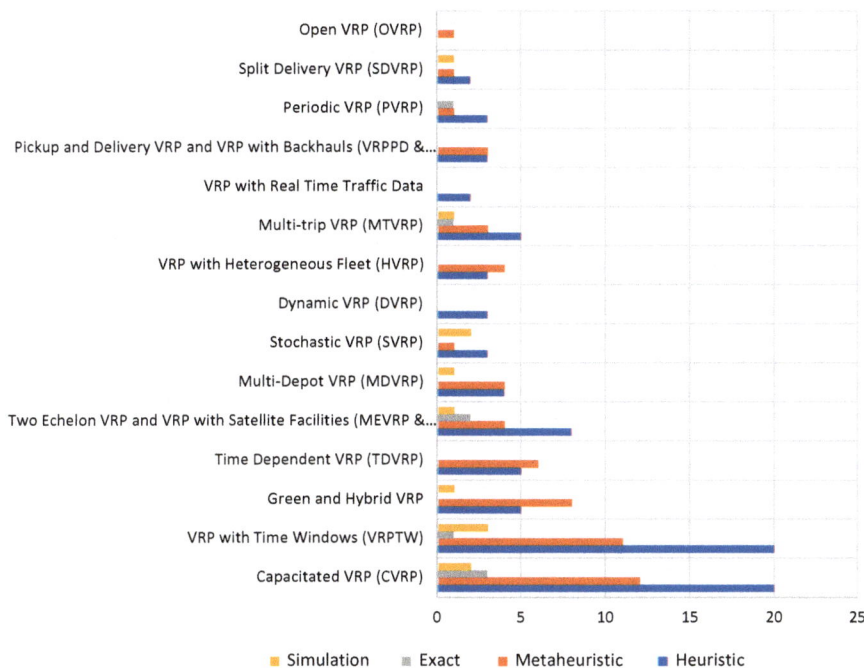

Fig. 4 Methods used per VRP variant

Table 6 Paper types

Paper type	Number of articles (total = 111)	Relative percentage
Computational Results or Test Data	80	72.07%
Propose/Develop Algorithm or Present/Describe Algorithm	59	53.15%
Case Study and Real-World Industrial Examples	27	24.32%
Literature Review or Survey	22	19.82%
Software or System	5	4.50%

4 Conclusions

A considerable number of papers have been written about the VRP for urban freight transportation, analyzing many different variants of it. Accordingly, many methods have been proposed for solving all the VRP variants. However, few research projects for the VRP have led to the real-life application of Decision Support Systems (DSS) or other Management Systems (MS). The papers of Zeimpekis et al. (2007, 2017) and Sun and Hu (2012) refer to Vehicle MS and DSS that endorse logistics managers by monitoring the status of deliveries in real time and suggesting optimal re-routing strategies whenever needed due to uncontrollable external events that cause perturbations in the schedule. The paper of Smirlis et al. (2012) presents a model which evaluates software products through the total performance/price criterion and proposes the proper solution as the selection of these systems has become increasingly difficult for decision makers due to a large number of software products available and the great variety of features and capabilities they offer. There are systems which are based on GIS (Geographical Information Systems) such as those described by Sicilia-Montalvo et al. (2013). Authors are also reporting the need for ITS (Intelligent Transportation Systems), offering the confrontation of high costs and environmental impact which is important especially in urban areas. Due to the need for lower costs, lower carbon emissions, and higher customer services, DSS and MS can lead to sufficient and feasible solutions.

This paper presents the results of an extensive literature review of the VRP for urban freight transportation. An initial group of 178 papers extracted from Scopus database, and it was further shorted to a group of 111 relevant papers, applying deselection criteria. Papers which are irrelevant with applied solutions of the various VRP variants for urban freight transportation were excluded from the analysis. A link to all 111 examined papers is given and the analysis is presented in six tables and four figures. This review offers a summary of the latest knowledge of this research field, and it can enhance the adaptation of appropriate methods in software solutions for freight transportation in cities.

References

Alexander, A., Walker, H., & Naim, M. (2014). Decision theory in sustainable supply chain management: A literature review. *Supply Chain Management: An International Journal, 19*, 504–522. https://doi.org/10.1108/SCM-01-2014-0007.

Angelelli, E., & Speranza, M. G. (2002). The periodic vehicle routing problem with intermediate facilities. *European Journal of Operational Research, 137*(2), 233–247. https://doi.org/10.1016/S0377-2217(01)00206-5.

Archetti, C., & Speranza, M. G. (2012). Vehicle routing problems with split deliveries. *International Transactions in Operational Research, 19*, 3–22. https://doi.org/10.1111/j.1475-3995.2011.00811.x.

Baldacci, R., Mingozzi, A., Roberti, R., & Calvo, R. W. (2013). An exact algorithm for the two-echelon capacitated vehicle routing problem. *Operations Research, 61*, 298–314. https://doi.org/10.1287/opre.1120.1153.

Ball, M. (1995). *Handbooks in OR and MS, Network routing* (Vol. 8). North Holland, Amsterdam: Elsevier.

Ball, M., Golden, B., Assad, A., & Bodin, L. (1983). Planning for truck fleet size in the presence of a common-carrier option. *Decision Sciences, 14*, 103–120.

Bard, J., Dror, M., Bard, J. F., et al. (1998). A branch and cut algorithm for the VRP with satellite facilities a branch and cut algorithm for the VRP with satellite facilities. *IIE Transactions, 30*, 821–834. https://doi.org/10.1023/A:1007500200749.

Beheshti, A. K., Hejazi, S. R., & Alinaghian, M. (2015). The vehicle routing problem with multiple prioritized time windows: A case study. *Computers and Industrial Engineering, 90*, 402–413. https://doi.org/10.1016/j.cie.2015.10.005.

Braekers, K., Ramaekers, K., & Van Nieuwenhuyse, I. (2016). The vehicle routing problem: State of the art classification and review. *Computers and Industrial Engineering, 99*, 300–313. https://doi.org/10.1016/j.cie.2015.12.007.

Cattaruzza, D., Absi, N., Feillet, D., & Vidal, T. (2014). A memetic algorithm for the multi trip vehicle routing problem. *European Journal of Operational Research, 236*, 833–848. https://doi.org/10.1016/j.ejor.2013.06.012.

Christofides, N. (1985). The vehicle routing. In E. L. Lawler, J. K. Lenstra, A. H. G. Rinnooy Kan, & D. B. Shmoys (Eds.), *The travelling salesman problem*. New York, NY: Wiley.

Clarke, G., & Wright, J. W. (1964). Scheduling of vehicles from a central depot to a number of delivery points. *Operations Research, 12*, 568–581. https://doi.org/10.1287/opre.12.4.568.

Crevier, B., Cordeau, J.-F., & Laporte, G. (2007). The multi-depot vehicle routing problem with inter-depot routes. *European Journal of Operational Research, 176*, 756–773. https://doi.org/10.1016/j.ejor.2005.08.015.

Dantzig, G. B., & Ramser, H. J. (1959). The truck dispatching problem. *Management Science, 6*(1), 80–91.

Eksioglu, B., Vural, A. V., & Reisman, A. (2009). The vehicle routing problem: A taxonomic review. *Computers and Industrial Engineering, 57*, 1472–1483. https://doi.org/10.1016/j.cie.2009.05.009.

Gayialis, S. P., & Tatsiopoulos, I. P. (2004). Design of an IT-driven decision support system for vehicle routing and scheduling. *European Journal of Operational Research, 152*(2), 382–398.

Golden, B., & Assad, A. (1986). Perspectives on vehicle routing: Exciting new developments. *Operations Research, 34*, 803–810.

Golden, B. L., & Assad, A. A. (Eds.). (1988). *Vehicle routing: Methods and studies*. North Holland, Amsterdam: Elsevier Science.

Gonzalez-Feliu, J., & Salanova-Grau, J.-M. (2015). VRP algorithms for decision support systems to evaluate collaborative urban freight transport systems. In M. Lauras, M. Zelm, B. Archimède, F. Bénaben, & G. Doumeignts (Eds.), *Enterprise interoperability: I-ESA'14, ISTEWILEY* (pp. 196–201). Hoboken: Wiley. https://doi.org/10.1002/9781119081418.ch27.

Huang, Y., Zhao, L., Van Woensel, T., & Gross, J.-P. (2017). Time-dependent vehicle routing problem with path flexibility. *Transportation Research Part B: Methodological, 95*, 169–195. https://doi.org/10.1016/j.trb.2016.10.013.

Kim, S., & Lewis, M. E. (2004). Optimal vehicle routing with real-time traffic information. *IEEE Transactions on Intelligent Transportation Systems, 6*, 178–188. https://doi.org/10.1109/TITS.2005.848362.

Laporte, G., & Osman, I. H. (1995). Routing problems: A bibliography. *Annals of Operations Research, 61*, 227–262.

Lysgaard, J., Letchford, A. N., & Eglese, R. W. (2004). Digital object identifier (a new branch-and-cut algorithm for the capacitated vehicle routing problem). *Mathematical Programming Section A, 100*, 423–445. https://doi.org/10.1007/s10107-003-0481-8.

Mancini, S. (2017). The hybrid vehicle routing problem. *Transportation Research Part C: Emerging Technologies, 78*, 1–12. https://doi.org/10.1016/j.trc.2017.02.004.

Montoya-Torres, J. R., López Franco, J., Nieto Isaza, S., et al. (2015). A literature review on the vehicle routing problem with multiple depots. *Computers and Industrial Engineering, 79*, 115–129. https://doi.org/10.1016/j.cie.2014.10.029.

Okhrin, I., & Richter, K. (2008). The real-time vehicle routing problem. *Operations Research Proceedings, 2007*, 141–146.

Pillac, V., Gendreau, M., Guéret, C., & Medaglia, A. L. (2013). A review of dynamic vehicle routing problems. *European Journal of Operational Research, 225*(1), 1–11.

Qian, J., & Eglese, R. (2016). Fuel emissions optimization in vehicle routing problems with time-varying speeds. *European Journal of Operational Research, 248*, 840 848. https://doi.org/10.1016/j.ejor.2015.09.00.

Renaud, J., Laporte, G., & Boctor, F. F. (1996). A tabu search heuristic for the multi-depot vehicle routing problem. *Computers and Operations Research, 23*, 229–235. https://doi.org/10.1016/0305-0548(95)O0026-P.

Rothlauf, F. (2011). *Design of modern heuristics: Principles and application, natural computing series*. Berlin, Heidelberg: Springer-Verlag. https://doi.org/10.1007/978-3-540-72962-4.

Sariklis, D., & Powell, S. (2000). A heuristic method for the open vehicle routing problem. *Journal of the Operational Research Society, 51,* 564–573. https://doi.org/10.105 //palgrave.jors.2600924.

Sicilia-Montalvo, J. A., Escuín-Finol, D., Royo-Agustín, B., & Larrodé-Peilicer, E. (2013). Smart system for freight distribution planning, based on variable neighbourhood search and tabu search metaheuristics. *Dyna, 88,* 414–423. https://doi.org/10.6036/5561.

Smirlis, Y. G., Zeimpekis, V., & Kaimakamis, G. (2012). Data envelopment analysis models to support the selection of vehicle routing software for city logistics operations. *Operations Research, 12,* 399–420. https://doi.org/10.1007/s12351-010-0100-4.

Sun, L., & Hu, X. (2012). A knowledge representation method for algorithms in dss for real-time vehicle routing in urban distribution. *International Journal of Innovative Computing, Information & Control, 8,* 5859–5872.

Teng, L., & Zhang, Z. (2016). Green vehicle routing problem with load factor. *Journal of Advaned Transportation Study, 3,* 75–82. https://doi.org/10.4399/978885489937707.

Wassan, N., & Nagy, G. (2014). Vehicle routing problem with deliveries and pickups: Modelling issues and meta-heuristics solution approaches. *International Journal of Transportation, 2,* 95–110. https://doi.org/10.14257/ijt.2014.2.1.06.

Zeimpekis, V., Giaglis, G. M., Tatarakis, A., & Minis, I. (2007). Towards a dynamic real-time vehicle management system for urban distribution. *International Journal of Integrated Supply Management, 3,* 228. https://doi.org/10.1504/IJISM.2007.012628.

Zeimpekis, V., Minis, I., Mamassis, K., & Giaglis, G. M. (2017). Dynamic management of a delayed delivery vehicle in a city logistics environment. *Dynamic Fleet Management, 197–217.* https://doi.org/10.1007/978-0-387-71722-7_9.

Development of a Framework for the Assessment of Soft Skills in the ICT Sector

Valasia-Anna Valavosiki, Emmanouil Stiakakis,
and Alexander Chatzigeorgiou

Abstract In modern times and during the recent global economic crisis, a paradox has emerged: the workforce becomes more and more skilled and trained, while unemployment rates remain very high. The new generation shows a clear tendency towards education, by obtaining various diplomas and certifications. This situation has created a highly educated generation and therefore the selection of the appropriate employee is becoming as difficult as ever. Moreover, it becomes more and more difficult for a candidate to stand out among so many other equally qualified individuals. The elements, which can really make a difference, are the skills a candidate possesses. Skills are divided into two broad categories: technical skills and non-technical or soft skills. Technical skills include all the aspects of formal learning, which results in obtaining degrees and certifications. Nevertheless, the skills that can make a candidate really stand out are non-technical or soft skills. These skills include many personal characteristics of the individual, which form a unique combination of assets. Soft skills are not developed exclusively within the context of formal education, but are mainly part of a wider process of lifelong learning. The aim of the present paper is the development of a framework for the assessment of both technical and non-technical skills in the Information and Communications Technology (ICT) sector. In this context, content analysis of online job ads was conducted, in order to determine the significance of each skill generally in the ICT sector, as well as in each of the 23 professions included in this sector. The results demonstrate that every ICT-related profession requires a different ideal combination of skills. The implications of the present research will lead to a new, automated, and reliable personnel selection process, which assesses both technical and non-technical skills for a specific profession or job offering.

Keywords Technical skills · Non-technical skills · Assessment of skills · ICT sector · Content analysis

V.-A. Valavosiki · E. Stiakakis (✉) · A. Chatzigeorgiou
Department of Applied Informatics, University of Macedonia, Thessaloniki, Greece
e-mail: stiakakis@uom.edu.gr

© Springer Nature Switzerland AG 2019
A. Sifaleras, K. Petridis (eds.), *Operational Research in the Digital Era – ICT Challenges*, Springer Proceedings in Business and Economics,
https://doi.org/10.1007/978-3-319-95666-4_8

1 Introduction

The introduction of the concept of skills in the workplace was introduced by McClelland (1973), who integrated the concept of skills as a criterion of choosing personnel in the US Information Agency. In the past, the US Information Agency had used various intelligence tests, which failed to predict the efficiency of the candidate employee. Thus, McClelland (1973) proposed the measurement of skills as an alternative model of predicting the candidate's efficiency. Specifically, he proposed as a case study the selection of qualified Foreign Intelligence Service employees. The results of this case study showed that skills, such as positive inter-cultural perceptions, management skills, and interpersonal sensitivity significantly differentiated the superior from the mediocre Information Offices (Dubois 1998).

Since then, skills in workplace have been studied by many researchers (Marrelli 1998; Dubois 1998; Boyatzis 1982; Peterson and Van Fleet 2004). According to Marrelli (1998), skills are presented as the measurable human capabilities, which are necessary for an effective performance at work. On the other hand, Dubois (1998) defined skills as those characteristics, pieces of knowledge, ways of thinking, and experiences, which can be used either individually or in various combinations and affect significantly the performance of the individual at work. In the same context, Boyatzis (1982) presents skills as the fundamental characteristics of the individual, which are causally associated with the efficient performance at work. Last, but not least, Peterson and Van Fleet (2004) approach skills as the ability of the individual to perform some specific behavioral task or some specific cognitive process regarding a particular task.

Over the past few years, youngsters who enter the international workforce tend to collect knowledge, as well as many relevant certifications. As a result, nowadays' workforce is characterized by highly educated individuals, who seek for the perfect job and yet this is not enough. In addition, from the enterprise perspective, the recruitment procedure aims to find the perfect employee for each position and most of the times this is a difficult, as well as time-consuming process. Especially, in the ICT sector, the demand for high-skilled professionals is rising, whereas the supply is relatively small. The component which can effectively determine which candidate is the best choice for each position is non-technical or soft skills. The contribution of the present paper is double: first of all, the highlighting of the importance of soft skills in the ICT sector and second, motivating individuals to emphasize on the development of soft skills.

The outline of the present paper was especially designed in order to present explicitly the framework for the assessment of soft skills in the ICT sector. First of all, a literature review is demonstrated regarding soft skills and their assessment, as well as the professions included in the ICT sector. Moreover, job ad analysis combined with content analysis is presented as the ideal methodology, which can delineate the demand for soft skills. Later on, the exact methodology that was followed is explained and the results of the research are demonstrated. Last, but not least, the benefits and practical implications of the this research are presented.

2   Literature Review

2.1   Technical and Non–technical Skills (Soft Skills)

In the past, technical skills, which are also widely known as hard skills, were the main criteria used in order to determine whether an individual had the appropriate qualifications for a job. Hard skills are commonly described as a science, the knowledge of processes, tools, and techniques (Sukhoo et al. 2005). Subsequently, technical skills are defined as the understanding or the ability for specific activities that require the use of special tools, methods, processes, techniques or knowledge. In general, technical skills can be considered special skills, which are required in order to perform a specific job or task. In fact, technical skills are related with the interaction of the individual with things rather than other persons (Katz 1955).

Non-technical skills refer to soft skills, general skills or life skills (Munce 1981) and are not found in the curriculum of formal education. These skills are not specific to a particular job and are not related to a particular work environment, however, they can be used in all tasks and duties assigned. Non-technical skills cannot be acquired in a short period of time, but they can be developed throughout the years and along with the professional experience of the individual (Sahandri and Kumar 2009).

2.2   The Assessment of Soft Skills

The ever-growing labor market requirements have made soft skills assessment a subject of research. However, there is not yet a wide acceptable way to assess the soft skills of a job candidate, although researchers agree that this procedure is crucial in order to find the most appropriate employee for a position, especially in the ICT sector (Purao and Suen 2010; Kechagias 2011; Gibb 2013; Rashidi et al. 2013; Zhang 2012; Migdalas et al. 2013).

Gibb (2013) recognizes and points out the need for assessing all the aspects of soft skills. More specifically, he identifies the following needs regarding the assessment of soft skills (Gibb 2013):

- The first need is the recognition that during the assessment of any skill there are various problems regarding the security of good data. So, the assessment of soft skills requires a completely different approach than the assessment of hard skills. The approach should be simple and the candidate should appreciate the role and the relevance of the soft skills in their job performance.
- On the other hand, the soft skills should be assessed separately and they should not be overshadowed by other topics, such as employability, leadership, and graduate employment.
- Another important need is to conduct inter-contextual research, which will include various domains and environments in which the assessment of the soft

skills actually takes place. This could include a soft skills assessment program or a soft skills development seminar.

- Last, but not least, there is a critical need to obtain longitudinal data. A relative example is that there is a wide variety of data, grades, marks, and qualifications for hard skills, but no such data exists about the formative assessment of soft skills.

The first organization that seems to understand the necessity of the assessment of soft skills is the Electronics and Information Technology Program at Torrens Valley TAFE, which began in 1991 and is widely recognized for the development of an approach of developing and assessing generic skills. This program also provides an Electrotechnology Training Package from certificate II to an advanced diploma. This approach focuses on the assessment of generic skills, which are defined as a group of five categories: problem solving, collection, analysis and organization of information, communication about ideas and information, teamwork, and plan and organization activities. Another important factor for the success of the program is the role of "validated self-assessment". Within this context the learner can assess his own competence in a particular generic skill. An individual has to meet two aspects in order to be certified. On the one hand, the individual has to meet the specified assessment criteria on the assessment sheet. In this case, according to the score of the individual, the student is considered to have successfully performed the key competency. On the other hand, the student should be explicitly aware of the key competence processes (Denton 2003).

Zhang (2012) designed a peer-assessment scale for both soft-skill and hard-skill evaluation. The appropriate data was collected from an IT course and then the method of factor analysis was used. More specifically, peer assessment refers to a process of assessment within which students are required to assess the work of others (Reese-Durham 2005). The assessment scale was administrated by the review of existing tools, and it involved 18 items, such as the attendance of a meeting, the on time completion of the assigned work, the effective communication with other members of the team, the leadership skills, the organization skills, the effective handling of conflicts, and other soft skills. Results indicated two dimensions of the peer-assessment scale: the soft skills and the hard skills dimension. This result supports the definition of soft skills that was presented in the previous section of this paper. In addition, the tool was tested and was proven to be valid. However, this study used a quite small size of 24 students, so the result has weak generalizability (Zhang 2012).

Purao and Suen (2010) designed a multi-faceted metric in order to evaluate soft skills. The research focused on the assessment of information system developers, who work in teams and may be involved in designing and building or extending software-intensive solutions for a company. The paper used a combination of meta-analysis of prior work and the analysis of data, which was gathered from both novice system developers and coding experts. This metric used a simple ordinal scale for the purpose of the assessment. It should also be noted that the soft skills were identified after data-driven discovery from the basis of the metric. For each

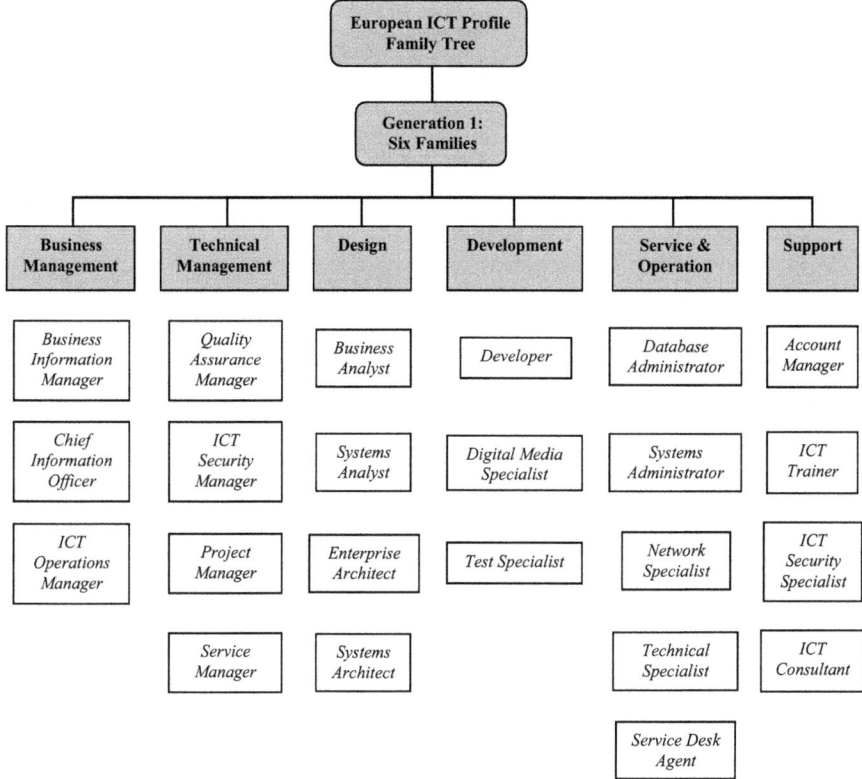

Fig. 1 European ICT profile family tree

behavior there is a suitable scenario, on which the candidate should respond to a presence/absence test. Then the answer is scored by an expert, such as an instructor. The metric was used in one semester and so far seems to give useful results. However, the disadvantage of this technique is that it requires a small number of candidates and takes time in order to give results (Purao and Suen 2010).

2.3 Defining ICT Professions

The first step for the development of an assessment framework for the soft skills in the ICT sector was the determination of the ICT jobs. During this attempt, two basic questions have emerged:

- How many ICT-related jobs are there?
- Which are the ICT-related jobs?

The answer to both questions was found in the European e-Competence Framework (2012), where the European ICT Professional Profiles are presented and analyzed. The European ICT Professional Profiles were developed in CEN Workshop Agreement (CWA) aiming to increase the transparency and to outline the European ICT landscape. During this workshop, 23 Professional Profiles were identified, which were later divided into six families, according to relevance. This framework was chosen as a trustworthy reference for the present research, mainly due to the European character of the study.

In Fig. 1 the above ICT profiles are presented, followed by a short summary statement (Table 1).

2.4 Job Ad Analysis for Skills Assessment

A common method for assessing skills is the analysis of job ads mainly because it offers the following benefits (Vieira da Cunha 2009; Schlee and Harich 2010; Beile and Adams 2000; Cullen 2000): (a) data is easily accessible, (b) data is organic and naturalistic, and (c) data can be converted to a useful supporting tool for job seekers.

In addition, job ads analysis enables the longitudinal comparison, as well as the intertemporal documentation of job trends (Albitz 2002). According to Todd et al. (1995) and Vieira da Cunha (2009), this methodology can be used as an indicator of change in a profession. Hence, the collection of job ads can produce a measurable and comparable set of research data, which can show long-term changes in a profession (Todd et al. 1995; Vieira da Cunha 2009).

Job ads analysis can be conducted through content analysis, which is a qualitative method leading to a subjective interpretation of text data. According to Krippendorff (2013, p. 24), "Content analysis is a research technique for making replicable and valid inferences from texts (or other meaningful matter) to the contexts of their use". This method is based on a systematic classification process that includes coding and the identification of various themes and patterns (Hsieh and Shannon 2005). This is mainly an empirical, methodological controlled approach, which focuses on the analysis of texts within their context of communication, and it is conducted by following predefined content analytic rules without rash quantification (Mayring 2000). The goal of the method is the data reduction through a sense-making effort of identification of basic consistencies and meanings (Patton 2002).

Content analysis can be compared to a typical empirical study, as both methods use numerical and categorical data. On the one hand, an empirical study uses variables in order to represent various measures in the dataset and, on the other hand, content analysis uses variables in order to represent the frequency of occurrence of specific keywords. Last, but not least, both methods include the following stages: (a) data collection, (b) design of the appropriate variables, and (c) analysis using these variables (Sodhi and Son 2010).

Regarding the implementation of content analysis, this method can be conducted either manually or with the use of appropriate content analysis software. Manual

Table 1 European ICT professions and short descriptions

European ICT profile title	ICT profile summary statement
Account Manager	Senior focal point for client sales and customer satisfaction
Business Analyst	Analyzes information system for improving business performance
Business Information Manager	Proposes plans and manages functional and technical evolutions of the information system within the relevant business domain
Chief Information Officer	Develops and maintains information systems compliant to business and organization's needs
Database Administrator	Designs and implements or monitors and maintains databases
Developer	Builds/codes ICT solutions and specifies ICT products according to the customer needs
Digital Media Specialist	Creates websites and multimedia applications combining the power of digital technology with effective use of graphics, audio, photographic, and video images
Enterprise Architect	Designs and maintains the enterprise architecture
ICT Consultant	Supports understanding of how new ICT technologies add value to a business
ICT Operations Manager	Manages operations, people, and further resources for the ICT activity
ICT Security Manager	Manages the information system security policy
ICT Security Specialist	Ensures the implementation of the organizations security policy
ICT Trainer	Educates and trains ICT professionals and practitioners to reach predefined standards of ICT technical/business competence
Network Specialist	Ensures the alignment of the network, including telecommunication and/or computer infrastructure to meet the organization's communication needs
Project Manager	Manages project to achieve optimal performance that conforms to original specifications
Quality Assurance Manager	Guarantees that information systems are delivered according to organization policies (quality, risks, Service Level Agreement)
Service Desk Agent	Provides first-line telephone or e-mail support to clients with technical issues
Service Manager	Plans, implements, and manages solution provision
Systems Administrator	Administers ICT system components to meet service requirements
Systems Analyst	Analyzes requirements and specifies software and systems
Systems Architect	Plans and is accountable for the implementation and integration of software and/or ICT systems
Technical Specialist	Maintains and repairs hardware and software on client premises
Test Specialist	Designs and performs testing plans

Table 2 Literature review on job ads analysis through content analysis

		Design	Analysis	
Researcher	Data collection	Set of keywords	Content analysis	Statistical analysis
Karanja et al. (2016)	200 online job ads	Structured	Manual	Relative frequency and x^2-test
Ahsan et al. (2013)	762 online job ads	Structured	Manual	Relative frequency
Lavy and Yadin (2013)	2000 job ads	Structured	Manual	Relative frequency
Ahmed et al. (2012)	500 online job ads	Structured	Manual	Relative frequency and Kendall coefficient and kappa statistics
Omar et al. (2012)	300 online job ads	Structured	Manual	Relative frequency
Wahl et al. (2012)	185 job ads	Structured	Manual	Relative frequency
Ayalew et al. (2011)	494 job ads	Unstructured	Manual	Relative frequency
Kennan et al. (2007)	400 online job ads	Structured	Computerized	Relative frequency and Jaccard's coefficient
Lee and lee (2006)	555 online job ads	Unstructured	Computerized	Relative frequency
Chao and Shih (2005)	484 online job ads	Unstructured	Manual	Descriptive analysis
North and worth (1996)	1000 job ads	Unstructured	Manual	Relative frequency
Todd et al. (1995)	1234 job ads	Structured	Manual	Relative frequency

analysis can be superior to computerized, mainly regarding the accuracy of the results as words can have various synonyms and homonyms and moreover can have different meanings in different contexts. However, computerized analysis is preferred for large amounts of data, as it offers an effective way of periodic analysis without excessive effort (Sodhi and Son 2010; Krippendorff 2013).

In this context, many researchers have used various approaches towards job ads analysis, which are presented in Table 2.

To conclude, content analysis is a useful scientific tool, which can provide new insights by enhancing the understanding of specific phenomena and informing about practical actions (Ayalew et al. 2011). As seen in Table 2, many different studies have applied content analysis for analyzing job ads, and it is often indicated that this method can help to identify skills in demand at present, as well as changes in this demand over time (Litecky et al. 2010; Todd et al. 1995).

3   Methodology

3.1   Job Ad Collection and Recording

For the collection of the job ads, electronic ads were chosen, mainly due to their variety, quantity, and easy accessibility. The first phase of the research requires the manual selection of a capable number of job ads for each of the 23 ICT professions. Later on, the ads are coded into a separate spreadsheet for each profession, which consists of the following fields:

- The date of the access to the job ad.
- The country of the job position offering.
- The hard skills required for the position.
- The soft skills required for the position.
- The electronic link of the job ad.

Bottom-Up approach consists of analyzing various forms of data, such as numbers, text, images, video, and voice in order to find relationships and patterns to gain knowledge from the data. Bottom-Up analysis has gained tremendous growth over the past few years. This type of analysis has spread to numerous sectors including finance, business, law enforcement, and defense indicatively. Data mining, machine learning, and big data are common representatives of Bottom-Up analysis (Berr and Linoff 1997).

In the present study, a form of data mining will be implemented through the record and the analysis of job ads.

3.2   The Construction of Non–technical Skills' Dictionary

The objective of the process is the categorization of the soft skills detected into the ads based on their relevance. More specifically, the synonyms and the soft skills with the same meaning will form each category. As a matter of fact, the present research uses the aforementioned Bottom-Up approach. During this process, data was inserted into Microsoft Excel. For this purpose, the following steps were accomplished:

1. Each ICT profession was examined separately; therefore, a different spreadsheet was created for each of the 23 ICT professions. The selection of the job ads was conducted through keywords search in major job-seeking websites. The keywords could be the official title of the job or an alternative relevant title.
2. The relevant job ads were scanned and the synonym terms and phrases were written down in separate columns. For example, the terms "you should have teamworking skills" and "it is essential for the candidate to be able to work excellently within a team" were placed in the same column as synonyms.

3. If a term or an exact phrase appeared more than once, then its frequency of appearance was declared next to the term in parenthesis. For example, if the term "you should have teamworking skills" appears three times throughout the ads gathered, then it should be written down as "you should have teamworking skills (3)" in the corresponding cell of the spreadsheet.
4. After the completion of the above procedure for each of the 23 ICT professions, each column was given a general title, which emerged from the most inclusive and brief term. In the context of the above example, a general title of the category could be "Teamworking Skills".

The result of the above procedure will be a "Soft-Skills Dictionary" for each profession of the ICT sector. Based on that dictionary, a program can be developed, which on the one hand will gather automatically new ads and on the other hand it will be capable of detecting soft skills in each of them.

3.3 Statistical Analysis

In order to fulfill the purpose of the present study, the relative frequency analysis was used in order to highlight the significance of soft skills for each profession, as well as for each category of professions in the ICT sector. The procedure was conducted manually following the steps demonstrated below:

1. The relative frequency of appearance for each category of soft skills was calculated.
2. The first twelve most appeared soft skills were extracted.
3. The ICT professions were divided into six categories according to the European e-Competence Framework (2012) respectfully: Business Management, Technical Management, Design, Development, Service and Operation, and Support.
4. The average relative frequency for each soft skill and for each family of the ICT professions was expressed as a percentage. This percentage also represents the possibility of each soft skill to be preferred by the employer.

4   Results

4.1 Soft Skills Demand for Each of the Six Families of Professions of the ICT Sector

Business Management ICT family includes the following professions: Business Information Manager, Chief Information Officer, and ICT Operations Manager. All the above professions combine Computer Science knowledge, as well as Business Management knowledge. As shown in Fig. 2, the most prominent soft skills are

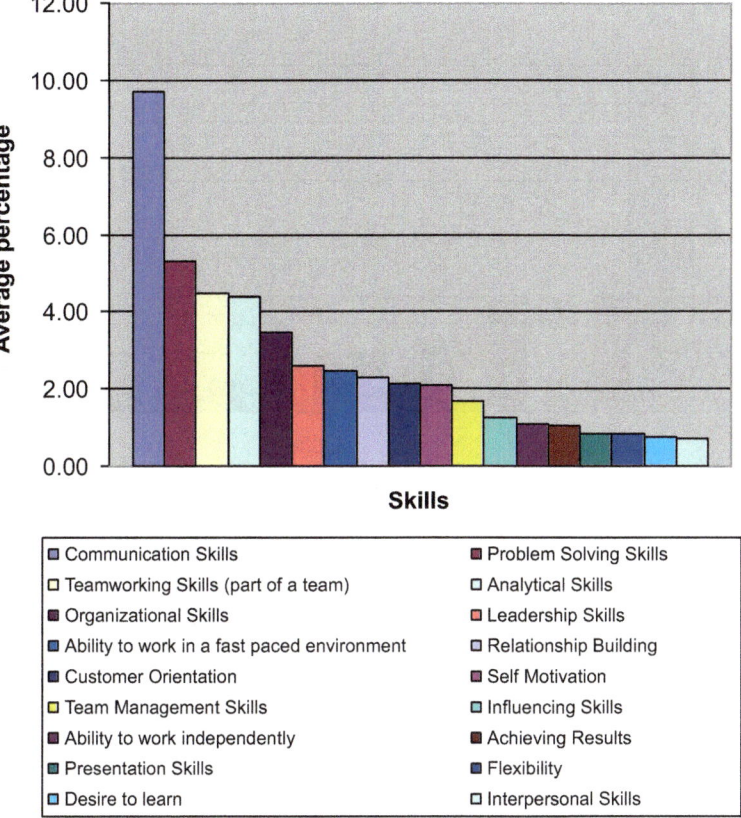

Fig. 2 Soft skills demand for Business Management-related ICT professions

Communication Skills, Problem Solving Skills, Team Working Skills, Analytical Skills, and Organizational Skills.

Technical Management ICT family includes the following professions: Quality Assurance Manager, ICT Security Manager, Project Manager, and Service Manager. The professions of this family combine Technical knowledge, as well as Management knowledge. The highlighted soft skills for this family (Fig. 3) are: Communication Skills, Organizational Skills, Analytical Skills, Problem Solving Skills, and Team Working Skills.

Design-related family includes the following professions: Business Analyst, Systems Analyst, Enterprise Architect, and Systems Architect. As demonstrated in Fig. 4, the most significant soft skills for this family of professions are the following: Communication Skills, Team Working Skills, Problem Solving Skills, Analytical Skills, and Presentation Skills.

Development-related family consists of the following professions: Developer, Digital Media Specialist, and Test Specialist. For these professions, employers seek

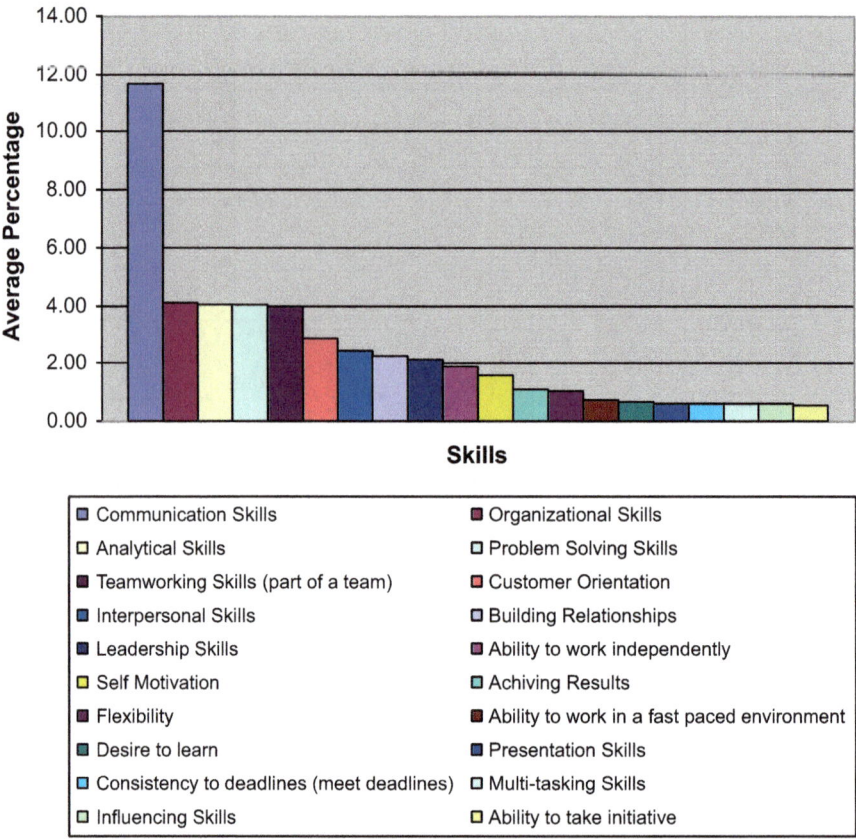

Fig. 3 Soft skills demand for Technical Management-related ICT professions

(Fig. 5): Communication Skills, Team Working Skills, Problem Solving Skills, Self-Motivation, Analytical Skills, and the Desire to learn.

Service and Operation family includes the following professions: Database Administrator, Systems Administrator, Network Specialist, Technical Specialist, and Service Desk Agent. The most prominent soft skills for this family of professions (Fig. 6) are: Communication Skills, Team Working Skills, Problem Solving Skills, Customer Orientation, and the Ability to Work Independently.

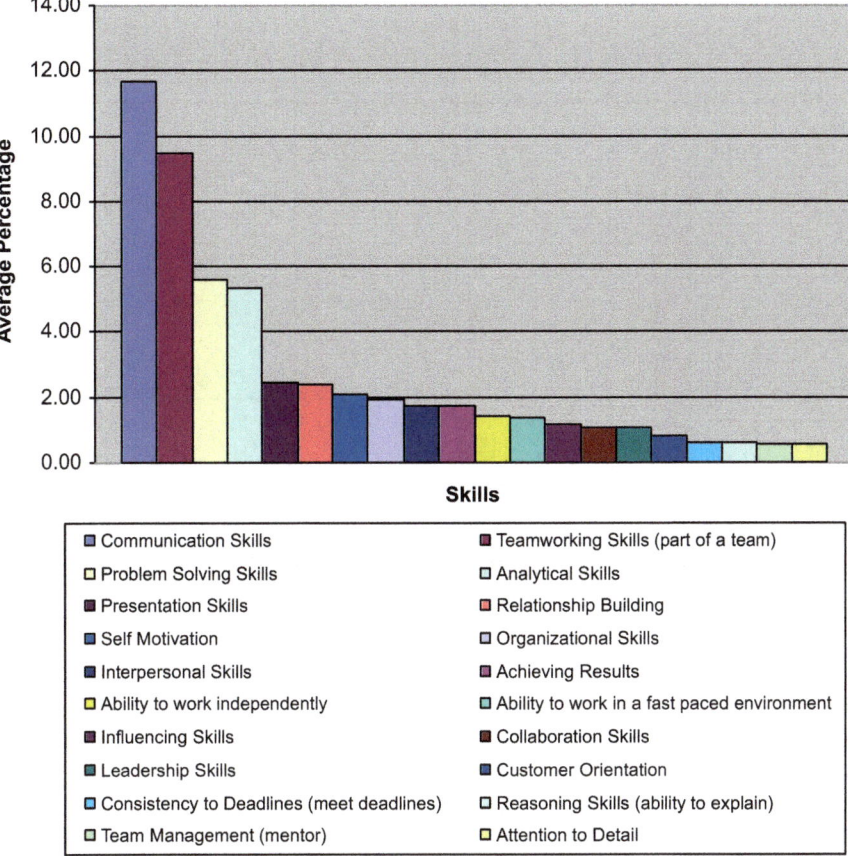

Fig. 4 Soft skills demand for Design-related ICT professions

The Support-related family consists of the following professions: Account Manager, ICT Trainer, ICT Security Specialist, and ICT Consultant. The required soft skills for this family of ICT professions are demonstrated in Fig. 7 and the most significant are the following: Communication Skills, Team Working Skills, Problem Solving Skills, Presentation Skills, and Self-Motivation.

5   Practical Implications

The systematic study of skills in the labor market shows many benefits for the individual, for businesses, as well as for the government and the community.

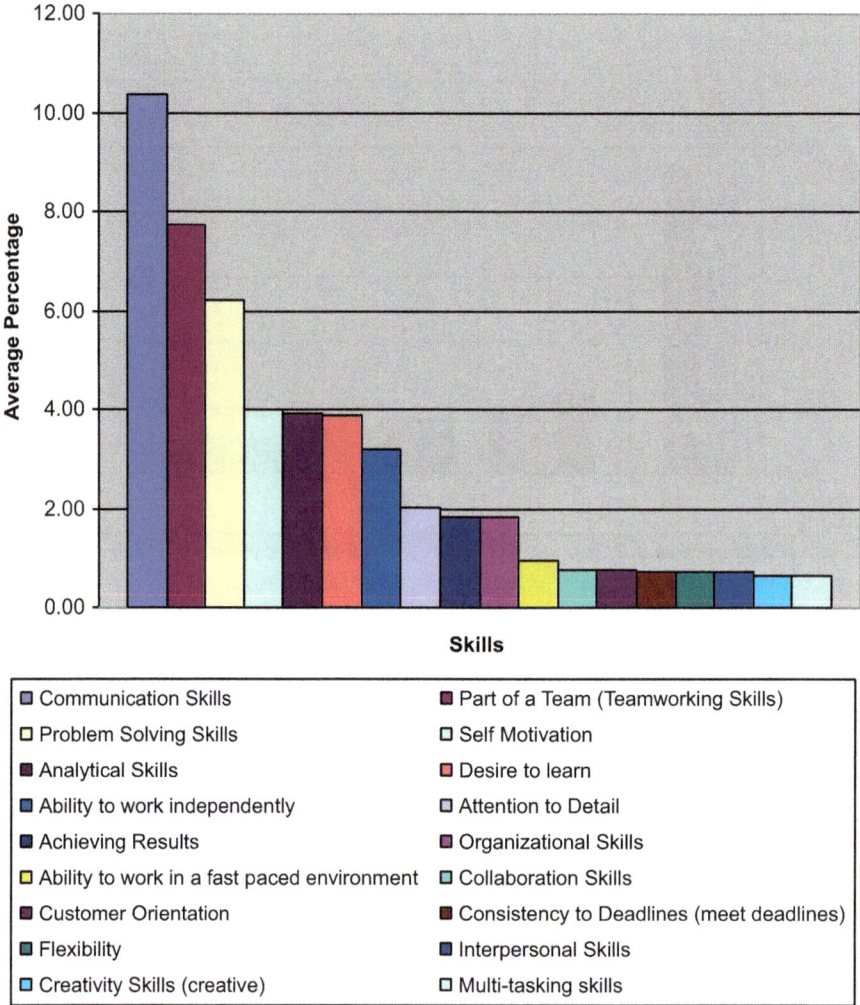

Fig. 5 Soft skills demand for Development-related ICT professions

Benefits for the individual:

- *Skills assessment*: The individual can recognize their skills as assets and detect the skills that are lacking and therefore should be further developed. Each profession requires different skills, so the individual can focus on the skills that are the most significant for their area of expertise.
- *Skills development*: The individual can attend seminars and training programs that aim to develop specific skills or can develop the preferable skills through lifelong learning and self-learning.
- *Vocational guidance*: Each individual can detect their strong skills and should be able to choose the most suitable profession.

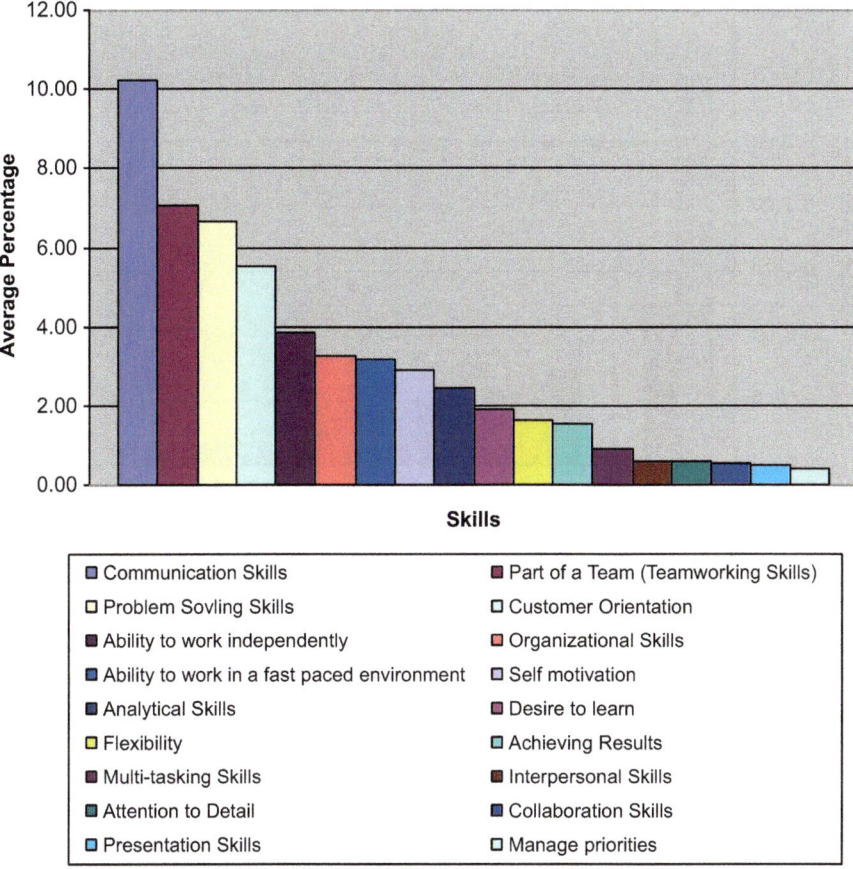

Fig. 6 Soft skills demand for Service and Operation-related ICT professions

- *Personal branding*: After acknowledging the possessed skills as strengths, the individual can highlight them in their resume. Personal branding plays a quite important role, as it is a vivid indication of the best an individual has to offer and simultaneously forms the expectations of the potential employer.

Benefits for the businesses:
- *The significance of specific skills for each industry and for each profession*. The study of skills and their significance in various contexts results in the recognition of which skills are required for each industry and each specific profession.
- *Selection of the most appropriate staff*. Through the recognition of the significance of specific skills for a specific profession, a linkage between the labor market and workforce takes place. Thus, each business can recruit the most qualified individual, in terms of both hard and soft skills, for a specific position. This fact can result in an increase in total productivity of the business.

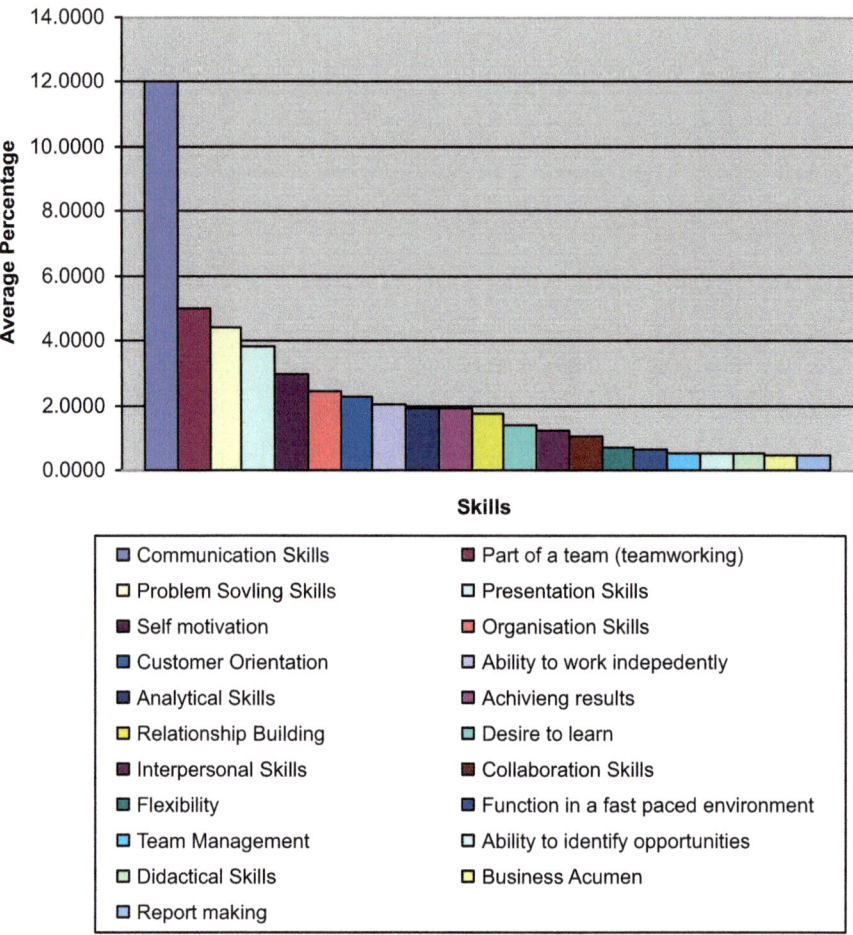

Fig. 7 Soft skills demand for Support-related ICT professions

- *Placement of the right people in the right positions within the corporation.* The assessment process can take place among the existing employees of a corporation.

Benefits for the government and the community:
- *Finding a job based on expertise and skills.* Nowadays, while the degree of specialization of employees is increasing, many individuals are unable to find a job in their area of expertise. On top of that, soft skills are neglected. The proposed system can contribute bridging the gap between human resources and labor market by finding the perfect position for an individual and conversely by finding the perfect individual for a specific position.

- *Implementation in the public sector.* Placing the right person in the right position can increase efficiency and productivity, while promoting a public sector which is characterized by transparency.

6 Conclusions

Over the past few years, the new generation shows a clear tendency towards education, by obtaining various diplomas and certifications. This situation has created a highly educated generation and therefore the selection of the appropriate employee is becoming as difficult as ever since there are many candidates with similar qualifications.

So, which is the element that can really make a candidate stand out from the crowd and dominate a job? The answer lies on soft skills. Nowadays, soft skills tend to gain more and more attention from researchers, as their importance is becoming visible in terms of employment and self-development. However, this field remains quite unclear and shadowy when it comes to the determination of soft skills, as well as their assessment.

The results of the present study, which will give new insights to the significance and the assessment of soft skills, are listed below:

- There are 23 ICT-related professions, which are divided into six distinct categories: Business Management, Technical Management, Design, Development, Service and Operation, and Support.
- There are many theories regarding soft skills. Therefore, there is a lack of a clear framework and categorization. However, soft skills are concisely described as the individual's abilities which are not related to typical education, such as teamworking skills, decision making skills, conflict management skills, organizational skills, and leadership skills.
- Ad analysis has been chosen as a research tool, mainly because it can provide a clear picture of the demands in soft skills. In this context, the collection of job ads for each of the 23 ICT professions is proposed as an initial step, in order to create a dictionary of soft skills. On this dictionary, an automatic collection and assessment program can be based.
- Communication Skills seem to be mandatory in the ICT workplace regardless of the profession. Other skills that are highly demanded by the employers are: Team Working Skills, Problem Solving Skills, Analytical Skills, Organizational Skills, Presentation Skills, Self-Motivation, Customer Orientation, the Ability to Work Independently, and the Desire to learn.

Last, but not least, content analysis of job ads is a useful method, which can demonstrate the current demand of skills, as well as changes and therefore their importance for specific professions.

In the future, this whole process can be automated by developing an innovative and dynamic platform, which will constantly collect and record job ads and assess the demand for soft skills. In addition, this process can also be implemented in other sectors, providing useful insights for other professions.

References

Ahmed, F., Capretz, F. L., Bouktif, S., & Campbell, P. (2012). Soft skills requirements in software development jobs: A cross-cultural empirical study. *Journal of Systems and Information Technology, 14*(1), 58–81.

Ahsan, K., Ho, M., & Khan, S. (2013). Recruiting project managers: A comparative analysis of competencies and recruitment signals from job advertisements. *Project Management Journal, 44*(5), 36–54.

Albitz, R. S. (2002). Electronic resource librarians in academic libraries: A position announcement analysis 1996–2001. *Portal: Libraries and the Academy, 2*(4), 589–600.

Ayalew, Y., Mbero, Z. A., Nkgau, T. Z., Motlogelwa, P., & Masizana-Katongo, A. (2011). Computing knowledge and skills demand: A content analysis of job adverts in Botswana. *International Journal of Advanced Computer Science and Applications, 2*(1), 1–9.

Beile, P. M., & Adams, M. M. (2000). Other duties as assigned: Emerging trends in the academic library job market. *College and Research Libraries, 61*(4), 336–347.

Berr, M. A., & Linoff, G. (1997). *Data mining techniques: for marketing, sales, and customer support*. Hoboken, NJ: Wiley Editions.

Boyatzis, R. E. (1982). *The competent manager: A model for effective performance*. New York: John Wiley and Sons Inc.

Chao, C. A., & Shih, S. C. (2005). Organizational and end-user information systems job market: An analysis of job types and skill requirements. *Learning, and Performance Journal, 23*, 1–15.

Cullen, J. (2000). A review of library and information service job advertisements: What do they tell us about work in the Irish library sector? *Journal of Information Science, 26*(4), 278–281.

Denton, R. (2003). *Down-to-earth key competencies assessment: A very practical student-centered perspective*. Retrieved June 8, 2017 from http://vuir.vu.edu.au/1841/1/Assessing_and_certifying_generic_skills.pdf

Dubois, D. (1998). *The competency casebook: Twelve studies in competency-based performance improvement*. Omaha: HDR Press Inc..

European e-Competence Framework. (2012). *European ICT professional profiles*. Retrieved June 15, 2017 from http://www.ecompetences.eu/ict-professionsl-profiles/

Gibb, S. (2013). Soft skills assessment: Theory development and the research agenda. *The International Journal of Lifelong Education, 33*(4), 455–471.

Hsieh, H. F., & Shannon, S. E. (2005). Three approaches to qualitative content analysis. *Qualitative Health Research, 15*(9), 1277–1288.

Karanja, E., Grant, D. M., Freeman, S., & Anyiwo, D. (2016). Entry level systems analysts: What does the industry want? *Informing Science: The International Journal of an Emerging Transdiscipline, 19*, 141–160.

Katz, R. L. (1955). Skills of an effective administrator. *Harvard Business Review, 33*(1), 33–42.

Kechagias, K. (2011). *Teaching and assessing soft skills*. School of Thessaloniki, Neapoli: MASS Project Report.

Kennan, M., Willard, P., Cecez-Kecmanovic, D., & Wilson, C. (2007). IS early career job advertisements: A content analysis. In: *11th Pacific-Asia Conference on Inf Sys Auckland*: 340–353. Retrieved November 14, 2016 from http://www.pacis-net.org/file/2007/1211.pdf

Krippendorff, K. (2013). *Content analysis: An introduction to its methodology*. Beverly Hills: Sage Publications.

Lavy, I., & Yadin, A. (2013). Soft skills – An important key for employability in the "shift to a service driven economy" era. *International Journal of e-Education, e-Business, e-Management and e-Learning, 3*(5), 416–420.

Lee, S., & Lee, C. (2006). IT managers' requisite skills. *Communications of the ACM, 49*(4), 111.

Litecky, C., Aken, A., Ahmad, A., & Nelson, H. (2010). Mining for computing jobs. *IEEE Software, 27*(1), 78–85.

Marrelli, A. F. (1998). An introduction to competency analysis and modelling. *Performance Improvement, 37*, 8–17.

Mayring, P. (2000). Qualitative content analysis. *Forum: Qualitative Social Research, 1*, 2 Retrieved November 19, 2016 from http://217.160.35.246/fqs-texte/2-00/2- 00mayring-e.pdf.

McClelland, D. (1973). Testing for competence rather than for intelligence. *The American Psychologist, 20*, 321–333.

Migdalas, A., Sifaleras, A., Georgiadis, C. K., Papathanasiou, J., & Stiakakis, E. (2013). Optimization theory, decision making, and operations research applications. In *Springer proceedings in mathematics & statistics* (Vol. 31). New York, NY: Springer.

Munce, J. W. (1981). *Toward a comprehensive model of clustering skills*. Washington, DC: NSIEE Occasional Paper.

North, A., & Worth, W. (1996). Trends in advertised entry-level technology, interpersonal, and basic communication job skills. *Journal of Employment Counseling, 33*(3), 98–105.

Omar, N., Abdul Manaf, A., Helma Mohd, R., Che Kassim, A., & Abd Aziz, K. (2012). Graduates' employability skills based on current job demand through electronic advertisement. *Asian Social Sciences, 8*(9), 103–110.

Patton, M. Q. (2002). *Qualitative research and evaluation methods*. Thousand Oaks: Sage Publications.

Peterson, T., & Van Fleet, D. (2004). The ongoing legacy of R. L. Katz: An updated typology of management skills. *Management Decision, 42*(10), 1297–1308.

Purao, S., & Suen, H. (2010). Designing a multi-faceted metric to evaluate soft skills. In *Proceeding Special Interest Group of Management Information Systems 'SIGMIS-CPR' 10, 48th annual conference on computer personnel research* (pp. 88–91). New York, NY: ACM.

Rashidi, A., Fakhrul, A. A. K., & Ilhamie, A. G. A. (2013). Integrating soft skills assessment through soft skills workshop program for engineering students at University of Pahang: An analysis. *International Journal of Research in Social Science, 2*(1), 33–46.

Reese-Durham, N. (2005). Peer evaluation as an active learning technique. *Journal of Instructional Psychology, 32*(4), 338–343.

Sahandri, M., & Kumar, S. (2009). Generic skills in personnel development. *The European Journal of Social Science, 11*(4), 684–489.

Schlee, R. P., & Harich, K. R. (2010). Knowledge and skill requirements for marketing jobs in the 21st century. *Journal of Marketing Education, 32*(3), 341–352.

Sodhi, M., & Son, B. (2010). Content analysis of OR job advertisements to infer required skills. *Journal of the Operational Research Society, 61*(9), 1315–1327.

Sukhoo, A., Barnard, A., Eloff, M. M., van der Poll, J. A., & Motah, M. (2005). Accommodating soft skills in software project management. *Issues in Informing Science and Information Technology, 2*, 691–703.

Todd, P. A., McKeen, J. D., & Brent, R. (1995). The evolution of IS job skills: A content analysis of IS job advertisements from 1970 to 1990. *MIS Quarterly, 19*(1), 1–27.

Vieira da Cunha, M. (2009). The information professional's profile: An analysis of Brazilian job vacancies on the internet. *Information Research, 14*(3), 5–16.

Wahl, H., Kaufmann, C., Eckkrammer, F., Mense, A., Gollner, H., Himmler, C., Rogner, W., Baierl, T., & Slobodian, R. (2012). Soft skills in practice and in education: An evaluation. *AJBE, 5*(2), 225–232.

Zhang, A. (2012). Peer assessment of soft skills and hard skills. *The Journal of Information Technology Education, 11*, 155–168.

Cloud Computing Adoption Decision in E-government

Ioannis Nanos, Vicky Manthou, and Efthimia Androutsou

Abstract Cloud computing is one of the latest ICT innovations, offering many advantages and leading to the digital transformation of private and public organizations. Despite the associated benefits, initiatives for cloud computing adoption in public administration are in early stage and relatively slow, comparing to initiatives for adoption in private organizations, due to various influencing factors. At the same time, academics and practitioners indicate that cloud computing not only has the potential to offer significant advantages in the public sector, but is also expected to be a fundamental part of e-government strategy in the upcoming years. The aim of this paper is to investigate the relationship between cloud computing and e-government, to highlight the importance of cloud computing adoption in public administration, and to offer insights on the way that cloud computing can contribute to the successful deployment of e-government services. Through the study of relevant theoretical models and frameworks, enabling and inhibiting factors for cloud computing adoption in the public sector are identified, classified, and analyzed. Furthermore, initiatives that have taken place so far in Europe and in Greece in the area of cloud computing and e-government are presented. The paper contributes to the knowledge domain of cloud computing adoption and e-government and indicates fields that can be further researched in this area.

Keywords Cloud computing adoption · E-government · Decision for cloud adoption in public sector

I. Nanos (✉) · V. Manthou
Department of Applied Informatics, University of Macedonia, Thessaloniki, Greece
e-mail: nanos@uom.edu.gr

E. Androutsou
Municipality of Thessaloniki, Thessaloniki, Greece

© Springer Nature Switzerland AG 2019
A. Sifaleras, K. Petridis (eds.), *Operational Research in the Digital Era – ICT Challenges*, Springer Proceedings in Business and Economics,
https://doi.org/10.1007/978-3-319-95666-4_9

1 Introduction

Cloud computing represents the emergence of a new computing paradigm (Vaquero et al. 2008; Cegielski et al. 2012), while at the same time it is a potential and rapidly developing issue for the evolution and innovation of the IT sector (Castells 2001). Despite the plethora of definitions in bibliography, it is difficult to find one-single definition that describes cloud computing precisely. According to Sultan (2011), cloud computing is "a model of delivering a range of IT services remotely through the Internet and/or a networked IT environment." The European Network and Information Security Agency (ENISA 2011) defines cloud computing as an "on-demand service model for IT provision, often based on virtualization and distributed computing technologies." A more complete and widely used definition is provided by the National Institute of Standards and Technology (NIST 2011), which defines cloud computing as "a model for enabling ubiquitous, convenient, on-demand network access to a shared pool of configurable computing resources (e.g., networks, servers, storage, applications and services) that can be rapidly provisioned and released with minimal management effort or service provider interaction."

Cloud computing offers significant advantages and can be applied to various sectors of the economy, leading to the digital transformation of private and public organizations and resulting in economic and other benefits. It is more than obvious that cloud computing is a growing market and a crucial driver for economic growth in Europe, with serious impacts for users of cloud computing services, providers, and the European society as a whole (European Commission 2017c).

A study conducted by Deloitte for the European Commission estimates that cloud computing could add a cumulative total revenue of €449 billion to the EU28 GDP, including the public sector (Deloitte 2016). As far as the European cloud computing market itself is concerned, estimates indicate that it will grow €44.8 billion by 2020, almost five times bigger than the market size in 2013 (€9.5 billion).

Therefore, and according to recommendations from several European bodies, countries should include cloud computing adoption in their e-government strategies and integrate it into the core of public sector innovation. By doing so, the EU policy can be delivered in a better, more efficient and more productive way, and countries will fully seize the opportunities offered by new and innovative technologies.

The aim of this paper is to further investigate the relationship between cloud computing and e-government, by highlighting the importance and the advantages of cloud computing adoption in the public sector and offering insights on the way that cloud computing can contribute to the successful deployment of e-government services. Models and characteristics of cloud computing are presented and advantages from cloud computing adoption in the public sector are analyzed. Recommendations for the selection of the proper cloud computing model are provided and possible factors that may inhibit cloud computing adoption are highlighted. Finally, initiatives that have taken place so far in Europe and in Greece in the area of cloud computing and e-government are discussed.

2   Cloud Computing and E-government

2.1   Cloud Computing Characteristics and Models

Following NIST's definition about cloud computing and according to Sosinski (2011), the features-characteristics of cloud computing that are identified in the various definitions and distinguish cloud computing from other computing models are:

- *Broad network access*, where cloud computing resources are accessible over the network by heterogeneous client platforms and regardless location and type of device.
- *Rapid elasticity*, where cloud computing resources can be scaled in and out automatically, whenever needed and as required.
- *Measured service,* where the cloud systems automatically monitor, control, optimize and report the usage of resources; thus, providing transparency for both cloud providers and clients.
- *On-demand self-service*, where the client can obtain and use cloud computing resources as needed, without the intervention of the cloud provider at any time.
- *Resource pooling*, where the cloud provider's physical and virtual computing resources (i.e., storage, processing, memory and network bandwidth) are pooled and utilized by multiple clients at the same time.

Based on the above characteristics, cloud computing models are categorized into: (a) *deployment models*, which refer to the structure of the cloud, its features, and the users who (can) have access to it and (b) *service models*, which refer to the type of cloud services offered (Höfer and Karagiannis 2011; Sosinski 2011; Hsu et al. 2014).

Deployment Models

- Public cloud: computing services offered by third-party providers over the Internet, making them available to anyone who wants to use or purchase them. Services may be free or sold on-demand, allowing customers to pay only per usage for the CPU cycles, storage, or bandwidth they consume.
- Private cloud: computing services offered only to selected users-organizations either over the Internet or a private internal network. Each private cloud is dedicated to a specific organization.
- Community cloud: computing services offered, for a specific use, to a specific set of users-organizations who share the same views and needs on issues such as security and politics.
- Hybrid cloud: combination of two or more of the above cloud deployment models. It can be used by different kinds of entities that actually use and share the same given technology.

Service Models

- Infrastructure as a Service (IaaS): provision of infrastructure such as networking, storage, servers, virtual machines and operating systems. In this model, users develop their own applications on the provided virtual machines and have total control and management over them.
- Platform as a Service (PaaS): provision of infrastructure (hosting options) and tools (programming frameworks, environments and languages) for users to design, develop and manage their own applications and services (middleware, runtime). In this model, the underlying physical infrastructure (storage, servers, operating systems, etc.) is also provided (as in the IaaS model), but users have no control over them.
- Software as a Service (SaaS): provision of software applications which support business related processes, from simple email messaging systems to more complex and integrated information systems, like Enterprise Resource Planning (ERP), Customer Relationship Management (CRM), and Supply Chain Management (SCM). In this model, users work on web-based applications through a web browser and they do not need to install software in their PCs. They do not manage or control the underlying infrastructure and they don't have access to application design, apart from some limited user-specific configuration on the web applications.

The differences between the main cloud service models (IaaS, PaaS, and SaaS) in comparison to the "traditional" IT model (where users control, own and manage everything, from servers to applications) are illustrated in Fig. 1.

Other cloud deployment models that are mentioned in the literature (Prakash et al. 2012; Firdhous 2014) are:

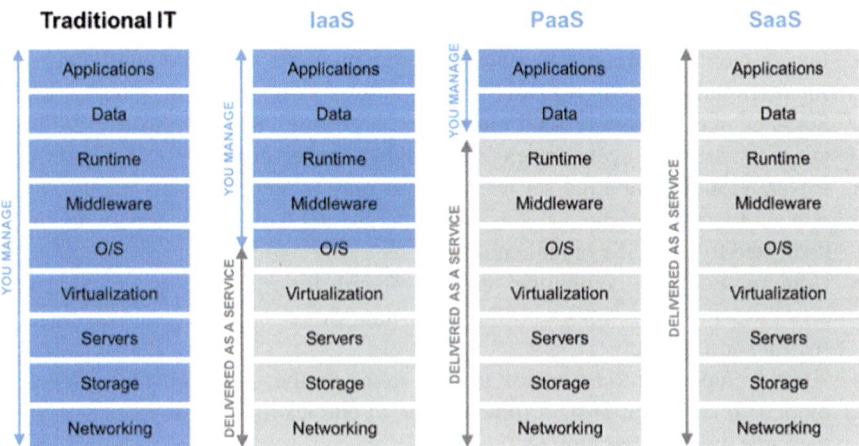

Fig. 1 Comparison between traditional IT and cloud service models *(Source: The economics of the cloud, Microsoft 2010)*

- Communication as a Service (CaaS): provision of Voice-over-IP (VoIP) solutions, videoconferencing and messaging systems, etc.
- Backup as a Service (BaaS): provision of data and systems backup.
- Disaster Recovery as a Service (DRaaS): data and systems recovery after disasters, etc.

It should be mentioned, though, that the above-mentioned CaaS, BaaS, and DRaaS models can be considered as subcategories of the IaaS model.

Finally, Mladenow et al. (2012) refer to the "Everything as a Service (XaaS) model" where X stands for a series of things like "X as a service" or "everything as a service." This acronym refers to an increasing number of services such as IT infrastructure, platforms, software, databases, and other IT resources provided over the Internet and can be accessed remotely (Winkler 2011).

2.2 Electronic Government (E-government)

Electronic government (e-government) is a multidimensional term (Ramaprasad et al. 2015) and can be defined as the application of information and communication technologies in public administration, in order to facilitate communication and interaction between governments, citizens and businesses (Yildiz 2007; Almarabeh and AbuAli 2010). E-government supports administrative processes, improves the quality of services offered, and increases internal public sector efficiency. Digital public services reduce administrative burden on businesses and citizens by making their interactions with public administration faster and efficient, more convenient and transparent, and less costly. In addition, "using digital technologies as an integrated part of governments modernization strategies can unlock further economic and social benefits for society as a whole" (European Commission 2017a). Moreover, global trends have made e-government a necessity for any country wishing to enter the twenty-first century (Brooks and Persaud 2015).

E-government models can be classified into the main following categories (Mosa et al. 2015):

- G2C (Government-to-Citizen): public services that refer to citizens (tax declarations, issuing of various certificates, social benefits-allowances, etc.) and public consultation with the citizens for various issues.
- G2B (Government-to-Business): public services that refer to businesses (tax declarations, social insurance for employees, government tenders, e-procurement, etc.)
- G2G (Government-to-Government): communication and cooperation between government departments, sharing of information.
- G2E (Government-to-Employee): provision of information on job opportunities and appointments in the public sector, etc.

Other e-government models mentioned in the literature are (Yildiz 2007):

- G2SC (Government-to-Civil Society Organizations): communication and coordination efforts after a disaster.
- G2N (Government-to-Non-Profit or Non-Governmental Organizations): communication and cooperation for voluntary or other social actions, and
- C2C (Citizen-to-Citizen): communication and interaction between citizens about public issues.

According to Ramaprasad et al. (2015), the essential entities-stakeholders in e-government are governments (in central/federal, provincial/regional/state and local/municipal levels), citizens, businesses, and intermediaries such as non-governmental organizations (NGOs).

Especially local governments (municipalities), which are close to the citizens and usually act as the first (and more often) point-of-contact for public service delivery (Wirtz et al. 2017), should become more innovative, embrace e-government, and adopt modern ICT capabilities like cloud computing.

2.3   Cloud Computing Adoption in E-government

According to OECD's Recommendation on Digital Government Strategies (OECD 2014) "today's technology is not only a strategic driver for improving public sector efficiency, but can also support effectiveness of policies and create more open, transparent, innovative, participatory and trustworthy governments."

Cloud computing not only has the potential to offer significant advantages in the public sector, but is also expected to be a fundamental part of e-government strategy in the upcoming years and lead to the digital transformation of governments (Microsoft 2017).

In this context and despite their bureaucracy, rigid structures and low degree of innovation adoption, public administration authorities and governments have begun to use some cloud computing services or consider to do so in the upcoming years (Zwattendorfer and Tauber 2013), in order to achieve cost reduction (to conform with tight and reduced budgets) without cutting essential services, increased utilization of human resources, high availability, scalability and efficiency of systems and services, and provision of improved services to citizens (Craig et al. 2009). Additionally, cloud computing can contribute, in the long run, to lower Total Cost of Ownership (TCO) and reduction in the overall carbon footprint of IT. In the UK, government officials stated that county councils could save millions from the public sector IT bill, by applying cloud services and adopting the "pay-as-you-go" model, rather than keep applying the traditional long-term IT contracts (Wall 2014).

However, due to the fact that cloud computing is a relatively new paradigm and still unknown for many governments, there are various factors that influence and inhibit its adoption, such as lack of awareness about cloud computing, lack of standards that will ensure compliance-compatibility with existing systems, internet availability and bandwidth, fear of loss in IT control, switching costs, immature

Table 1 Rewards and risks of cloud computing (Jones et al. 2017)

Classification	Rewards	Risks
Strategic	• Centralization of infrastructure • Increased resilience • Device and location independence • Release internal IT resources • Better citizen services • Green technology	• Unproven financial business case • Loss of governance • Lack of trust on providers • Security and privacy issues
Tactical	• Improved business continuity and disaster recovery • Improved agility and empowerment • Faster implementation • Improved security • Scalability • Easier application migration	• Portability restrictions • Lack of data ownership • Integration restrictions
Operational	• Reduced costs • Reduced maintenance and support • Flexibility of work practices • Utilization and efficiency improvements • Shared services • Increased peak-load capacity	• Poor performance • Limited storage capacity • Financial pressures • Loss of control • Lack of detailed information about data locations • Disaster recovery restrictions • Lack of service availability • Difficult to customize

cloud providers market and risk in the selection of the appropriate cloud provider, data integrity, security and privacy, and concerns about operations and systems continuity (Buyya et al. 2009; Paquette et al. 2010; Zissis and Lekkas 2011; Alshomrani and Qamar 2013; Shin 2013).

A detailed mapping-classification of anticipated rewards and risks of cloud computing into strategic, tactical, and operational is performed by Jones et al. (2017) and is presented in Table 1.

Initiatives for cloud computing adoption in the public sector are in early stage and relatively slow, comparing to similar (and even other IT-related) initiatives in the private sector. Krogstie and Veld (2015), based on a literature review and on a survey performed in Norwegian organizations, argue that there is a significant difference between private and public organizations, whereas private organizations are more able to successfully adopt value-adding IT activities.

Furthermore, there is a differentiation between cloud computing adoption in the various levels of government. More specifically and according to data from UK's Governmental Digital Service (GDS), adoption at the local government level is markedly slower than the adoption at the central level, mainly due to the fact that central government authorities are mandated to adopt cloud, while the wider public sector is not. Local governments are more autonomous comparing to central government authorities and in many cases follow their own agenda (Donnelly 2017). Also, there is a lack of best practices and a well-documented list of risks and rewards that local councils could take into account in their decision-making process in order to proceed to cloud computing adoption (Jones et al. 2017).

2.4 Decision for Cloud Computing Adoption in the Public Sector

According to El-Gazzar and Wahid (2015) and Schneider and Sunyaev (2016), the decision for cloud computing adoption in public sector requires an extensive and systematic analysis about the appropriate cloud deployment and service model that will be selected (private, public, community, hybrid/IaaS, PaaS, Saas), taking into account the characteristics, advantages, and disadvantages of each model. Moreover, it requires proper analysis of requirements and priorities of the specific public authority, the overall IT workload, and the applications that will be migrated into cloud, since all applications may not be able to operate properly in the cloud. Issues concerning security, privacy, integrity, availability, and compliance to existing laws and regulations should be examined (ENISA 2011). Finally, the selection of the cloud provider (or providers, in the case that the public authority decides to spread workload components across multiple clouds) is of great importance and appropriate Service Level Agreements (SLAs) should be signed and followed.

As far as cloud deployment models are concerned (private, public, community and hybrid), the European Agency for Network and Information Security (ENISA 2011) recommends the use of "private cloud" and "community cloud" models, as they allow more control and incorporate more security and privacy features. Zwattendorfer and Tauber (2013) state that the dominant cloud deployment model for governmental services is the so-called G-Cloud, a combination of "private" and "community" cloud model, that offers better compliance possibilities with national regulations and legislations than public clouds. The "public cloud" model can be deployed in the case of non-sensitive data and low risk e-government applications, mainly due to its low cost. The "hybrid cloud" model (e.g., combination of private and public cloud) can also be adopted by public organizations, but it usually requires data separation, as sensitive data should not be stored in a public cloud.

Regarding the adoption of cloud service models (IaaS, PaaS, or SaaS) by a public authority, all models are acceptable (Zwattendorfer and Tauber 2013). For example, the IaaS model can be used to store and backup e-government data and systems. The PaaS model can be applied to the development of custom public domain applications in the cloud. In this case, specialized public sector services may include specific national or regional services such as tax or electronic delivery of services or simple services of submitting applications to be processed by public authority's back-office. Finally, the SaaS model could be used within collaborative frameworks, workflow management systems of electronic documents, business and citizen information services, or any other "X" service model (Nedev 2014).

Before deciding to adopt cloud computing and integrate its capabilities into everyday operational procedures, public authorities at all levels (central, regional, and local) should formulate an e-government strategy, where cloud computing will be a key element of this strategy. Furthermore, a detailed cost-benefit analysis should be carried out, including a complete and documented list of anticipated risks and rewards, together with a detailed plan for the alignment of cloud computing capabilities with existing culture and infrastructure.

2.5 E-government and ICT Implementation in Europe and in Greece

The European Commission eGovernment Action plan, the Digital Agenda for Europe, and the European Cloud Computing Strategy have set the effective exploitation of the benefits of information and communication technologies (ICT) as one of their main goals, where the use of cloud computing is being promoted for the creation of more agile, trustworthy, and transparent administrative services.

In this context, Greece has deployed a national e-government strategy for the upcoming years, where the main vision is "in the next years using ICT as a catalyst of development and modern governance tool, the Greek Public Administration will regain the trust of society and become more efficient and productive by providing citizens, and business user – centric online service that will be constantly upgraded" (European Commission 2017a). According to the action plan for e-government, the most important models that will be adopted include IaaS and SaaS, so as to make the best use of governmental cloud technologies (G-Cloud) through the completion of catalyst projects (eGov Now, IT Public Policy, etc.).

However, according to the 2017 European Digital Economy and Society Index (European Commission 2017b), which measures progress of member states in internet connectivity, human capital, use of internet, integration of digital technology, and digital public services (e-government), Greece (EL) ranked 26th and did not make much progress compared to other EU member states (Fig. 2). Especially in the area of digital public services, Greece has made a slight progress, but is still lagging from other European Countries.

As far as the use of digital public services in Greece is concerned, a recent study by the National Statistical Authority shows that, although the percentage of population (persons 16–74 years old) using e-government services has significantly increased in the period between 2010 and 2016, in 2017 the percentage was decreased by 3.1% (Fig. 3).

There are several barriers that hinder efficient implementation of ICT actions in Greece, thus leading to the low digital maturity of the country. According to studies carried out by the Foundation for Economic & Industrial Research (2014) and by Accenture in cooperation with the Hellenic Federation of Enterprises (2017), these barriers are identified and categorized as following:

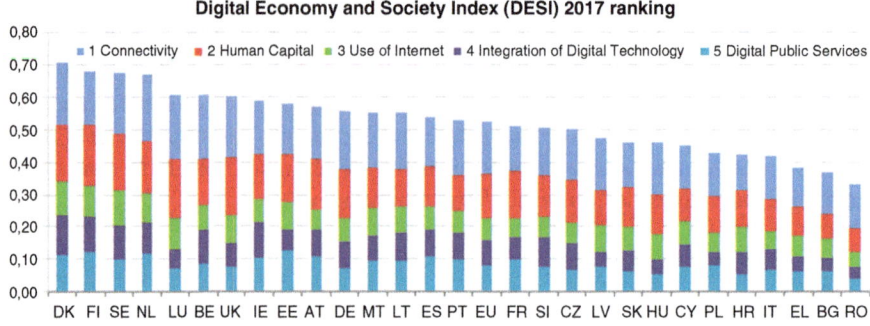

Fig. 2 European digital economy and society index *(Source: European Commission* 2017b)

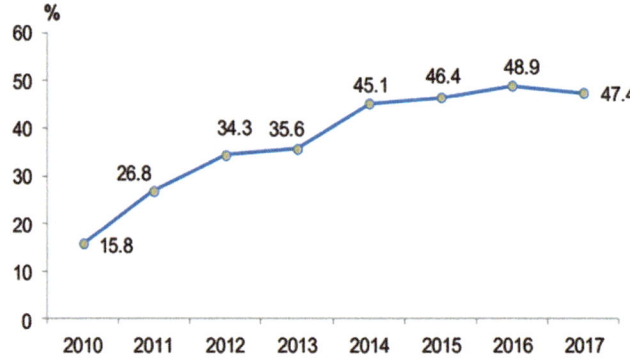

Fig. 3 Use of e-government services in Greece, 2010–2017 *(Source: Hellenic Statistical Author-ity* 2017)

Policy-driven limitations

- Lack of national digital vision and limited political willing to stimulate digital growth and e-government.
- Inefficient mechanisms of horizontal government schemes.
- Discontinuity of adopted policies at every governmental change.
- Delay in the deployment of a national e-government strategy, with clear tactics, metrics, and monitoring frameworks.
- Outdated laws and regulations about data protection that do not follow the rapid pace of technological progress.

Weaknesses related to technical design and planning

- Lack of interoperability and interconnection among the information systems of the public sector.
- Lack of a common architecture in public sector computing, absence of common standards, and compliance policies for ICT use.

- Complexity and lack of simplification in the relevant institutional and regulatory framework.

  Obstacles to efficient implementation of ICT adoption

- Time-consuming public procurement processes (due to significant delays in the stages of tendering, auctions, awarding, etc.) overcoming the lifecycle of procured ICT products/services, resulting to the introduction of old-fashioned products and services.
- Lack of efficient monitoring, evaluation and feedback in ICT activities.
- Lack of motivation to public servants, serving in ICT roles, to be engaged in the process and effectively support the whole process.

2.6   Initiatives for Cloud Computing Adoption in Europe

The European Commission's strategy on cloud computing was established on 27/09/2012, with the official report (communication) entitled "Unleashing the Potential of Cloud Computing in Europe" (European Commission 2012a). The aim of the strategy is to accelerate and increase the adoption and use of cloud computing in Europe, and is part of the Digital Single Market Strategy for Europe, which "aims to open up digital opportunities for people and business and enhance Europe's position as a world leader in the digital economy" (European Commission 2012b).

The European Commission identified three key actions-initiatives to be undertaken in order to speed up cloud computing uptake in Europe: (1) development of safe and fair model contract terms and conditions, (2) development of a standardization framework, that will ensure interoperability, data portability, and reversibility, and (3) establishment of a European Cloud Partnership that will bring together private and public sector to work together on common requirements for cloud computing and help Europe's public authorities to adopt cloud products and services.

In this context, European countries have already incorporated cloud computing adoption in their digital strategies, both in central and in regional/federal and local level and are using or planning to use some form of cloud computing services.

For example, in **Germany**, one of the Federal Government's action programmes is to accelerate the development and introduction of cloud computing facilities both in private and in public sector (BMWi 2010), although there are concerns that, with the existing models, cloud computing may increase the technological dependence on global IT corporations (Federal Ministry for Economic Affairs and Energy 2014). Therefore, cloud computing adoption should be carried out through the exploitation of innovation and market potential, the provision of informational guidance, and the creation of comprehensive regulatory frameworks for increased security, privacy standardization, and interoperability (BMWi 2010; Federal Ministry for Economic Affairs and Energy 2014).

In **Austria**, there is no evident cloud strategy, but there are already some initiatives and projects currently implemented at local level or in specific sectors (ENISA 2014).

In **Nordic countries** (Denmark, Finland, Norway, and Sweden) cloud strategy has already been formulated and aligned to the European strategy, and the potential of cloud computing utilization in the public sector is great. **Denmark** is considered as one of the leading countries in cloud adoption, and a number of initiatives have been implemented, both in central and in local level. For example, a procurement organization moved procurement services into the cloud and some municipalities use Google Apps Services, such as calendar and email, in their school systems (ENISA 2014).

In **Finland**, a unique and very interesting initiative has been implemented, under the title Forge Service Lab. It is actually a cloud service development laboratory, where software and services can be tested with customers before the deployment in production within commercial cloud service providers' environments, under the coordination of a non-profit company consisting private companies, universities, and public bodies (ENISA 2014).

In **Italy**, there is no high-level cloud strategy, but some interesting initiatives and services are already running. For example, the Department of Treasury of the Ministry of Economy and Finance operates a cloud platform that provides services which can be used internally and by other public administrations, while the Ministry of Foreign Affairs has developed a private cloud to ensure service continuity for Italians living abroad. In regional level, the region of Tuscany developed a new cloud data center for providing services (IaaS, PaaS, and SaaS) to local municipalities (Strategic 2014).

In **France**, a nationwide governmental cloud (G-Cloud) was implemented in 2011, based on the IaaS cloud service model. One of the main objectives of this G-Cloud (named Andromeda) is the compliance of all governmental authorities with national law in terms of data protection and security (ENISA 2014).

In **Spain**, legislation concerning cloud computing is aligned to the European one and a private governmental cloud has been established (named Red SARA), for the connectivity and collaboration of public administration. Red SARA connects 16 ministries, 17 autonomous communities, 2 autonomous cities, and over 3708 local entities (Zaharia-Rădulescu and Radu 2017). Another interesting initiative, in regional level, comes from the regional government of Castilla-La Mancha, which includes 919 municipalities and employs more than 70.000 people. By implementing a cloud strategy, Castilla-La Mancha sought to extend reach and accelerate the rollout of e-government (pensions, tax, passports, driving licenses, vehicle registration, etc.) while also developing Papás 2.0, an innovative Web portal connecting over 100 educational centers with online learning and virtual classroom services (VCE 2011).

In **Cyprus**, despite the existence of a Digital Strategy for some years (since 2012), until now there is no clear-evident cloud computing strategy and no relevant cloud initiatives or governmental cloud experiences reported so far (ENISA 2014).

In the **UK**, which can be considered as "a long time champion in Europe in the use of ICT to increase the efficiency of public services" (Zaharia-Rădulescu and Radu 2017), a national cloud strategy has been formulated for years and several cloud computing initiatives and projects have been successfully implemented, both in central and in local level. The most important one is the Governmental G-Cloud, which aimed at the introduction and use of cloud services into government departments, local authorities, and the wider public sector (ENISA 2014). G-Cloud platform consists of: (1) a series of framework agreements with suppliers, from which public sector organizations can call for services without needing to run a full tender or competition procurement process and (2) an online store—the "CloudStore" or "Government Application Store"—that allows public sector bodies to search for services that are covered by the G-Cloud frameworks (Strategic 2014).

As seen above, the landscape of the governmental cloud adoption in European countries seems heterogeneous and several variations exist between countries. According to the European Union Agency for Network and Information Security (ENISA 2013), European countries can be classified into different groups, regarding: (a) the existence of a policy background to support the implementation of cloud computing in administrative systems, i.e., national cloud strategy or digital agenda and (b) the phase of the governmental cloud implementation (design, implementation, projects running, etc.). The groups of countries are given in Table 2.

A more recent study by the same organization (ENISA 2015) claims that not many changes have been noted since the previous study, where the state of deployment of governmental cloud computing in European countries seemed to be at a very early stage (with the exceptions of some countries). The inhibiting factors for the low (in general) cloud computing adoption among European countries are security

Table 2 Classification of EU Countries concerning adoption of governmental cloud (adapted from ENISA 2013)

Group	Countries	Characteristics
Early adopters	United Kingdom, Spain, and France	• Existence of a cloud strategy • Specific decisions on how to implement the governmental cloud • A number of initiatives already running
Well-informed	The Netherlands, Germany, Republic of Moldova, Norway, Ireland, Finland, Slovak republic, Belgium, Greece, Sweden, and Denmark	• Existence of a cloud strategy • Implementation is still at design or prototype stage • Planning to implement cloud computing massively in the following years
Innovators	Italy, Austria, Slovenia, Portugal, and Turkey	• No high-level cloud strategy, but some cloud-based services are already running • Cloud implementation is forthcoming
Hesitants	Malta, Romania, Cyprus, and Poland	• No governmental cloud strategy • No relevant cloud initiatives or governmental cloud experiences • Plan to implement cloud in the future

and privacy issues, compliance with national and European rules and regulations, interoperability and data portability, identity and access management, adaptability and availability, risk management, etc. (ENISA 2015). Other factors-barriers to government cloud adoption are: the cost of migration from the existing-traditional infrastructure to the cloud, the national data sovereignty in the case where cloud storage servers may be far away from national boundaries, fast, reliable, and stable internet connectivity-accessibility, and institutional readiness of public sector authorities planning to adopt cloud (Tweneboah-Koduah et al. 2014).

Concerning security and privacy of data and compliance to European and national laws and regulations, which are critical factors that affect cloud computing adoption decision in e-government, a very useful tool has been deployed, in European level: the Cloud Privacy Check and Data Privacy Compliance in the Cloud, implemented by Eurocloud, which is an independent no-profit organization for disseminating information for the development and growth of cloud computing in the European Union. Through the website https://cloudprivacycheck.eu, anyone can be informed about the date protection rules-laws in 33 European countries and compare this information between countries. By applying this method, anyone can check the legality of using a particular cloud solution and determine the appropriate legal action that is required by the law.

2.7 Initiatives for Cloud Computing Adoption in Greece

In Greece, as mentioned above, cloud computing is a part of the national e-government strategy and some initiatives for adopting cloud services have already been implemented and discussed below.

OpenGov Private Cloud

In 2010, the Greek eGovernment and ICT Group decided to create a private cloud, based on the IaaS cloud service model, in order to host and manage governmental websites and applications and to save costs by using infrastructure (servers) that in most cases utilized no more than 5% of its power. The virtualization solution that was developed (consisting of 144 virtual machines in 20 servers) resulted to the increase of servers utilization from 5 to 90%, improved energy efficiency, rapid development of new services, easier disaster recovery procedures, and increased resource pooling and elasticity.

The private cloud that was created hosted a number of governmental websites (Greek Presidency, Office of Prime Minister, and several Ministries), applications (email services for the General Secretariat of Government), information systems (like Diavgeia and Apografi), and platforms for public consultation (Greek eGov and ICT Group 2012). All systems were supported until June 2012, where the Greek eGovernment and ICT Group stopped its operation.

GRNET Cloud Computing Services

Since 2013, GRNET (Greek National Network for Research and Technology—
"EΔET" in Greek) offers innovative cloud computing services (dynamic and
on-demand available computing/network/storage resources) to all members of
the research and academic community. The services are offered in the form of
Infrastructure as a Service (IaaS) model, under the brand name ~okeanos. By
using ~okeanos, any academic user can create a multi-layer virtual infrastructure,
combining simple virtual building blocks: hundreds of virtual machines can be
activated in just a few seconds through virtual networks on random topologies, while
data storage is feasible either on virtual drives or on cloud object storage (GRNET
2017).

It is worth noting that one of GRNET's data center is built on the banks of the
river Louros, in the area of Philippiada, next to the hydroelectric dam of PPC (Public
Power Corporation S.A.—"ΔEH" in Greek). In this innovative data center that hosts
200 latest generation servers, cooling systems are powered from the river's cold
waters thus eliminating the need for use of traditional power supplies. This data
center works also as a disaster recovery center, for the main data center that is
located in Athens, about 360 kms away (DigitalPlan 2017).

G-Cloud

Greek G-Cloud is a 15 M€ undergoing project, for the development and creation
of a private governmental cloud that is based on the Iaas service model. The
aim of the G-Cloud is to provide hosting infrastructure for information systems
of General Secretariat of Information Systems (GSIS) and other governmental
agencies (DigitalPlan 2015). The most recent implementation within the G-Cloud
is the Integrated Healthcare Information System for the allowance of healthcare
subsidies (in total 680 M€ annually) to over 200,000 beneficiaries, through a
network of about 1400 active users–employees in municipal and regional authorities
all over the country. The previous infrastructure was outdated and could not support
efficiently the volume of users and daily transactions, and the risk of system failure
and data loss was very high. After migrating to the cloud, the risk of system failure
is eliminated, the availability and response time is higher, the productivity of users
is increased, and the overall provision of services to citizens is improved (Business
News 2017).

Storm Clouds

Concerning the adoption of cloud computing in municipalities, the municipality of
Thessaloniki city participated in the European Project Storm Clouds (http://storm-
clouds.eu), together with the cities of Águeda (Portugal) and Valladolid (Spain). The
project was implemented in 2015 and focused on exploring the shift to a cloud-based

paradigm for deploying services that public authorities currently provide, based on their internal ICT infrastructure. The aim of the project was to define useful guidelines on how to implement the process of moving applications to the cloud, by suggesting a model that consists of four stages for the cloud migration process. These stages include actions regarding (a) the selection of applications/services to be migrated to the cloud, (b) addressing technical or procedural challenges, (c) migration to the pre-production cloud, and (d) moving applications to the production cloud (Panori et al. 2016).

In the case of Thessaloniki, the political priority was to cloudify applications related to entrepreneurship and quality of life in the city of Thessaloniki, such as (Tarani 2016):

- Improve My City: enables the citizens to report non-emergency local problems such as potholes, illegal trash dumping, and faulty street lights through web, Android, and iOS applications.
- Cloud Funding: supports local communities to collect money for social and charitable purposes.
- City Branding: promotes the identity of the city using virtual tours while connects the commons with local shops and services providers.
- Virtual Mall: enables every commercial enterprise located in the city center to create its own virtual shop.

These applications would be available through a platform that supported all cloud deployment models (i.e., private, community, public, and hybrid), as well as two of the cloud service models (PaaS and IaaS).

The application that was finally selected was the Virtual City Mall. Although the initial numbers of participating enterprises (62) and users-visitors (3893) were satisfactory (for a pilot project like this) and promising, the project seems to be abandoned, possibly due to obstacles to efficient implementation of ICT in e-government (as mentioned above). The initial web link for the application (https:// smartcity.thessaloniki.gr/index-en.html) cannot be reached anymore, and through the municipality's portals (http://thessaloniki.gr and https://opengov.thessaloniki.gr) there is no evident-working link to the Virtual Mall.

However it should be noted that, according to Panori et al. (2016), it was a pilot project and the results should be received as a helpful experience for municipalities or other public authorities that are willing to adopt cloud computing for e-government applications in the following years. Panori et al. (2016) also indicate another factor for the successful migration of public services to the cloud: the participation of users-citizens, especially when the cloud applications refer to Government-to-Citizens services. When users become an active part of the technological evolution of their city, they will realize that their city is essentially interested in covering their needs in the best possible way.

Novoville

Novoville (http://novoville.com) is an innovative cloud-based project, implemented by a Greek private company, including a free mobile application for citizens and a web-based application for local authorities to track citizen needs, preferences and views. It is based on the SaaS cloud service model, where local authorities use and manage the web-based application through a web browser, without installing software in their PCs.

By using the app, citizens are able to report issues on the move, receive real-time updates as the issue gets fixed, be notified about important news, announcements and city-related events, access city services directly from their mobile phone, respond to polls, participate in discussions and shape the future of the city, find answers to frequently asked questions, and finally find points of interest. Through the web dashboard, authorities manage incidents in real time, have access to interactive maps, communicate with citizens through any available medium, and leverage data to define priorities and make data-driven decisions.

Up to now and according to the data provided by http://novoville.com, thirty-five local governments (municipalities) are using novoville and receive notices from their citizens on issues mainly referring to rubbish, lighting, potholes, etc. The results seem quite impressive, as 77% of citizens that downloaded the app use it every week, 91% of reports submitted have been resolved, and 78% of all submitted issues are resolved in less than a week.

3 Conclusions

Cloud computing represents a new paradigm shift for e-government, since it enables the digital transformation of public authorities through the use of innovative and cost-effective models and services. However, initiatives for cloud computing adoption in public administration are still in early stage, especially in Greece, due to various influencing-inhibiting factors such as policy-driven limitations, weaknesses related to technical design and planning, and obstacles to efficient implementation of ICT innovations adoption. Although in European level there are some countries with successful cloud implementation that can be characterized as early adopters, the majority of countries are still in the investigation, planning or prototype phase.

The decision for cloud computing adoption in the public sector requires an extensive and systematic analysis about the appropriate cloud deployment and service model that will be selected, taking into account the characteristics, advantages and disadvantages of each model as well as the anticipated risks and rewards. Moreover, it requires proper analysis of requirements and priorities of the specific public authority and careful selection of the applications that will be migrated into the cloud, taking into account compliance with regulations as long as data security and privacy issues. Up to now, the trend in cloud deployment models for governmental services is the G-Cloud, which supports all types of e-government models (G2C, G2B, G2G, etc.) and has already been implemented in some European countries.

In Greece, as in other European Countries, cloud computing will be an integral part of e-government strategy in the following years and some initiatives for cloud computing adoption have already been implemented with notable results in the areas of cost savings, energy efficiency and green computing, increased utilization of resources, increased productivity, elimination of system failure risk, provision of improved services to citizens, and increased citizens engagement. The experience from these pilot projects is expected to act as a guide for future cloud computing implementation in the public sector, together with further theoretical and empirical investigation on appropriate frameworks, decision support models and critical success factors.

Future work at the area of cloud computing adoption in e-government may include a study and classification of European countries, concerning the adoption of cloud computing initiatives, based on recently implemented projects. This classification may lead to the assessment of every country regarding its readiness to adopt cloud computing and the categorization of the decisions that can be taken in every stage-level of cloud adoption. Finally, the analysis and study of best practices regarding cloud adoption in the public sector can assist public authorities that are still in the investigation, planning or prototype phase to formulate and/or modify accordingly their cloud computing strategy, as long as the decision-making process.

References

Accenture and Hellenic Federation of Enterprises (in Greek "ΣΕΒ"). (2017). *Digital Greece: the road for growth* (in Greek "Η ψηφιακή Ελλάδα: ο δρόμος προς την ανάπτυξη"). Retrieved May 24, 2017 from http://www.sev.org.gr/uploads/Documents/Digital_Greece_060517_full_hi_res.pdf.

Almarabeh, T., & AbuAli, A. (2010). A general framework for e-government: Definition maturity challenges, opportunities, and success. *European Journal of Scientific Research, 39*(1), 29–42.

Alshomrani, S., & Qamar, S. (2013). Cloud based e-government: Benefits and challenges. *International Journal of Multidisciplinary Sciences and Engineering, 4*(6), 1–7.

BMWi. (2010). *ICT strategy of the German Federal Government: Digital Germany 2015.* Federal Ministry of Economics and Technology (BMWi), Public Relations/L2. http://www.bmwi.de.

Brooks, L., & Persaud, A. (2015). Comparing local e-government websites in Canada and the UK. In: E. Tambouris et al. (Eds.), *IFIP International Federation for Information Processing 2015* (Vol. 9248, pp. 291–304). EGOV 2015, LNCS. https://doi.org/10.1007/978-3-319-22479-4_22.

Business News. (2017). *Until the end of March the G-Cloud project* (in Greek "ΚτΠ: Μέχρι τέλος Μαρτίου το έργο G-Cloud"). Retrieved February 10, 2017 from http://www.businessnews.gr/article/63431/ktp-mehri-telos-martioy-ergo-g-cloud.

Buyya, R., Yeo, C. S., Venugopal, S., Broberg, J., & Brandic, I. (2009). Cloud computing and emerging IT platforms: Vision, hype, and reality for delivering computing as the 5th utility. *Future Generation Computer Systems, 25*(6), 599–616.

Castells, M. (2001). *The internet galaxy: Reflections on the internet, business, and society.* Oxford: OUP.

Cegielski, C. G., Jones-Farmer, A., Wu, L. Y., & Hazen, B. T. (2012). Adoption of cloud computing technologies in supply chains: An organizational information processing theory approach. *The International Journal of Logistics Management, 23*(2), 184–211.

Craig, R, Frazier, J, Jacknis, N, Murphy, S, Purcell, C, Spencer, P, & Stanley, J. (2009). *Cloud computing in the public sector: Public manager's guide to evaluating and adopting cloud computing.* White Paper, Cisco Internet Business Solutions Group. Retrieved June 12, 2017 from http://www.cisco.com/c/dam/en_us/about/ac79/docs/wp/ps/Cloud_Computing_112309_FINAL.pdf.

Deloitte. (2016). *Measuring the economic impact of cloud computing in Europe: A study prepared for the European Commission DG Communications Networks, Content & Technology.* Retrieved June 30, 2017 from http://ec.europa.eu/newsroom/dae/document.cfm?doc_id=41184.

DigitalPlan. (2015). *G-Cloud node of the Greek General Secretariat of Information Systems* (in Greek "Κόμβος G-Cloud της ΓΓΠΣ"). Retrieved February 18, 2017 from http://www.digitalplan.gov.gr/portal/resource/Kombos-G-Cloud-ths-GGPS.

DigitalPlan. (2017). *Green data center on the banks of the river Louros* (in Greek "Πράσινο Κέντρο Δεδομένων στις όχθες του ποταμού Λούρου"). Retrieved April 10, 2017 from http://www.digitalplan.gov.gr/portal/resource/Prasino-Kentro-Dedomenwn-stis-ohthes-toy-potamoy-Loyroy.

Donnelly, C. (2017). *Barriers to adoption: Why are local councils holding back on G-Cloud?* Retrieved May 13, 2017 from http://www.computerweekly.com/feature/Barriers-to-adoption-Why-are-local-councils-holding-back-on-G-Cloud.

El-Gazzar, R. F., & Wahid, F. (2015). *Strategies for cloud computing adoption: insights from the Norwegian public sector.* In: Proceedings of the 12 European, Mediterranean & Middle Eastern Conference on Information Systems (EMCIS 2015).

ENISA (European Agency for Network and Information Security). (2011). *Security & resilience in governmental clouds.* Retrieved March 20, 2017 from https://www.enisa.europa.eu/act/rm/emerging-and-future-risk/deliverables/security-and-resilience-in-governmental-clouds/at_download/fullReport.

ENISA (European Agency for Network and Information Security). (2013). *Good practice guide for securely deploying governmental clouds.* Retrieved July 7, 2015 from https://www.enisa.europa.eu/publications/good-practice-guide-for-securely-deploying-governmental-clouds.

ENISA (European Agency for Network and Information Security). (2014). *Annex good practice guide for securely deploying governmental clouds.* Retrieved January 28, 2016 from https://www.enisa.europa.eu/topics/cloud-and-big-data/good-practice-guide-for-securely-deploying-governmental-clouds-annex/view.

ENISA (European Agency for Network and Information Security). (2015). *Security framework for governmental clouds.* Retrieved February 3, 2016 from https://www.enisa.europa.eu/publications/security-framework-for-governmental-clouds.

European Commission. (2012a). *Unleashing the potential of cloud computing in Europe.* Retrieved June 10, 2017 from http://eur-lex.europa.eu/LexUriServ/LexUriServ.do?uri=COM:2012:0529:FIN:EN:PDF.

European Commission. (2012b). *European cloud strategy 2012.* Retrieved June 15, 2017 from https://ec.europa.eu/digital-single-market/en/european-cloud-computing-strategy.

European Commission. (2017a). *eGovernment in Greece.* Retrieved May 15, 2017 from https://joinup.ec.europa.eu/sites/default/files/ckeditor_files/files/eGovernment_in_Greece_March_2017_v2_00.pdf.

European Commission. (2017b). *Digital economy and society index 2017.* Retrieved April 30, 2017 from https://ec.europa.eu/digital-single-market/digital-economy-and-society-index-desi.

European Commission. (2017c). *Measuring the economic impact of cloud computing in Europe.* Retrieved June 30, 2017 from https://ec.europa.eu/digital-single-market/en/news/measuring-economic-impact-cloud-computing-europe.

Federal Ministry for Economic Affairs and Energy. (2014). *The Federal Government: Digital Agenda 2014–2017.* Retrieved June 6, 2017 from https://www.digitale-agenda.de/Content/DE/_Anlagen/2014/08/2014-08-20-digitale-agenda-engl.pdf?__blob=publicationFile&v=6.

Firdhous, M. (2014). A comprehensive taxonomy for the infrastructure as a service in cloud computing. In: *Advances in computing and communications (ICACC), 2014 Fourth International Conference on: 158–161.* IEEE. https://doi.org/10.1109/ICACC.2014.45.

Foundation for economic & industrial research (in Greek "IOBE"). (2014). *ICT adoption and digital growth in Greece.* Retrieved January 10, 2016 from http://iobe.gr/docs/research/RES_03_10062015_REP_ENG.pdf.

Greek e-Gov and ICT Group. (2012). Retrieved February 6, 2017 from http://egovict.blogspot.gr/.

GRNET. (2017). *okeanos.* Retrieved March 5, 2017 from https://grnet.gr/en/services/computing-and-storage-services/okeanos/.

Hellenic Statistical Authority. (2017). *Survey on the use of Information and Communication Technologies by households and individuals: 2017.* Press Release 10 November 2017. Retrieved November 14, 2017 from http://www.statistics.gr/documents/20181/699091de-a065-4cbc-98b3-fdc368ca0830.

Höfer, C. N., & Karagiannis, G. (2011). Cloud computing services: Taxonomy and comparison. *Journal of Internet Services and Applications, 2*(2), 81–94. https://doi.org/10.1007/s13174-011-0027-x.

Hsu, P., Ray, S., & Li-Hsieh, Y. (2014). Examining cloud computing adoption intention, pricing mechanism, and deployment model. *International Journal of Information Management, 34,* 474–488.

Jones, S., Irani, Z., & Sivarajah, U.. (2017). Risks and rewards of cloud computing in the UK public sector: A reflection on three Organisational case studies. *Information Systems Frontiers,* 1–24. https://doi.org/10.1007/s10796-017-9756-0.

Krogstie, J., & Veld, T.K. (2015). Information systems evolution efficiency – Differences between the public and the private sector, innovation and the public sector. In: E. Tambouris et al. (Eds.), *Electronic government and electronic participation* (Vol. 22, pp. 216–223). https://doi.org/10.3233/978-1-61499-570-8-216.

Microsoft. (2010). *The economics of the cloud.* Retrieved June 10, 2017 from https://news.microsoft.com/download/archived/presskits/cloud/docs/The-Economics-of-the-Cloud.pdf.

Microsoft. (2017). *Using cloud services to advance digital transformation in government.* Retrieved March 28, 2017 from http://www.govtech.com/library/papers/Using-Cloud-Services-to-Advance-Digital-Transformation-in-Government-81067.html?promo_code=GOVTECH_web_library_list.

Mladenow, A., Kryvinska, N., & Strauss, C. (2012). Towards cloud-centric service environments. *Journal of Service Science Research, 4*(2), 213–234.

Mosa, A., El-Bakry, H., & AbuElkheir, M. (2015). Cloud computing in e-government: A survey cloud computing in e-government: A survey. *International Journal of Advanced Research in Computer Science & Technology, 3*(2), 132–139.

Nedev, S. (2014). Exploring the factors influencing the adoption of cloud computing and the challenges faced by the business. *Enquiry-The ACES Journal of Undergraduate Research, 5,* 1.

NIST (National Institute of Standards and Technology). (2011). *US government cloud computing technology roadmap volume III technical considerations for USG cloud computing deployment decisions.* Retrieved February 23, 2017 from https://www.nist.gov/sites/default/files/documents/itl/cloud/NIST_cloud_roadmap_VIII_draft_110111-v3_rbb.pdf.

OECD (Organisation for Economic Co-operation and Development). (2014). *Recommendation on digital government strategies.* Retrieved April 10, 2017 from http://www.oecd.org/gov/digital-government/recommendation-on-digital-government-strategies.htm.

Panori, A., González-Quel, A., Tavares, M., Simitopoulos, D., & Arroyo, J. (2016). Migration of applications to the cloud: A user-driven approach. *Journal of Smart Cities, 2,* 1. https://doi.org/10.18063/JSC.2016.01.005.

Paquette, S., Jaeger, P. T., & Wilson, S. C. (2010). Identifying the security risks associated with governmental use of cloud computing. *Government Information Quarterly, 27*(3), 245–253. https://doi.org/10.1016/j.giq.2010.01.002.

Prakash, S., Mody, S., Wahab, A., Swaminathan, S., & Paramount, R. (2012). *Disaster recovery services in the cloud for SMEs*. In: Cloud Computing Technologies, Applications and Management (ICCCTAM), 2012 International Conference on: 139–144. https://doi.org/10.1109/ICCCTAM.2012.6488087.

Ramaprasad, A., Sanchez-Ortiz, A., & Syn, T. (2015). An ontology of eGovernment, IFIP International Federation for Information Processing 2015. In: E. Tambouris et al. (Eds.), *EGOV 2015, LNCS* (Vol. 9248, pp. 258–269). https://doi.org/10.1007/978-3-319-22479-4_20.

Schneider, S., & Sunyaev, A. (2016). Determinant factors of cloud-sourcing decisions: Reflecting on the IT outsourcing literature in the era of cloud computing. *Journal of Information Technology, 31*(1), 1–31. https://doi.org/10.1057/jit.2014.25.

Shin, D. H. (2013). User centric cloud service model in public sectors: Policy implications of cloud services. *Government Information Quarterly, 30*(2), 194–203.

Sosinski, B. (2011). *Cloud computing bible*. Indianapolis: Wiley Publishing Inc..

Strategic. (2014). *Report on stakeholders requirements. Public deliverable of a European project under the competitiveness and innovation framework Programme.* Retrieved February 3, 2016 from http://strategic-project.eu/wp-content/uploads/STRATEGIC_D2.-1_Report-on-Stakeholders-Requirements_v1.0-public.pdf.

Sultan, N. A. (2011). Reaching for the "cloud": How SMEs can manage. *International Journal of Information Management, 31*(3), 272–278.

Tarani, P. (2016). *STORM CLOUDS' pilot cities move to the Cloud: The Thessaloniki case.* Retrieved May 15, 2017 from http://storm-clouds.eu/2016/12/06/storm-clouds-pilot-cities-move-to-the-cloud-the-thessaloniki-city-case/.

Tweneboah-Koduah, T., Endicott-Popovsky, B., & Tsetse, A. (2014). Barriers to government cloud adoption. *International Journal of Managing Information Technology (IJMIT), 6*(3), 1–16. https://doi.org/10.5121/ijmit.2014.6301.

Vaquero, L. M., Rodero-Merino, L., Caceres, J., & Lindner, M. (2008). A break in the clouds: Towards a cloud definition. *ACM SIGCOMM Computer Communication Review, 39*(1), 50–55.

VCE. (2011). *Regional government creates new collaborative cloud model.* Retrieved March 11, 2016 from http://www.vce.com/asset/documents/castillalamancha-casestudy.pdf.

Wall, M. (2014). *Councils 'wasting millions' ignoring government IT cloud.* BBC. Retrieved September 12, 2016 from http://www.bbc.com/news/business-27618218.

Winkler, V. J. (2011). *Securing the cloud: Cloud computer security techniques and tactics.* Waltham, MA: Elsevier.

Wirtz, B. W., Mory, L., Piehler, R., & Daiser, P. (2017). E-government: A citizen relationship marketing. *The International Review on Public and Nonprofit Marketing, 14*, 149–178.

Yildiz, M. (2007). E-government research: Reviewing the literature, limitations, and ways forward. *Government Information Quarterly, 24*, 646–665.

Zaharia-Rădulescu, A. M., & Radu, I. (2017). Cloud computing and public administration: Approaches in several European countries. *Proceedings of the International Conference on Business Excellence, 11*(1), 739–749.

Zissis, D., & Lekkas, D. (2011). Securing e-government and e-voting with an open cloud computing architecture. *Government Information Quarterly, 28*(2), 239–251.

Zwattendorfer, B., & Tauber, A. (2013). The public cloud for e-government. *International Journal of Distributed Systems and Technologies (IJDST), 4*(4), 1–14.

A Unified Framework for Decision-Making Process on Social Media Analytics

Nikolaos Misirlis and Maro Vlachopoulou

Abstract Data analysis originated from social media presents huge interest among researchers and practitioners. In order to understand better and clarify notions and methodologies used regarding social media analytics, a framework is needed with clear classification schemes and procedures. The objective of this paper is to develop a unified framework that clusters the possible categories of data and their interactions. Furthermore, the proposed framework indicates the procedures that have to be followed in order to achieve the most optimized choice of social media analytics (SMA) methodology, initiating the 4P's procedure (People, Purpose, Platform, and Process). Next, the methodologies used on SMA, in specific the structural and content-based analysis, as well as their sub-methodologies (community and influencers' detection, NLP, text, sentiment, and geospatial analysis) are indicated. The proposed framework will facilitate researchers and marketers on the decision-making process by clarifying each step, regarding the objectives, the involved parties, the social media platform, and the analysis process that can be chosen.

Keywords Social media · Social media analytics · SMA framework · Social data · SMA methodologies · Decision making

1 Introduction

Social media provide practitioners and researchers with the relevant communication tools to customers and vice versa. Consumers, in that way, acquire a voice that marketers use in order to convert social media data into useful marketing insights. On January 2017, Facebook counts more than 1.8 billion active users and Google more than 415 million. We upload 10,000 photos on Instagram and we perform over 20,000 times of Skype calls every second. Internet produces 31,500 GB of

N. Misirlis (✉) · M. Vlachopoulou
Department of Applied Informatics, School of Information Sciences, University of Macedonia, Thessaloniki, Greece

© Springer Nature Switzerland AG 2019
A. Sifaleras, K. Petridis (eds.), *Operational Research in the Digital Era – ICT Challenges*, Springer Proceedings in Business and Economics,
https://doi.org/10.1007/978-3-319-95666-4_10

data every second (www.internetstats.com). If Facebook was a country it would be bigger than China or India, two times bigger than Europe, ten times bigger than Russia, and 1.8 million times bigger than Vatican City (esa.un.org). Kaplan and Haenlein (2010) define social media as a group of Internet-based applications that build on the ideological and technological foundation of Web 2.0 and that allow the creation and exchange of user-generated content (UGC). In 2010 social media represented a revolutionary way for companies to do business and could be seen as the most remarkable innovation penetrating the everyday life. Five years later, more than 70% of marketers use Facebook to successfully gain new customers in a total of 93% of marketers who use social media for business matters (shortstack.com). Forrester Research, Inc. predicts that social media will be the second-fastest growing marketing channel in the USA in 2016 (Gandomi and Haider 2015). Constantinides and Fountain (2008) claim that Internet of Things and Web 2.0 will offer endless possibilities in the business world. Social media, also as a part and sub-category of big data platforms, will contribute to such possibilities, as well. As a result of these innovative web models and technologies on the social media landscape, considerable research issues and questions arise, regarding social media analytics and big data technologies: How to render actionable the large datasets from social media? How to classify all the relevant techniques? How to capitalize all the existing information? The objective of this study is to approach the above research issues regarding several social media types, social media analysis methodologies in a precise unified framework, based on literature review and Internet search. Our proposed framework will facilitate the decision-making process of practitioners and researchers. Each part of the framework is explained and composed of the relevant literature. Therefore, a specific procedure of well-analyzed steps is followed in order to take the best decision of which will be the best methodology, data, or tool to use.

The article is structured as follows. Next, we perform a full report of social media landscape, presenting three main classification suggestions for social media. Furthermore, we analyze social media on marketing and its research options. In the following section we present the main definitions for social media analytics analyzing further different approaches in analysis, dividing in structural and content-based approach. All the above literature review and discussion leads to a unified framework suggested for the SMA procedure. Finally, we provide with concluding remarks and future research implications.

2   The Social Media Landscape

The assemblage of the extrapolated social data is the main subject for further analysis. In order to study social media analytics (SMA), analysts need to understand fully the complete social media landscape. Current literature consists of diverse theories and frameworks regarding social media taxonomy. Constantinides and Fountain (2008) present a five-group classification system composed from: Blogs, social networks, content communities, forums, and content aggregators. Respects to the

Table 1 Main classifications of social media

Authors	Social media categories
Constantinides and Fountain (2008)	Blogs, social networks, content communities, forums, content aggregators
Kaplan and Haenlein (2010)	Collaborative wikis, blogs, social content, virtual communities
Mangold and Faulds (2009)	Social networking sites, creativity work sharing sites, users sponsored websites, company sponsored cause, invitation-only social networks, business networking sites, collaborative websites, virtual worlds, commerce communities, podcasts, news delivery sites, educational material sharing sites, open-source software communities, social bookmarking sites

same authors, back in 2008, blogs were the most known and fastest-growing category of Web 2.0 applications. Today the scenery is completely different, with social media, and especially Facebook, to be the dominant platform, followed by Google+, Twitter, and Pinterest (www.pewresearch.org). Kaplan and Haenlein (2010) divide social media on collaborative wikis, blogs, social content, and virtual communities. Mangold and Faulds (2009) separate social media on social networking sites, creativity work sharing sites, user sponsored websites, company sponsored cause, invitation-only social networks, business networking sites, collaborative web sites, virtual worlds, commerce communities, podcasts, news delivery sites, educational material sharing sites, open-source software communities, and social bookmarking sites (Table 1).

3 Social Media Marketing and Analytics Research Options

SMA is the practice of gathering data from social media platforms and applications and analyzing that data to make effective business/marketing decisions. The most common use of SMA is to mine customers' sentiment, support marketing and customer service activities.

In specific, research on social media marketing and analytics is divided into three areas, according to the point of focusing the involved entities and their roles. Therefore, social media analytics can be approached from several perspectives, related to the different involved entities: the users'/customers' perspective, the platform and application providers' perspective, and the suppliers'/organizations' one. Therefore, consumer-centric studies generally focused on social media use and their impact on consumer behavior. Researchers need to study several perspectives of usage alternatives. For example, which is the specific platform and application used, how often used, how and when or what do they seek, what is their demographics and which is the specific field of interest (e.g., health, tourism, general info, travel, sports, games, etc.). This research analysis leads to large volumes of data, here and after known as CustomerData or *CD* that constitute valuable resource for the marketing strategy related to the decision making of several organizations. On the other side, *platforms* and applications of social media concentrate also on the interest of researchers posing a series of questions, like: which are the appropriate or most preferred platforms and applications, what data they record, which is the relationship between platforms and customers. We call these data, PlatformData or *PD*. The third perspective is consisted of the supplier-related social media studies, focusing on the specific use of social media by several organizations/brands (e.g., TripAdvisor, Skyscanner, Uber, Booking, Trivago, etc.). Companies may have doubt as to whether their investments in social media marketing could turn into business or how much resources they should invest in several social media platforms/applications. These research questions can be answered based on data collected and analyzed in order to provide clues or directions for their future marketing strategy. The ultimate goal of the organizations for employing several social media is to convert social media visitors to actual customers, using social media platforms for information dissemination—sharing, brand awareness, engagement, advocacy, and direct sales. The companies' social media sites are the intermediates between platforms and customers, combining useful, but different data from alternative sources and media (also known as Suppliers'/BusinessData or *SD*), rendering these data actionable for business insights and decision-making procedures. The raised challenge for marketers and data analysts is what to do with this amount of user-generated data, and how exactly to analyze these data in order to be more effective (Kobielus 2010).

According to Smith, Pilecki, and McAdams (2014) social media analytics should be used, in order to make the emerging social data actionable based on the following four P's procedure: People (assign responsibilities, clarify tasks, and identify skills), Purpose (set goals and metrics in continuous way), Platform (determine the exact platform—source of data—to use), and Process (identify and distribute the insights to the involved entities).

The first step in a social media analytics initiative is to determine which business goals data gathered and analyzed will benefit. Typical objectives include brand awareness and engagement, increasing revenues, reducing customer service costs, getting feedback on products and services, and improving public opinion of a particular product or business division. Once the business goals have been identified, specific metrics (e.g., key performance indicators—KPIs) for objectively evaluating the data should be defined. SMA refers to the approach of collecting data from social media platforms and evaluating that data to support business decisions.

4   Social Media Analytics

Social media constitute a source of data, information, and knowledge, which analysis leads to understanding real-time consumer choices, intentions, and sentiments. The most prevalent application of social media analytics is to get to know the

Table 2 SMA definitions

Authors	SMA definition approaches
Daniel, Hsinchun, Lusch, and Shu-Hsing (2010)	[. . .] developing and evaluating informatics tools and frameworks to collect, monitor, analyze, summarize, and visualize social media data, usually driven by specific requirements from a target application
Yang, Kiang, Ku, Chiu, and Li (2011)	[. . .] developing and evaluating informatics tools and frameworks to measure the activities within social media networks from around the web. Data on conversations, engagement, sentiment, influence, and other specific attributes can then be collected, monitored, analyzed, summarized, and visualized
Mayeh, Scheepers, and Valos (2012)	[. . .] scanning social media to identify and analyze information about a firm's external environment in order to assimilate and utilize the acquired external intelligence for business purposes
Grubmüller, Götsch, and Krieger (2013)	[. . .] social listening and measurements [. . .] based on use generated public content (such as postings, comments, conversations in online forums, etc.)
Sterne and Scott (2010)	SMA is the study of social media metrics that help drive business strategy
Nielsen (2012)	SMA is the ability to analyze performance of social media initiatives and social data for business intelligence
Bensen Connie—Dell Company (con-niebensen.com)	[. . .] consist on web analytics, engagement and revenue generated from social media
Awareness (2012)	[. . .] an evolving business discipline that aggregates and analyzes online conversation (industry, competitive, prospect, consumer, and customer) and social activity generated by brands across social channels. SMA enable organizations to act on the derived intelligence for business results, improving brand awareness and reputation, marketing and sales effectiveness and customer satisfaction and advocacy

customer base on a more emotional level to help better target customer service and marketing. As we notice, the social media environment is complex enough with a plethora of definitions and classifications. As a consequence, SMA is also not yet fully clarified. Many researches argue that there is a scientific gap concerning the taxonomy of the field of SMA and the relative techniques/methodologies. Next we provide with several definition approaches for SMA, four from scientific journals and four from the business world. Thus, understanding the field exactly will help us to choose the appropriate sub-category related to the SMA objectives (Table 2).

Next, we classify SMA in main methodologies and sub-methodologies. More analytically, SMA can be divided into two main methodologies—each one following by further sub-divisions: (a) structural analysis and (b) content-based analysis.

5   SMA Methodologies

With the emergence of social data and the advance of analytical technologies and methodologies, organizations can apply SMA in order to create a competitive advantage within their markets. Studying several approaches on SMA, we conclude that there is not a specific choice suitable for every decision, but it is common the combined use of several analyses. In specific, according to the literature, SMA can be divided into structural and content-based. Each of them contains different subcategories of analyses. Through structural analysis we conduct community and/or influencer detection. With content-based analysis we conduct sentiment, text, geospatial analysis, and natural language processing. Next figure summarizes the above-mentioned processes and their interactions. More analytically, we present each analysis methodology, based on the existing literature.

5.1   Structural Analysis

Structural analysis is performed mainly by graphs. It is the base notion for two important techniques: community and influencers' detection (Gandomi and Haider 2015). Community detection is capable of revealing homophily and shared characteristics among users, as well as personality's correlations with social media. Behavioral patterns of community can also be detected from graphs (Aggarwal 2011). Influencers' detection is also another useful technique on structural analysis and graphs. By counting, for example, the number of edges of a node, analysts understand which user is more active, who interacts with whom, who posts more item, etc. Community and influencers' detection is strongly correlated with behavioral analytics and social science and represents a field of study for many researchers (Amichai-Hamburger and Vinitzky 2010; Bishop 2007; Kaptein et al. 2009; Moore and McElroy 2012; Ryan and Xenos 2011).

5.2   Content–Based Analysis

Content-based analysis is the most complete type of analysis on social media. This sub-category contains all the data mining techniques based on statistics, computing, engineering, and machine learning. Generally, the content-based analysis focuses on user-generated content, whether this content is text, video, images, and/or geospatial data. This type of data is mostly unstructured, noisy, and dynamic. Today, 2.5 billion GB of unstructured content (sensors, social media posts, and photos) is created every day, while only a 1% of the data is finally analyzed. Unstructured data represent the 90% of all data available (IBM n.d.; Syed et al. 2013; Valkanas and Gunopulos 2013).

Four sub-analysis processes are included in content-based analysis:

1. *Natural Language Process* (NLP). In this type of analysis, data mining is performed on text, trying to produce meaningful outcomes. NLP is related to computer–human interaction, artificial intelligence, and linguistics. After studying relevant definitions, we conduct that text analysis is supplementary for NLP. Text analysis conducts lexical analysis by recognizing patterns and word frequencies (Bello-Orgaz et al. 2016; Gandomi and Haider 2015).
2. *Sentiment analysis.* This type of analysis applies the NLP outcomes in order to extract users' sentiments and opinions on a subject. Sentiment analysis adapts tools from machine learning, such as automatic procedures for determining opinions and extracting subjective information from users (Batrinca and Treleaven 2015).
3. *Text analysis.* The text data are commonly related to information associated with context and content. In order to obtain better outcomes from the text analysis, Aggarwal (2011) suggest that the analysis techniques must be extended, incorporating also context in the analysis. Regarding social media, text analysis refers to the lexicon analysis of posts, comments, even photos.
4. *Geospatial analysis.* This type of analysis includes four types of diverse data such as: (a) both location and time sensitive data (e.g., foursquare), (b) location sensitive only data (e.g., yelp), (c) time sensitive only data (e.g., Facebook status updates and tweets), and (d) neither location nor time sensitive data (YouTube videos and Wikipedia entries).

Next we propose a unified framework that collects both existent and original schemes for SMA. In order to summarize the SMA process we use the Smith et al. (2014) model of 4 P's together with this article's proposed models of Data Interaction and SMA methodologies. In Fig. 1, the correlations and the process from one model to another are shown. In the previous paragraphs we explained all the mid-processes analytically. Figure 1 shows the alternate usage among the different proposed frameworks. More analytically, after clarifying People involved, the Purpose of the research, the social media Platform used, and the Process chosen, the study has to be focused on the Data Interaction and Gathering. Consequently the framework indicates the internal interactions among all SMA methodologies. We notice that every item of the proposed framework is correlated with the others, interchanging measurable data or techniques. We can notice this interchangeable nature also in Table 3, where diverse methodologies are used in common according to the literature review, since several of the research articles use techniques and methods that are mutual.

Lastly, Table 3 summarizes for each sub-methodology proposed, the relevant literature. This table will provide researchers and practitioners the necessary information for further research of the methodologies, depending on their specific choice.

As we notice, articles are almost equally distributed in each category. This can be explained by the fact that it is difficult to use only one methodology without consider the others, nor use them. So if a researcher studies one method, it is common to

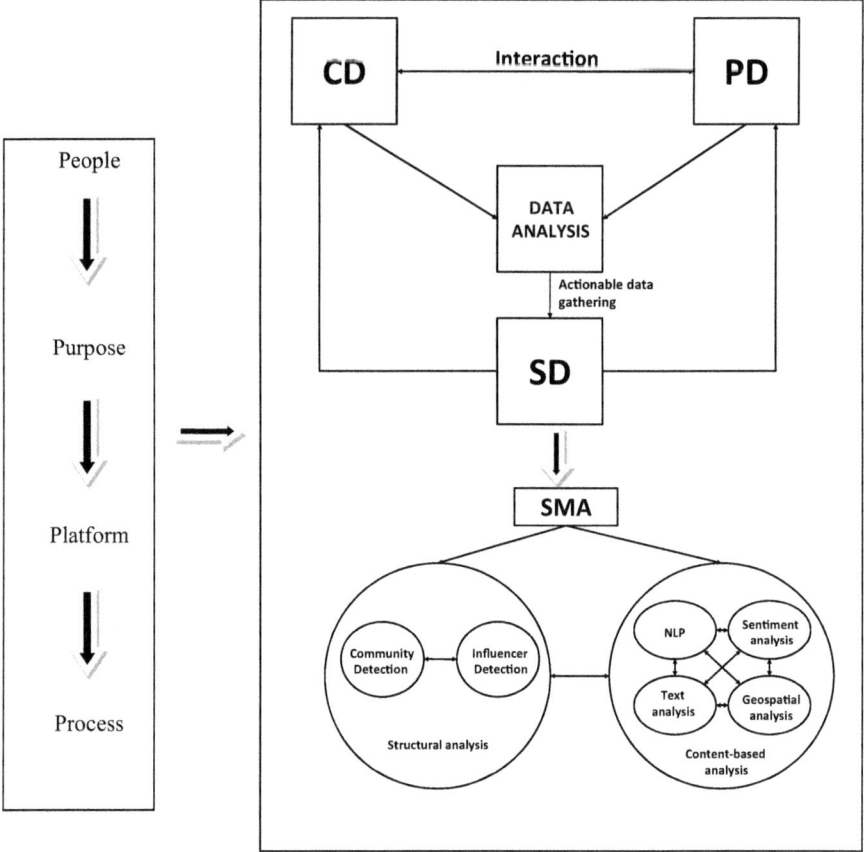

Fig. 1 A unified framework for social media analytics procedure

consider and further methodologies. Even though, in order to classify the articles, the most used method of each article was taken into consideration, although other methods may have been mentioned.

Additionally, we provide an index with related software in order to perform each sub-methodology, together with the relative links, where applicable (Table 4). We notice that same tools are used for different methodologies, since many times, these are being used interchangeably. An exception is noticed on community detection methodology. In this case, we provide with the main algorithms that are used for this type of analysis and not only the software used.

We observe that multinational big companies like IBM, Hootsuite, Apache, and Google produce software that is capable of analysis in multiple fields and sub-methodologies. On the other hand, smaller companies are limited in one or two methodologies but they are available for free usage or even for open source edit.

Table 3 Literature review for SMA related articles

Main SMA methodology	Sub-methodology	Articles
Structural analysis	Community detection	Amichai-Hamburger and Vinitzky (2010); Bishop (2007); Kaptein et al. (2009); Moore and McElroy (2012); Ryan and Xenos (2011); Aggarwal (2011); Gandomi and Haider (2015)
	Influencer detection	Fan and Gordon (2014); Leong, Ooi, Chong, and Lin (2013); Taneja, Vitrano, and Gengo (2014)
Content-based analysis	NLP	Bello-Orgaz et al. (2016); Gandomi and Haider (2015); Koohikamali, Peak, and Prybutok (2017)
	Sentiment analysis	Batrinca and Treleaven (2015); Amjad and Wood (2009); Hajli, Shanmugam, Powell, and Love (2015); Mandilas, Karasavvoglou, Nikolaidis, and Tsourgiannis (2013); Tang, Chen, Yang, Chung, and Lee (2016)
	Text analysis	Agner et al. (2014); Asur and Huberman (2010); Bollen et al. (2011); Gayo-Avello et al. (2013); He et al. (2013); Liu and lee (2010); O'Connor and Paunonen (2007)
	Geospatial analysis	Al-Debei, Al-Lozi, and Papazafeiropoulou (2013); Bozionelos and Bennett (1999); Mandilas et al. (2013)

6 Conclusion

With social media we produce a vast amount of data, introducing data analysis procedures in the big data era. Marketing science, together with information technology and statistics have great interest on understanding and analyzing social media, and managing data. Even if SMA can be considered on its early stages of maturity, organizations and other involved entities can capitalize on social media turning them to their advantage. This can be succeeded by using right and scientifically the different methodologies, by creating the right strategies, turning SMA in actionable insights, and by employing the right technology. The findings are expected to benefit researchers and marketers by supporting them better understand what has been hitherto achieved. In addition, both researchers and practitioners can use as a main guide our proposed model in order to make the procedure towards the choice of the appropriate method.

Social media analytics present a series of advantages facilitating businesses. By analyzing social media, digital marketers can enlarge the potential audience of enterprises, encourage sharing content, increase brand loyalty, and uncover important insights and outcomes. On the very opposite, negative feedback is a major disadvantage for companies and analysts. Furthermore, social media analysis can be time intensive, since it is necessary from specialized personnel to monitor continuously each network, read feedback, and answer questions. It is a fact that there is no unique approach on social media analytics. Researchers need to consider all possible methodologies, many times combining them, in order to succeed more useful insights. Since this combination is necessary, a comparison

Table 4 Software for different types and techniques of analysis

Main SMA methodology	Sub-methodology	Related software
Structural analysis	Community detection	Algorithms: *Infomap, Label propagation, Multilevel, Walktrap, Spinglass, Edge betweenness* Software: *Gephi, NodeXL, MIT's senseable* (http:// senseable.mit.edu/community_detection/)
Content-based analysis	Influencer detection	Upfluence (search.upfluence.com), followerwonk (moz.com/followerwonk), Buzzsumo (buzzsumo.com), Kred (home.kred/), Klout (klout.com/home), Klear (klear.com), Traackr (traackr.com), Linkdex (linkdex.com), brandwatch (brandwatch.com/audiences), Inkybee (inkybee.com)
	NLP	IBM SPSS Text Analytics for Surveys, Google Translate API, IBM Watson Conversation, Epic, BLLIP Parser, Apache cTAKES, OdinText, NVivo, ClearTK, CogComp NLP, Colibri Core, Cortical.io, CRF++, Deeplearning4J, FACTORIE, FoLiA, Google Cloud Natural Language API, CoreNLP (stanfordnlp.github.io/CoreNLP), Apache Open NLP (opennlp.apache.org)
	Sentiment analysis	PeopleBrowsr (peoplebrowsr.com), Google analytics (www.google.com/analytics), hootsuite (hootsuite.com), TweetStats (tweetstats.com), Facebook Insights, Unified (unified.com), Socialmention (socialmention.com), DatumBox (datumbox.com/machine-learning-framework)
	Text analysis	RapidMiner, KH Coder, Coding analysis toolkit (CAT), TAMS (tamsys.sourceforge.net), Apache Mahout, Natural Language Toolkit (nltk.org), DatumBox, TwinWord (twinword.com), Apache UIMA, LingPipe (alias-i.com/lingpipe), Gensim (radimrehurek.com/gensim), GATE (gate.ac.uk), IBM Watson Analytics
	Geospatial analysis	Hootsuite, ElasticSearch.co, IBM Watson Analytics

among methodologies may not be practical for researchers and practitioners. On the contrary, deep knowledge of all methodologies and tools is essential in order to determine the percentage and the necessity of each methodology.

By knowing how to effectively measure the social media value, companies and individuals can produce insights that allow them to improve and promote their products and services, or even themselves (for individuals). Paraphrasing Peter Sondergaard from Gartner Research, data analysis, big data, and social media are the oil of the twenty-first century and social media analytics, the combustion engine.

References

Aggarwal, C. (2011). An introduction to social network data analytics. In C. C. Aggarwal (Ed.), *Social network data analytics* (pp. 1–15). New York, NY: Springer.

Agner, S. C., Rosen, M. A., Englander, S., Tomaszewski, J. E., Feldman, M. D., Zhang, P., et al. (2014). Computerized image analysis for identifying triple-negative breast cancers and differentiating them from other molecular subtypes of breast cancer on dynamic contrast-enhanced MR images: A feasibility study. *Radiology, 272*(1), 91–99. https://doi.org/10.1148/radiol.14121031.

Al-Debei, M. M., Al-Lozi, E., & Papazafeiropoulou, A. (2013). Why people keep coming back to Facebook: Explaining and predicting continuance participation from an extended theory of planned behaviour perspective. *Decision Support Systems, 55*(1), 43–54.

Amichai-Hamburger, Y., & Vinitzky, G. (2010). Social network use and personality. *Computers in Human Behavior, 26*(6), 1289–1295. https://doi.org/10.1016/j.chb.2010.03.018.

Amjad, N., & Wood, A. M. (2009). Identifying and changing the normative beliefs about aggression which lead young Muslim adults to join extremist anti-Semitic groups in Pakistan. *Aggressive Behavior: Official Journal of the International Society for Research on Aggression, 35*(6), 514–519.

Asur, S., & Huberman, B. A. (2010). *Predicting the future with social media.* Paper presented at the Proceedings of the 2010 IEEE/WIC/ACM International Conference on Web Intelligence and Intelligent Agent Technology, (Vol. 01).

Awareness, I. (2012). *Actionable social analytics: From social media metrics to business insights.* Retrieved December 14, 2015 from http://igo2group.com/wp-%C2%AD%E2%80%90content/uploads/2012/10/Actionable-%C2%AD%E2%80%90Social-%C2%AD%E2%80%90Analytics.pdf

Batrinca, B., & Treleaven, P. (2015). Social media analytics: A survey of techniques, tools and platforms. *AI & SOCIETY, 30*(1), 89–116. https://doi.org/10.1007/s00146-014-0549-4.

Bello-Orgaz, G., Jung, J. J., & Camacho, D. (2016). Social big data: Recent achievements and new challenges. *Information Fusion, 28*, 45–59. https://doi.org/10.1016/j.inffus.2015.08.005.

Bishop, J. (2007). Increasing participation in online communities: A framework for human–computer interaction. *Computers in Human Behavior, 23*(4), 1881–1893. https://doi.org/10.1016/j.chb.2005.11.004.

Bollen, J., Mao, H., & Zeng, X. (2011). Twitter mood predicts the stock market. *Journal of Computational Science, 2*(1), 1–8. https://doi.org/10.1016/j.jocs.2010.12.007.

Bozionelos, G., & Bennett, P. (1999). The theory of planned behaviour as predictor of exercise: The moderating influence of beliefs and personality variables. *Journal of Health Psychology, 4*(4), 517–529.

Constantinides, E., & Fountain, S. J. (2008). Web 2.0: Conceptual foundations and marketing issues. *Journal of Direct, Data and Digital Marketing Practice, 9*(3), 231–244.

Daniel, Z., Hsinchun, C., Lusch, R., & Shu-Hsing, L. (2010). Social media analytics and intelligence. *Intelligent Systems, IEEE, 25*(6), 13–16. https://doi.org/10.1109/mis.2010.151.

Fan, W., & Gordon, M. (2014). *Unveiling the power of social media analytics.* Communications of ACM.

Gandomi, A., & Haider, M. (2015). Beyond the hype: Big data concepts, methods, and analytics. *International Journal of Information Management, 35*(2), 137–144. https://doi.org/10.1016/j.ijinfomgt.2014.10.007.

Gayo-Avello, P. T. M., Mustafaraj, E., Strohmaier, M., Schoen, H., Peter Gloor, D., Schoen, H., et al. (2013). The power of prediction with social media. *Internet Research, 23*(5), 528–543. https://doi.org/10.1108/IntR-06-2013-0115.

Grubmüller, V., Götsch, K., & Krieger, B. (2013). Social media analytics for future oriented policy making. *European Journal of Futures Research, 1*(1), 1–9. https://doi.org/10.1007/s40309-013-0020-7.

Hajli, N., Shanmugam, M., Powell, P., & Love, P. E. (2015). A study on the continuance participation in on-line communities with social commerce perspective. *Technological Forecasting and Social Change, 96*, 232–241.

He, W., Zha, S., & Li, L. (2013). Social media competitive analysis and text mining: A case study in the pizza industry. *International Journal of Information Management, 33*(3), 464–472. https://doi.org/10.1016/j.ijinfomgt.2013.01.001.

IBM. (n.d.). *What is big data*. Retrieved December 15, 2015 from www.01.ibm.com/software/in/data/bigdata/

Kaplan, A. M., & Haenlein, M. (2010). Users of the world, unite! The challenges and opportunities of social media. *Business Horizons, 53*(1), 59–68. https://doi.org/10.1016/j.bushor.2009.09.003.

Kaptein, M., Markopoulos, P., de Ruyter, B., & Aarts, E. (2009). Can you be persuaded? Individual differences in susceptibility to persuasion. In T. Gross, J. Gulliksen, P. Kotzé, L. Oestreicher, P. Palanque, R. Prates, & M. Winckler (Eds.), *Human-computer interaction – INTERACT 2009* (Vol. 5726, pp. 115–118). Berlin, Heidelberg: Springer.

Kobielus, J. (2010). *Social media analytics: you will still need actual analysts in the loop*. Retrieved from http://blogs.forrester.com/james_kobielus/10-07-16-social_media_analytics_you_will_still_need_actual_analysts_loop

Koohikamali, M., Peak, D. A., & Prybutok, V. R. (2017). Beyond self-disclosure: Disclosure of information about others in social network sites. *Computers in Human Behavior, 69*, 29–42.

Leong, L. Y., Ooi, K. B., Chong, A. Y. L., & Lin, B. (2013). Modeling the stimulators of the behavioral intention to use mobile entertainment: Does gender really matter? *Computers in Human Behavior, 29*(5), 2109–2121.

Liu, F., & Lee, H. J. (2010). Use of social network information to enhance collaborative filtering performance. *Expert Systems with Applications, 37*(7), 4772–4778. https://doi.org/10.1016/j.eswa.2009.12.061.

Mandilas, A., Karasavvoglou, A., Nikolaidis, M., & Tsourgiannis, L. (2013). Predicting consumer's perceptions in on-line shopping. *Procedia Technology, 8*, 435–444.

Mangold, W. G., & Faulds, D. J. (2009). Social media: The new hybrid element of the promotion mix. *Business Horizons, 52*(4), 357–365. https://doi.org/10.1016/j.bushor.2009.03.002.

Mayeh, M., Scheepers, R., & Valos, M. (2012). Understanding the role of social media monitoring in generating external intelligence. In *Paper presented at the Australasian Conference on Information Systems (23rd: 2012: Geelong, Victoria)*. Victoria: Geelong.

Moore, K., & McElroy, J. C. (2012). The influence of personality on Facebook usage, wall postings, and regret. *Computers in Human Behavior, 28*(1), 267–274. https://doi.org/10.1016/j.chb.2011.09.009.

Nielsen, J. K. (2012). *Actionable social analytics: From social media metrics to business insights* (Vol. 2015).

O'Connor, M. C., & Paunonen, S. V. (2007). Big five personality predictors of post-secondary academic performance. *Personality and Individual Differences, 43*(5), 971–990. https://doi.org/10.1016/j.paid.2007.03.017.

Ryan, T., & Xenos, S. (2011). Who uses facebook? An investigation into the relationship between the big five, shyness, narcissism, loneliness, and Facebook usage. *Computers in Human Behavior, 27*(5), 1658–1664. https://doi.org/10.1016/j.chb.2011.02.004.

Smith, A., Pilecki, M., & McAdams, R. (2014). *How to make social media data actionable*. Retrieved from https://www.forrester.com/How+To+Make+Social+Media+Data+Actionable/fulltext/-/E-RES56563

Sterne, J., & Scott, M. D. (2010). *Social media metrics: How to measure and optimize your marketing investment*. Hoboken, NY: Wiley.

Syed, A. R., Gillela, K., & Venugopal, C. (2013). The future revolution on big data. *International Journal of Advanced Research in Computer and Communication Engineering, 2*(6).

Taneja, A., Vitrano, J., & Gengo, N. J. (2014). Rationality-based beliefs affecting individual's attitude and intention to use privacy controls on Facebook: An empirical investigation. *Computers in Human Behavior, 38*, 159–173.

Tang, J. H., Chen, M. C., Yang, C. Y., Chung, T. Y., & Lee, Y. A. (2016). Personality traits, interpersonal relationships, online social support, and Facebook addiction. *Telematics and Informatics, 33*(1), 102–108.

Valkanas, G., & Gunopulos, D. (2013). A UI prototype for emotion-based event detection in the live web. In A. Holzinger & G. Pasi (Eds.), *Human-computer interaction and knowledge discovery in complex, unstructured, big data* (Vol. 7947, pp. 89–100). Berlin, Heidelberg: Springer.

Yang, M., Kiang, M., Ku, Y., Chiu, C., & Li, Y. (2011). Social media analytics for radical opinion Mining in Hate Group web Forums. *Journal of Homeland Security and Emergency Management, 8*, 1–17.

Author Index

© Springer Nature Switzerland AG 2019
A. Sifaleras, K. Petridis (eds.), *Operational Research in the Digital Era – ICT Challenges*, Springer Proceedings in Business and Economics,
https://doi.org/10.1007/978-3-319-95666-4

Subject Index

© Springer Nature Switzerland AG 2019
A. Sifaleras, K. Petridis (eds.), *Operational Research in the Digital Era – ICT Challenges*, Springer Proceedings in Business and Economics,
https://doi.org/10.1007/978-3-319-95666-4

Printed by Printforce, the Netherlands